The
Backyard Homestead,
Mini-Farm and Garden
Log Book

The Backyard Homestead, Mini-Farm and Garden Log Book

by John Jeavons,
J. Mogador Griffin and Robin Leler

10 Ten Speed Press

Edited by Jackie Wan

Food from Your Backyard Homestead by Robin Leler and John Jeavons

Mini-Farming by John Jeavons, J. Mogador Griffin and Ecology Action Staff

Crop-Testing by J. Mogador Griffin, John Jeavons and Ecology Action Staff

The Herbal Lawn by John Jeavons, Robin Leler and J. Mogador Griffin

Planning Your Garden and Keeping Records by J. Mogador Griffin and John Jeavons

ILLUSTRATIONS

Pedro J. Gonzalez: pages 53–57, 62–65, 70, 72, 82–115, 123–129 and 132–144

Betsy Jeavons: pages 5–8, 10, 12, 15 and 48

Jane Rockwell: pages 9, 19, 43, 71, 147 and 151

Eskimo art on page 2 reproduced from *American Indian Design and Decoration* by Le Roy H. Appleton, Dover Publications, New York, NY. Reprinted by permission of the publisher.

Illustration on page 58 by Eric Brewer.

Maps on pages 148–150 reproduced from *Climates of the United States* by John L. Baldwin, U.S. Dept. of Commerce, Washington, D.C. Reprinted by permission of the publisher.

TEN SPEED PRESS
P O Box 7123
Berkeley, California 94707

You may order single copies direct from the publisher for $8.95 plus $1.00 for postage and handling (California residents add 6% state sales tax; Bay Area residents add 6½%).

Library of Congress Catalog Card Number: 83-070116
ISBN: 0-89815-093-0

Book Design by Hal Hershey
Cover Design by Brenton Beck
Cover Illustration by Pedro J. Gonzalez

Printed in the United States of America

10 9 8 7 6 5 4 3 2 1

635
JEA

1. Vegetable gardening
2. Gardening
3. Organic gardening

Contents

PART TWO
Planning Your Garden and Keeping Records

Annual Planning Charts: When to Plant What *page 147*

THE GARDENING YEAR   FROST MAPS
DETERMINING MAXIMUM SUNLIGHT IN YOUR YARD
PLANNING CALENDARS — 90-DAY THROUGH 240-DAY

Planning Guide: Determining How Much of Each Crop to Plant *page 162*

Planning Map: Laying Out the Garden *page 165*

Monthly Calendars and Logs:
Charting Daily Activities and Keeping Notes and Records *page 166*

Resource Guide *page 190*

Preface

Your backyard mini-farm begins with a seed and the joy of tending tiny green shoots as they grow and flourish into lush green bearers of tomatoes, corn and melons. That first garden eleven years ago had us hooked! We soon outgrew mere vegetables, though, as we tried to figure out how much of a total diet could be produced in a small yard. When we were introduced to the biointensive growing approach of Alan Chadwick we soon saw the potential offered for feeding hungry people. Our interest blossomed into a full-time profession as we began testing the limits of this highly productive way of raising food. Our back-yard expanded to include chickens, goats, bees and a small orchard. Land was also leased by Ecology Action from the Syntex Corporation in Palo Alto for detailed testing of biointensive yields, water requirements, fertilizer use and many other topics. For almost ten years we tested the intensive growing of vegetables for market, grains from wheat to rice, herbs, flowers and even cotton and flax for cloth. Some experiments failed, while others still need fine tuning. Each chapter of this book was originally pub-lished as a booklet in response to inquiries about different aspects of the research. By and large our greatest expectations have been fulfilled, convincing us that this method can fill the food needs of even the poorest people worldwide.

The research garden has now moved to a larger, more rural site in northern California where tests continue on the many areas suggested in this compendium: tree crops, animal fodder, cover crops, complete diets and market gardening especially. We expect to continue this type of work for the next fifty years and you will notice much of what we share here is necessarily experimental. We raise as many questions as we answer and have found many answers through correspondence with individuals working all over the world. If you welcome exciting challenges, consider this book an invitation—the result could well be an agriculture that can really feed people even in their own backyards.

Robin Leler
January 1983

Introduction

For over ten years, Ecology Action has been working with the biodynamic/French intensive method of food and plant raising, trying to discover the smallest amounts of land necessary to provide for the nutritional requirements of people while caring for and nurturing the earth. This work has included both research and education. Our hope has been to enable people to enrich their lives by increasing their level of self-reliance in their own backyards. A personal agriculture which seeks to work with the natural elements and living forces that make up this world is an exciting adventure truly within each person's reach.

Throughout the years, many people have written to us at Ecology Action. Some have wanted personalized training sessions, others wanted more detailed data, some sought help in setting up their own mini-farms, and many have wanted to know just how the use of the biodynamic/French intensive method could help them — in their gardens, on their smallholdings, and on their farms. Out of our responses grew a series of booklets, which is the basis for this book.

Here we hope to answer some of these questions and to show how people can begin — it does not matter how small — to take some responsibility in providing for themselves in a way that is ecologically sound, intellectually and physically stimulating, emotionally satisfying, and, above all, fun. You can do it alone, with your family, and with your neighbors or your whole community. Think of it as a "mini-course" in self-reliance. By beginning very small — perhaps with a bed or two — you can start learning the dynamics of this growth in your own climate and soil.

Knowing what is needed for an abundant and sustainable food raising system makes possible a re-examination of our attitudes and approaches toward the world and the life it contains. We are a part of the earth — instead of apart from it. This wholeness can be expressed as a practical part of our lives: in experiencing, once again, what it is to be one with the earth!

John Jeavons
January, 1983

PART ONE

After Candide and his friends returned from their remarkable adventures in which everything that could possibly go wrong did go wrong, they came upon a farmer and his family and were invited to share a meal which was quite exquisite.

After dinner Candide remarked to the man, "You must have a vast and magnificent estate?"

"I have only twenty acres," replied the man. "I cultivate them with my children. Work keeps away three great evils: boredom, vice, and need."

As Candide went back to his farm, he reflected deeply on the man's remarks. He said to his friends, "That good old man seems to me to have made himself a life far preferable to that of the six Kings with whom we had the honor of having supper."

One of his friends, agreeing with Candide, began listing quite a number of kings and emperors who met with ill fate. Candide cut him short saying, "I also know that we must cultivate our garden."

This same friend replied, "You are right. For when man was put in the Garden of Eden, he was put there **ut operaretur eum**, to work; which proves that man was not born for rest."

They then gathered their little group of friends and began gardening on Candide's little parcel of land—each bringing their own particular talents to fruition. And the little piece of land produced much.

Every now and then his philosopher friend would bring up the subject of Candide's misadventures and how "all events are linked together in the best of all possible worlds." And then he litanized all the terrible things which befell Candide and how it all resulted in bringing Candide and his friends together on this piece of land.

"That is well said," Candide would reply, "but we must cultivate our garden."

And they did.

Based on **Candide (or Optimism)**
Voltaire, 1759

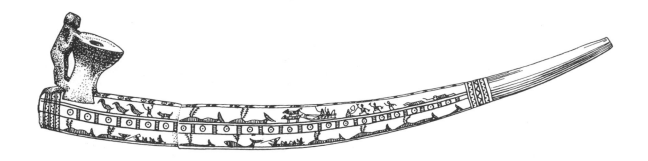

People of the Deer

Not very long ago, there lived a civilization of inland Eskimo peoples known as the Ihalmiut. Their home extended across the northern territories of Canada. They called themselves the "People of the Deer" and their lives revolved around the twice-yearly migration of the vast herds of caribou which once roamed the wide expanse of northern North America.

They were discovered by fur traders who wished to provide furs for distant markets. The Ihalmiut said that they were "People of the Deer" and lived with and because of the deer—not from fur-trapping. But the fur trader, knowing how they depended on the caribou migrations and how they herded and killed the caribou, explained how he could ease their burden so that they could have all the caribou they needed **and** still be able to get furs for him. He showed them a rifle.

The "People of the Deer" were very impressed with the rifle and agreed to help the fur trader. In exchange for the furs that they were to bring to a pre-ordained place, they would be provided with rifles and bullets, flour, tobacco, and foodstuffs. This arrangement went on for some years. Once a year, they brought the furs that they had trapped to the trader's cabin and the trader would give them more ammunition and foodstuffs.

The "People of the Deer" thought this arrangement very good. They enjoyed trapping. They did not have to work as hard herding and killing the caribou. They did not have to make bows and arrows. And they even got food, tea, tobacco, and other things, besides. To them it was a very good deal.

It was very good—until the market dropped out of the fur trade! The "People of the Deer", of course, had no idea that the market had folded. They returned at the appointed time that year and waited for the trader to arrive. They waited and waited until they could wait no longer. And they headed back to their respective areas, communities, and families. They did not think to be worried. Sometimes things like this happened and the fur trader was late in coming. Besides, they still had some bullets left for the rifles they possessed.

The next year, the Ihalmiut returned to the trader's cabin with new furs, and again, they waited for the fur trader to come back. Again—he did not. After a while, they left. They were now out of bullets. And that year, many "People of the Deer" died.

The next year came and went, and still no fur trader arrived. But even worse, they were not quite sure how to work the caribou or make bows-and-arrows anymore. Also, the deer had altered their migration patterns and because they had not been paying attention, they lost the ability to fend for themselves. It had been but two generations and the "People of the Deer" had become so dependent on the outside support that they did not ever think of the day when there might not be that support anymore, and their inner strength and skills had deteriorated.

Attempts were made to revive the old ways, but the older people had died and the old ways were lost. When Farley Mowat authored **The People of the Deer** (on which this synopsis is based) in 1951, only 49 "People of the Deer" were left—out of a civilization that numbered in the thousands only years earlier.

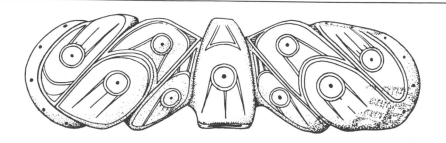

Food From Your Backyard Homestead

A small-scale, bio-intensive approach to providing more food for the family

A Perspective

How much different are we from the "People of the Deer" with our dependence on a system that is so complex — much more complex than the simple manufactured goods that the Ihalmiut needed? While the farmers who grow our food and fiber make up only 3% of the American people, and an additional 20% of the American people work in food related industries and support systems, very few people know how to raise food in a way that supports themselves and their families.

In our search for "the good life", it seems as if we have rearranged our priorities. Instead of giving our

---

Man, despite his artistic pretensions, his sophistication, and many accomplishments, owes the fact of his existence to a six-inch layer of topsoil — and the fact that it rains.

ANONYMOUS

---

houses and food-raising gardens the scrutiny they deserve to assure their sustainability, we are living more and more outside our home gardens. Instead of tending our own "gardens" — both literally and figuratively — we seem to hope a local regulatory agency, government, organization or someone else will "put the house in order". Actually, and logically, *responsibility* has to begin with the individual.

Self-Sufficiency

How self-sufficient can we be? This question, more than any other, has activated Ecology Action's biointensive mini-farming research and education program. We have found that 100 square feet can easily produce all the vegetables for one person in a 6-month growing season. On the average, each person in the United States eats 322 pounds of vegetables and soft fruits such as melons and strawberries each year. Our research has shown that a 100 square foot garden, in other words, the average suburban backyard, can easily produce that — up to 1.8 pounds per day, assuming you are an average gardener with a working knowledge of the biodynamic/French intensive method. As your skills increase, and your soil improves, the yields may be even greater.

If you are new to mini-farming, begin small — and take the time to learn to build up your soil and your expertise. We have been researching and demonstrating for eleven years, and we are still learning from our successes and failures. We do not claim to know all the answers, but want to share with you what we have learned so far in our test gardens, and in our backyard homestead.

Biodynamic/French Intensive Gardening

Throughout this chapter — throughout this book, for that matter — we assume all your efforts will be based on a thorough knowledge of the biodynamic/French intensive method of gardening, as this is the key to achieving high yields in the small spaces described.

The backbone of the method can begin with double-digging a 5-by-20 foot bed, and *incorporating compost* into the soil. Double-digging the first year is the hardest part of "the method" — subsequent years become easier as the soil becomes more friable. In fact, the Irish call them "lazy beds." Double-digging and the addition of compost serve to increase air penetration and increase the capacity of the soil to both absorb and hold moisture throughout the plants' root environment.

Afterwards, *the plants are spaced closely and evenly throughout the bed surface,* so that when the plants are mature, their outer leaves will touch. This has the effect of creating a "living mulch" by shading the ground, keeping the moisture in, and cutting down unwanted weed growth. In addition, it helps to create the plants' own 'mini-climate' and allows more optimal

Original Common Ground Garden, Palo Alto, California.

PHOTO: AUDREY ROSS, SILVER CITY, NM

Figure 1. Each bed is 5 by 10 feet.

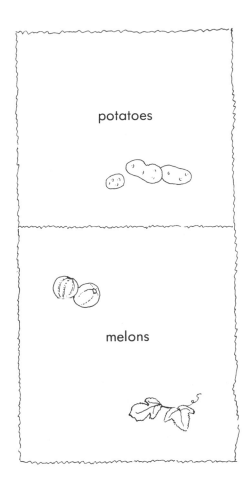

Table 1. Basic 100 square foot garden, yielding 1.4 pounds per day for 6 months assuming a good gardener with reasonable soil. Higher yields, up to 1.8+ pounds per day can be obtained by very good gardeners with excellent soil.

Crop	Square Feet	Approximate Initial Yield in Pounds	Followed by:	Yield in Pounds
cucumbers	2.5	8	spinach	2.5
peppers	2.5	2	parsnips	5.0
green beans	5.0	4	cabbage	10.0
strawberries	10.0	16		
winter squash	5.0	5		
zucchini + herbs	5.0	15		
tomatoes	10.0	20		
salad vegetables	10.0	20	broccoli	4.0
potatoes	25.0	50	salad vegetables	50.0
peas	25.0	14	melons (or corn)	25.0 (15-20 ears)
	100 feet	154 pounds		plus 96.5 lbs. = 250.5 lb.

air and moisture circulation in the critical area 2 inches above and 2 inches below the ground — very important areas to healthy growth.

Overhead watering is done daily during the summer and, depending on the sun's intensity, may be done twice — early in the morning and late afternoon. Overhead watering with a fan-type nozzle, simulating a gentle rainfall, washes the leaves and carries air-borne nutriments to the soil.

This is a brief description of the method. For complete instructions, refer to the basic manual on biodynamic/French intensive gardening: *How to Grow More Vegetables Than You Ever Thought Possible On Less Land Than You Can Imagine,* by John Jeavons. Published by Ten Speed Press, 1974, 1982.

The mainstay of most backyard homesteads is the vegetable garden, crops that can be grown quickly, with little money invested, and a harvest enjoyed the same year seeds are sown. Figure 1 shows a sample 100 square foot garden that will yield 1.4 pounds per day for 6 months, assuming a good gardener with reasonable soil. Table 1 gives appropriate yields from this basic garden. Higher yields, 1.8+ pounds per day, can be obtained by very good gardeners with excellent soil. For other garden plans and an extensive table of appropriate yields, consult *How to Grow More Vegetables.*

The crops you select to plant will be determined by your own situation. Your family's dietary preferences and the climate in your location are two factors to consider. If your yard is small, you'll probably want crops that are space efficient (squash instead of corn, for instance). If you want crops that are high in protein yield, your choices will again be different. Protein efficient crops are discussed later in this chapter and in Chapter Two (see page 11 and page 43).

Small Livestock

Vegetables are but a small part of the food picture. Hardly anyone starts out growing food without dreaming about fruit trees, a few chickens or rabbits, perhaps even a goat or cow.

We added six laying hens to our backyard almost immediately. Their space requirements are very small — as little as 4 square feet per chicken for night protection and room to move around in, although we recommend that each chicken have a run area of at least 20 square feet as well. Their food requirements are another matter. Feed must be provided at the rate of 100 pounds per year per chicken to produce approximately 230 eggs a year. Growing 100 pounds of feed (for example 50 pounds of corn and 50 pounds of wheat) would require about 500 to 1,000 square feet per hen!

Fortunately, hens will thrive on foods that are not so space-costly to grow. Feed requirements drop 50% if hens are allowed to run in the garden and scavenge for insects, weeds, and other forage during part of the day. Special forage can be grown for them such as high-protein comfrey leaves, alfalfa, clover, and sunflower seeds. We cut the need for purchased food by giving them extra milk from our goat, but the high space requirement for feeding laying hens does limit their use for someone aiming at total self-sufficiency in a very small space.

Goats proved to be much more efficient than laying hens. One goat needs as little as 200 square feet for a pen, including a 24 square foot shelter. One goat consumes 3/4 ton of alfalfa (1,500 pounds baled dry weight) *plus* approximately 400 pounds of grain per year. The alfalfa requires 2,500 to 3,000 square feet of growing area, assuming three cuttings per year. Up to six cuttings are possible in some localities with long growing seasons, which could reduce this area to 1,250 to 1,750 square feet. The grain requires 2,000 to 4,000 square feet to grow. Feed requirements then total up to 3,250 to 7,500 square feet (1/12 to 1/6 acre), but a good milking doe produces up to 1-1/2 gallons of milk a day, or enough for six to twelve people.

At least two goats should be kept, normally, since solitary goats often suffer from loneliness. A pair of goats could easily become a neighborhood project, supplying six families with milk, with the responsibility of providing feed shared by all.

Feed requirements can be reduced by using many suburban waste products such as untreated grass clippings, unsprayed tree trimmings, shrub prunings and weeds. Leaves, especially, are high in trace minerals and can increase milk production 10% to 20%. In addition to producing a high quality protein food, goats will bless your garden with a rich and inoffensive manure.

Honeybees are an exceptional investment for any backyard. They are easy to keep, requiring attention only two to six times a year, and need very little space. A hive can even be kept on a rooftop. Usually no extra food needs to be provided, especially in suburban areas where landscaping, herbs, flowers, hedges and gardens provide abundant and diverse nectar and pollen sources. Friends and neighbors confirm that a honey yield of 50 to 120+ pounds per hive is extracted each year. Bees are also essential for pollination of 1/3 of our food crops in the United States.

Fruit Trees

Fruit trees should have a high priority in every backyard homestead. One dwarf tree takes only about 60 square feet of space, and can yield up to 100 pounds of fruit per year. A small orchard can be planted intensive style, with dwarf trees 8 feet apart in hexagonal or offset spacing to provide shade. A "living fence" can be grown using trees for the "posts" and berry vines for the "fencing" between. Edible fruit trees also make especially good public plantings in schools, churches, parks, and along streets.

Once established, trees are easier to take care of than vegetables, requiring only seasonal attention. They do, however, require a higher level of gardening skill. Planting mistakes may not seem apparent for several seasons, and improper pruning may also take its toll.

For more information, see the tree section in Chapter Three on page 67.

Special consideration should be given to fruits not commonly seen in the grocery. Figs produce two crops a year; persimmons produce very late in the

Table 2. Some fruits and vegetables that benefit from insect pollination.

Almond	Mango
Apple	Muskmelons
Apricot	Pawpaw
Avocado	Passion fruit
Blackberry	Peach and nectarine
Blueberry	Pear*
Broadbean	Peppers
Chayote	Persian melon
Cherry	Plums and prunes
Chinese gooseberry (kiwi apple)	Pumpkin
Cucumber	Quince
Currant	Raspberry
Eggplant	Scarlet runner-bean
Gooseberry	Squash
Honeydew melon	Strawberry*
Lima bean	Tangelo
Macadamia	Tangerine
	Watermelon

* Some varieties

season when little other fresh fruit is available; *Rosa rugosa* roses make a fine hedge and produce large rose hips that are high in Vitamin C.

Backyard Ecology

At this point we should consider the synergistic effects of all these elements. Not only can we produce vegetables, fruit, eggs, milk, cheese and honey for the table: any homestead encourages an intricate web of interrelationships.

In our backyard the chickens were let out an hour before sunset to scratch and consume insects (which are more active in the evening and early morning), weeds and, of course, some of our garden plants. Hens love slugs, earwigs, snails and other garden pests which are harder to control by other means. They provide good manure as well as eggs and are allowed free access to compost piles and the goat pen area where they feast on table scraps and keep flies under control.

Our goat eats corn and sunflower stalks, shrub clippings, apple cores, carob pods and even whole branches of our wild plum trees. She provides manure in neat, inoffensive form and milk for humans, several cats, a dog and the chickens.

Fruit trees offer shade to the goat and the compost bins, roosts to the chickens, food to the goat, some firewood and a place for the children to climb, hang swings and build forts, as well as plums, figs, apricots and other fruit.

The garden welcomes many unexpected tenants. Toads burrow into the moist soil and feast on many garden insects such as flies, earwigs, ants, aphids and small slugs. Lizards would also be good pest controllers in drier climates and even hedgehogs are used for snail control in England. Pineapple sage and bottle brush, with their red flowers, attract hummingbirds which stay and consume many insects, while blue flowers attract bees for pollination and honey. Cosmos and sow thistle attract other birds. Many flowers, especially the compositae, harbor other insect predators and parasitizers such as the tiny braconid wasp which is harmless to humans but paralyzes cabbage worms for its larvae to feed on.

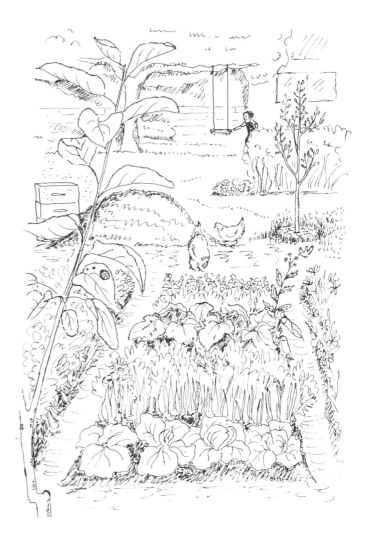

Food Produced — A Personal Example

How self-sufficient can we be? For six months of the year or more we fed four people largely from part of our suburban backyard. Below is a sampling of the foods we ate. Italicized foods are those we did not produce on site before we moved to a small farm. Once we are established, we expect to grow almost all of our food there.

BREAKFAST: Eggs, *toast,* fresh fruit or *cooked grains* with milk

LUNCH AND/OR SNACKS: Stir-fried vegetables, milk, potatoes, milk-fruit shakes, fresh goat cheese, honey *cookies,* fresh fruits, fresh vegetables with dip, pumpkin and squash seeds

DINNER: Curried cheese and onion pie, marinated beets, steamed broccoli, *apple cake*

Veggie "meatballs" in tomato sauce, mashed potatoes, fresh green salad, custard

Hearty bean soup, muffins, corn on the cob, fruit salad

The time involved in growing this food was still small — we spent about an hour a day, 1/2 in the garden and 1/2 with the animals.

The layout shown evolved over the last 25 to 30 years, or ever since the houses were built. There is plenty of room for future experiments.

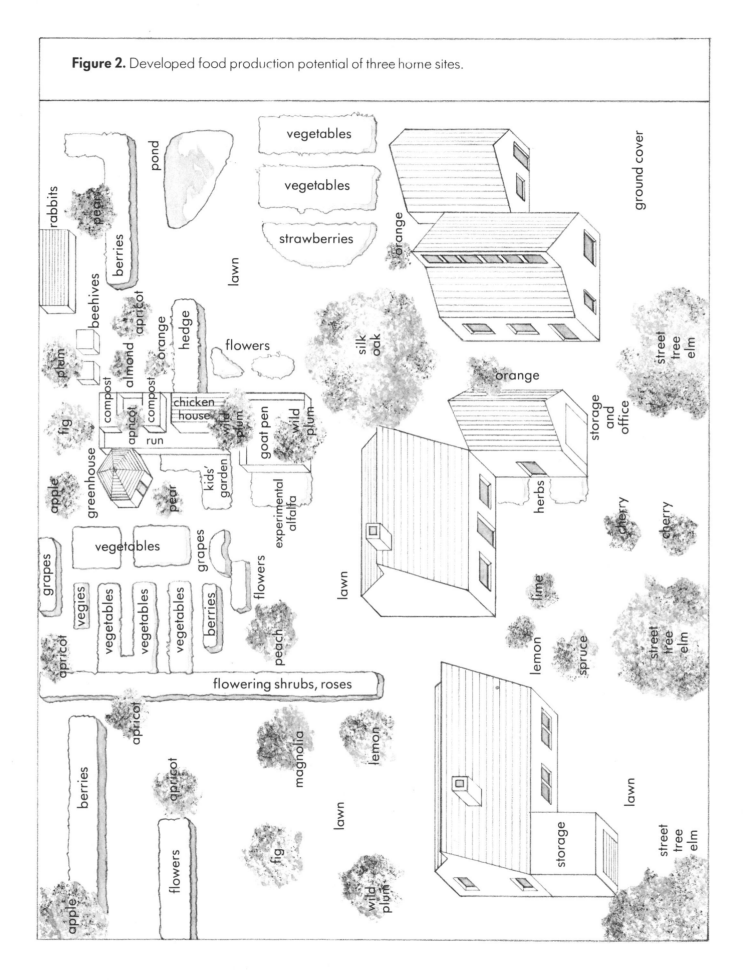

Figure 2. Developed food production potential of three home sites.

Fruit-producing bushes and nut trees could go in front. The grass lawn could become an herbal lawn or even grow grains and animal fodder. The pond which is now decorative could grow fish or valuable food plants. In short, the garden is expected to change and grow.

The major outside inputs were animal feeds and grains (wheat, oats, dried beans, and so on). This is naturally our most intensive area of research. By our current biointensive food raising practices we would need 500 to 1,000 square feet to:

> produce alfalfa and grain for the goat for 6 to 8 weeks
>
> OR raise 100 pounds of grain for one chicken
>
> OR grow 100 pounds of wheat, oats or possibly dried beans for human use.

We currently have several experimental plots for these crops and as we learn to grow them well, will use more of the lawn for their production.

More Backyard Products

We have talked only about food, yet many plants suitable for backyard culture can provide much more: CLOTHING from cotton and flax; BASKETS from honeysuckle and pine needles; BEER from barley and hops; WINE from grapes and other fruits; MEDICINES from horehound, willow, St. John's Wort, calendula and aloe vera; FLOWERS and FRAGRANCE, COSMETICS, TOYS, even ENERGY. Garden waste can be distilled into alcohol fuel. Jojoba and gopher plants may some day produce oil alternatives. Trees and shrubs can channel the sun's heat, block wind, and/or provide shade to the home and yard, reducing energy needs substantially.

The honey locust and carob trees produce large amounts of food (beans and pods), fuel and building material (wood), and fertilizer (leaves laden with trace minerals and other nutriments brought up from the soil's depths by deep probing roots). Pearl millet, alfalfa, comfrey, fava beans, cylindra beets and clovers provide large amounts of fertilizers, organic matter and nitrogen to build up the soil when grown as cover crops in season or afterwards. Each person will have his or her own special projects to undertake!

Towards a Complete Diet

In order to achieve self-sufficiency, it is essential to grow crops that will supply enough high-quality protein to meet dietary requirements. The Recommended Daily Allowance for healthy Americans is 44 to 56 grams of protein per day. Checking the data in Table 3 will give you some idea of how much space it would take to provide your needs using various protein sources. The protein listings in Table 3 are for 1/3 to 1/4 this amount. A variety of food needs to be consumed to supply each nutrient, especially in the case of protein where quality and amino acid completeness is just as important as quantity. Furthermore, protein is only one of many important factors in diet. Also, a diet designed to use nutrients most efficiently may need only *one-half* the square feet described here.

Nut Trees

Nuts are an excellent source of protein, and for this reason can be a worthwhile addition to your backyard scheme. One nut tree can yield as much protein per square foot as does a goat (see Table 3). Almond trees on 16.5 -foot spacings yield up to 12 pounds of nuts (shelled) per tree. Filberts on 15-foot spacings can yield up to 60 pounds of nuts (shelled) per tree, producing even more protein per unit of area.

It will take several years from the time you plant a nut tree before you can harvest a reasonable crop. (The same holds true for fruit trees, of course.) At this rate, grains and beans provide more protein in a smaller space, though nut trees offer the advantage of permanency and less work. Certainly, more research needs to be done in this area, and Ecology Action would welcome comments on your experience with these trees.

The honey locust tree offers great promise as a protein source. A single tree is said to yield up to 1,000 pounds of high-protein (16%) beans annually. It could be invaluable as a source of survival food, as one tree can theoretically supply 200 grams of protein for a daily diet, or enough for three to five people. The pods as well as beans are edible, making this a versatile food for humans and livestock. Honey locust trees are planted 40 feet apart, so each requires

Table 3. Comparative Space Requirements for Different Protein Sources. To obtain this much protein **per day** — you need to grow this much **per year**. 1 oz. = 28 grams

Source Per Day	Protein	Per Year	Square Feet
2 eggs	13 g	3 hens 120–300 lb. grain	600–3000
2 cups milk	15.4 g	1/8 goat 188 lb. alfalfa plus 50 lb. grain	563–938 (156–438 250–500)
1.6 oz. soybeans	15.4 g	36.5 lb.	183–365
2.66 oz. peanuts	13.3 g	61 lb. (in shell)	222–763
5.3 oz. almonds	14.3 g	121.7 lb. (in shell)	811–1521 1 tree = 272 sq. ft.
4 oz. filberts	14.3 g	91 lb. (in shell)	371–737 1 tree = 225 sq. ft.
4 oz. wheat (assuming 13% protein)	15 g	91 lb. (dry weight)	455–910
3.2 oz. honey locust	14.5 g	73 lb. "beans" (dry weight)	117–235 1 tree = 1600 sq. ft.
1 lb. collards	14 g	365 lb.	100–200
5.5 oz. millet	14.9 g	125 lb. (dry weight)	625–1250
4 oz. sunflower seeds	14.7 g	91 lb. (in shell)	455–910

about 1,600 square feet. Their light leaf structure also allows sunlight to fall on the ground underneath where additional fodder crops can be grown in a form of *two-storied agriculture.* Our own research with these trees is just beginning as we develop our permanent site to continue long-term testing.

Protein Efficient Crops

Growing seeds such as wheat, millet, beans and sunflowers appears to be more efficient in terms of yield per square foot than is the cultivation of most nut trees or the raising of small livestock (see Table 3). Although there is a large variation in the area required per unit yield, we assume that yields of 10 pounds per 100 square feet are obtainable for most grains and beans, and that further testing will show yields of 20+ pounds per 100 square feet can be obtained for most protein crops.

Collards are also a surprisingly efficient source of protein, though it would be difficult to eat enough collards (3 to 4 pounds daily) to satisfy one's protein needs. Still, they can make a valuable contribution to the diet. In addition to a high protein content, collards are 50% to 100% higher in calcium than milk and are an excellent source of iron.

Soybeans and peanuts are good sources of protein, but their cultivation is limited to warmer climates. (In this respect, goats, because they and their fodder can adapt to a wider climatic range, have a marked advantage as protein producers.) Consult your county agriculture agent on the feasibility of growing soybeans and peanuts in your particular area.

Grain Self-Sufficiency — The Current Picture

Grain and fodder self-sufficiency for a small family still seems a long way off since meeting a family of four's protein needs of 172 to 224 grams per day would require:

> growing 1/2 the food for one goat
>
> PLUS the feed for six chickens
>
> PLUS 600 pounds of grains and beans for direct human consumption,

for a total of 8,250 to 15,750 square feet or 6,750 to 12,750 square feet if the chickens are allowed to forage for 1/2 their feed. Some people may have up to 6,750 square feet in lawn (about 1/6 of an acre) but this would assume the very best biointensive yields and, of course, no recreational area. Those homes with the more realistic 12,750 square feet (or about 1/3 of an acre) needed for food production could possibly come close to food self-sufficiency.

Ecology Action's Ongoing Grain Research

Some exciting breakthroughs may make backyard grain production more viable. In a 100 square foot growing bed, use of current U.S. standard-type growing methods would generally produce about 4 to 8 pounds of grain. Ecology Action has tested wheat in biointensive beds for seven years, varying the spacing distance and other factors. Yields obtained in 1979 per 100 square feet were as high as 21 pounds. Perhaps most amazing is that the protein content of the wheat increased simultaneously with increase in yield! Usually an increase in yield is obtained only by a decrease in protein content and a great increase in fertilizer and water requirements. Our research shows a more ecological result is possible.

Testing of grain yields is still in its beginning stages. We feel confident that yields will increase more with further improvements in the soil and in our grain-growing knowledge. If 26 pounds of wheat can be grown per bed consistently in a large area and two crops a year grown (perhaps with miniature greenhouses), we will be able to produce enough wheat for a 1-pound loaf of bread every week of the year in only 100 square feet. Results like these can put self-sufficiency at the vegetarian level well within many people's reach—about 5,400 square feet would be required during a 4-to 6-month growing season for a year's supply of grains, vegetables, herbs and fruits for a family of four.

Similar testing continues for other protein crops, especially soybeans. People are encouraged to send for Ecology Action's mini-teaching booklet on soybean testing and become part of the research effort. *You* could be the one who makes the breakthrough with this and other important crops. A backyard gardener in England, for example, grew a potato crop yielding 7.8 pounds per square foot, three times higher than Ecology Action's highest yield to date, and potatoes provide a large percentage of the calories, protein and calcium eaten worldwide!

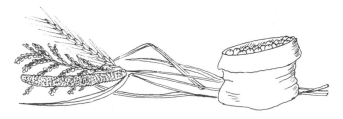

Chapter Three explains how to initiate a 5-crop test that includes lettuce, tomatoes, beets, wheat and soybeans. You can incorporate this into your backyard homesteading plans.

In addition to increasing yields, three research directions have a great potential for increasing self-sufficiency. First, *increasing the protein content and quality of crops* such as wheat, corn, rice and others would *decrease* the land required to obtain protein from those crops. Second, some exciting results are emerging from work with the *use of protein from new sources such as honey locust and grain amaranth.* Third, the space required to keep small livestock may be decreased by the *use of uncommon fodders with higher yields and/or higher nutritive value per unit of weight,* such as comfrey or carob pods. All these fields offer fertile ground for individual research.

Why Self-Sufficiency?

The personal benefits of "growing your own" are at least fourfold: substantial savings in money spent for food, increased freshness and nutritive value of the food consumed, the spiritual and healthful satisfactions of spending time in the fresh air with living and growing things, and a more ecologically-sound relationship with the earth. Producing food on site greatly reduces pollution of our air and water, the amount of garbage we generate and the amount of water, energy and purchased fertilizer we consume.

Though it may not always be so the first year, time in the garden with a reasonable amount of skill and an improved soil can yield vegetables and soft fruits for a family of four worth about $750. But the savings are more than monetary when we consider the other factors involved in putting food on the table. Think of the time we spend in the grocery when we could be outdoors growing the food, or how much of each work day is spent earning the money to pay for our car, gasoline and maintenance so we can go to the grocery? Spending less for food and transportation means spending less time at a job, freeing up more time for the important work in each of our lives.

The food you grow has more flavor. A homegrown tomato is a delight to all the senses. The sugar in the corn begins turning to starch within 12 minutes after being picked so optimum flavor can only come from ears grown close to home. A potato from the backyard has a flavor that can never be matched by store-bought spuds. Homegrown will naturally be fresher and fresh food is higher in vitamins.

Food that must be harvested by machine, trucked long distances and stored before purchase is bred for

toughness, not for nutriments, flavor or texture. The food grown is also "cleaner": it need not carry pesticide residues, wax coatings (apples, cucumbers), artificial colors (oranges) or growth retardants (potatoes).

Take a look inside a household garbage pail. You will probably find, as we did, that at least half is food packaging: milk cartons, cereal boxes, bottles, cans and plastic bags. Recycling bottles and cans to a processing center and organic waste to the compost pile may reduce substantially the amount that must go to the dump. But producing food in the backyard drastically reduces the amount of packaging that comes into the home in the first place. Food grown just outside your doorstep does not need to be transported across continents and oceans.

If our vast food network is reduced, as a nation we save tremendous amounts of fuel and reduce the resulting pollution. A decentralized food system is much less vulnerable to man-made and natural disasters. For example, France has been able to recover much faster after wars than many other countries because of her strong system of localized farms and markets.

Soil: A Case for Small-Scale Farming

We are blessed here in the United States with areas of very rich, fertile soil created over thousands of years. Such soil allows for plenty of abuse, but under the worst conditions can be depleted in as little as 50 to 100 years. It is not too surprising, then, that we are just starting to see signs of stress in our agricultural system. The Dustbowl of the 1930s comes to mind almost immediately. The soil's organic matter became so depleted that it could not hold precious moisture, and when drought hit for eight years the soil just blew away.

Similarly, today in corn growing, we are using up 2 bushels of topsoil for every bushel of corn harvested. Some estimate a much higher loss. Chemical fertilizers that initially boost agricultural yields also deplete soil life and fertility in the long run. To maintain high yields increasing amounts of fertilizer must be added. Between 1948 and 1969, there was a tenfold increase in chemical fertilizers applied to Illinois corn — with only a twofold increase in corn yields.

Furthermore, water requirements for plants increase in soil depleted of organic matter since it cannot hold moisture as well. In many areas water is

being pumped out of natural underground reservoirs faster than it can be replenished. As a result, parts of the Arizona landscape have sunk several feet. In California's San Joaquin Valley, where 25% of all the table food and 40% of all the vegetables and fruits consumed in the United States are grown, irrigation and chemical fertilization are causing a significant salt build-up. This fertile valley is in the initial stages of turning into a desert similar to the Sahara.

A biointensive, small-scale approach to food production can bypass all of these problems. When organic matter is recycled back to the soil, its texture and microbiotic life are improved. Such soil soaks up water like a sponge and holds it where it is accessible to the plants. The biointensive techniques being researched at Ecology Action use 1/3 to 1/16 the water to produce the same amount of food as commercial agriculture. Currently, agriculture uses 80% of the nation's water, and shortages of clean water are expected in the mid-1980s. Furthermore, while most agricultural systems deplete the soil, studies of test bed soil by University of California soil scientists show that the biodynamic/French intensive system may actually build up the soil. This potential for reclaiming marginal land and desert areas would be an exciting advantage.

Small Scale Efficiency

The claim is made that an organic agriculture is not viable today. It is claimed that the modern American farmer feeds himself and 70 others. The next time you hear this statement, two elements need to be considered. First, our food is produced at a tremendous energy loss. Including the fertilizer and pesticide used, and oil and gasoline to run the various pieces of farm equipment, the modern wheat farmer uses 8 calories of energy to produce 1 calorie of food. Part of this energy cost comes from making the wheat into bread, transporting it to market, packaging and so on. Second, the number of people who process, package, transport and sell our food, as well as those involved in manufacturing, transporting and selling seeds, fertilizer, pesticides and farm equipment, swells the number of people involved in the food industry to approximately 1 in 4. Taken as a whole then, one person in the food industry feeds him- or herself and *three* others. The increasing cost of petroleum-based energy will soon make mechanized agriculture economically unviable in most of the world's countries. During mid-1980, the U.S. Department of Agriculture released a study showing that in an age of fuel scarcity, organic approaches look increasingly important.

Small-scale agriculture produces more food per acre because it can afford to recycle nutriments and enrich the soil. Modern U.S. agriculture feeds at most two people from one acre given current U.S. diets, while biointensive farming would be able to feed at least 7.5 people per acre assuming the same diets. Sim van der Ryn, formerly Director of the California Office of Appropriate Technology, has estimated that, if the biointensive yields can be maintained, all the food in the U.S. could be grown on our 19 million acres of lawn. So building the health of ourselves and the environment can truly begin in our backyards!

Diversity

An important but sometimes overlooked advantage of a small-scale food production system and especially a backyard approach is that it can encourage and preserve genetic diversity in plants. Increasingly vast acreages are planted to just one crop, and only to the "best" variety of that crop. As the genetic base narrows, our food crops are more vulnerable to disasters such as the potato famine in Ireland or the spread of wheat stem rust in 1954. Immune varieties are used to breed resistances into future crops, but fewer and fewer of these potentially valuable varieties are grown.

Many of these "heirloom" seeds may not be valuable for agricultural interests but do have important characteristics for backyard gardeners and small farmers. At Ecology Action we have been experimenting with an "Early Stone Age Wheat," seeds of which go back thousands of years. This wheat produces up to 96 seed heads and high yields per plant with less water consumption. It also possesses a protein content of 18.3%, whereas modern wheats possess a much lower average protein content.

The Most Important Art

In a very real sense, the preservation of our earth starts in our backyard! We help keep alive important plant varieties, build the soil, conserve water, reduce energy needs, and increase human health and stability with a personally caring approach.

... ere long the most valuable of all arts will be the art of deriving a comfortable subsistence from the smallest area of soil. No community whose every member possesses this art can ever be the victim of oppression in any of its forms.

ABRAHAM LINCOLN, 1859

2

Mini-Farming

A practical guide to becoming more economically independent on a small holding

We need to re-orient our minds, and remember three basic things about the soil, the land, the country-side. The first is the fact that it is our home, and that our mental and physical well-being is dependent on its condition. The second is that it is our only source of food... And the third... is that we're stuck with this world for a long time...

E. F. SCHUMACHER

Maps can be useful things to have. They explain such things as the lay of the land, or the movement of the stars. They can tell you how far you are from Main Street or how close to Long Swamp, Pennsylvania. Maps indicate the depth of an ocean, the direction of a current. Some maps have even led people to buried treasure.

The accuracy of a map rests with the mapmaker's ability to adequately convey the area being represented. But even the most accurate chart is useless unless those acquiring it are able to read it, to understand what is depicted and what all the lines and figures mean. And the map itself becomes inaccurate if the reality it depicts changes... whether it is something as minor as the change of a street name, or as major as an earthquake or volcanic eruption.

We would like you to consider this chapter as a kind of map with the broad outlines depicted and many details yet to be added. The outline is one of the world as it is now in terms of resource and environmental problems. It also shows how these "boundaries" may change in the future. Included are ideas and suggestions on how to begin mini-farming which will enable you to begin charting your path on the world map.

This chapter, then, is written for new pioneers who are beginning to take on the responsibility of sustaining the world for ourselves, our families and communities, and for the generations which, hopefully will follow. As the late Dr. E. F. Schumacher has said, it is time to "inform ourselves, support others, and initiate changes in our own lives... to dream, to think, and to act."

Ecology Action's primary aim has always been to research and test the parameters of the biodynamic/ French intensive method of farming — to find out just how much can be grown in a limited space, while measuring the inputs and the effects on the soil. One branch of the research that became a major undertaking was the mini-farming project. We wanted to establish how much land it would take to provide a living income—or to provide all one's food needs—in other words, to be totally self-sufficient.

We developed a mini-farming scenario in which it might be possible for one person to make $5,000 to $20,000 net per year (based on wholesale prices) on only 1/8 of an acre (including paths), working 40 hours per week for 8 months, and then taking a 4-month vacation. Having established this scenario, we then set up various projects to see if it could be done, and how to best go about doing it. One of the crops we tested as a cash crop was cucumbers. The results of that series of tests are well-documented in our first mini-series booklet *Cucumber Bonanza.*

We also began testing for "complete diet mini-farming." Our estimate for the smallest potential area needed to grow one's food is 2,800 square feet in a 4-month growing season; and 1,400 square feet in an 8-month growing season. This assumes a 2,500 calorie diet containing 37 to 65 grams of protein and 800 mgs. of calcium. If a 400 mg. daily calcium intake is assumed instead (as many nutritionists indicate is adequate) the total areas required for complete diet growing may be reduced 25% to 50%. A 25% reduction is possible since approximately that area is required to grow the 400 mg. of calcium not eaten. Another 25% reduction in area may be possible, if higher yielding, calcium concentrating plants low in oxalic acid are used. Collards are one example. Collards produce 6 to 8 times the calcium yield and the same amount of protein yield per unit of area compared to milk produced from fodder grown on an area of the same size. Therefore, a complete diet may eventually be grown on as little as 1,400 square feet in a 4-month growing season, or 700 square feet in an 8-month growing season.

The mini-farm project came to a temporary end when we lost our original Common Ground garden site, but in 8 years' time we had learned a great deal. Later sections of this chapter will detail much of that experience.

Many people have been concerned that we not make these projections at this time because:

Ecology Action has some time to go *before actually operating* a successful economic mini-farm.

The many failures incurred during the initial testing period call into question projections based upon the successes.

Economic mini-farming when fully developed may not work as well as these projections.

However, we feel it is important to share the evaluations at this time because, considering world food and resource shortages, it would not be responsible to withhold information about the biointensive mini-farming potential.

We have begun again at a new site in northern California, and wish to encourage others to consider mini-farming, too. We feel that small-scale farming holds great promise for feeding the world in the future, particularly in light of the increasing number of problems commercial agriculture faces at this time.

Problems Inherent In Current Agricultural Practices

Former secretary of Agriculture Robert Bergland was asked on "Face the Nation" in November, 1978: "Can we continue our present *energy* and chemical intensive agricultural production without eventually wearing out our resources?" His answer was that we cannot, that we are:

on a collision course with disaster, in that context. Our water supplies are being reduced; we have whole watersheds where the ground reserves are being depleted; and we have mined our soil. In fact, the erosion of America's farm land today is probably at a record rate, and this simply cannot go on.

USDA Agricultural Research Administrator Terry Kinney also noted that "if we continue with conventional agriculture, we are going to lose our soils, our water supply, our resource base."

The statistics are indeed alarming. *Population pressures, high levels of resource consumption, economic demands, and non-optimal agriculture practices* are using up increasingly larger quantities of land and materials. Previously, in the United States and elsewhere, land made less productive could be abandoned for newer, more fertile areas. Today, there are fewer, if any, new places to relocate. A recent United Nations' study indicates that by the year 2000 about one-third of the world's present agricultural land will probably be changed into desert if current land management practices remain unchanged. (Only about 10.5% of the earth's land surface is agricultural land.) It can also be inferred from U.N. data that up to 90% of Third World agricultural land may not be farmable by the year 2000 due to desertification, salinization, urbanization, suburbanization, deforestation, and poor agricultural land practices. If this loss occurs, the 80% of the world's population living in those areas would only have one-half the farmland necessary to grow their food (even assuming the high yields obtained by Japanese commercial agriculture with its high energy, water, fertilizer, and special seed inputs).

Let's take a look at some of the facts and figures:

☐ In 1978, 14.7 million people died from starvation or malnutrition-caused diseases. In 1981, this figure climbed to 21.2 million people — an increase of 44%. This figure may well go higher as the world population increases, as food supplies dwindle, and as production becomes more tenuous.

☐ The current farming picture in the United States is one of fewer and fewer farmers working less and less land. While the annual production has not suffered in the short run, the situation is less clear for the future. The average age of the U.S. farmer is about 57... near retirement age. Few young people choose to become farmers and with good reason. The average on-farm income in 1979 was $12,600 from 300 acres of land with over $300,000 capital investment required to begin. Given that it is a job that requires a good deal of skill and work, it is not surprising that farming attracts few people.

☐ Modern commercial farming methods produce remarkable results, it is true, but this so-called "Green Revolution" is highly mechanized, depends on heavy use of chemical fertilizers, pesticides, water and special seeds. Increasing energy costs are making the "Green Revolution" no longer cost-effective in many areas. Commercial farming techniques utilize energy inputs equal to the amount of energy tied up in plant photosynthesis on the same commercial croplands. This is an amazing amount of energy, and means 6 calories of energy (or more) are needed to produce 1 calorie of food. If the whole world produced, marketed, and consumed food as we do in the U.S., by the year 2000 it would take 2-1/2 times the present *total* world energy consumption just to keep the food-supplying process going.

Figure 3. Losing Ground. From the 1977 United Nations State of the World Environment Report.

The world's soil loss by erosion in the last 100 years (estimated).

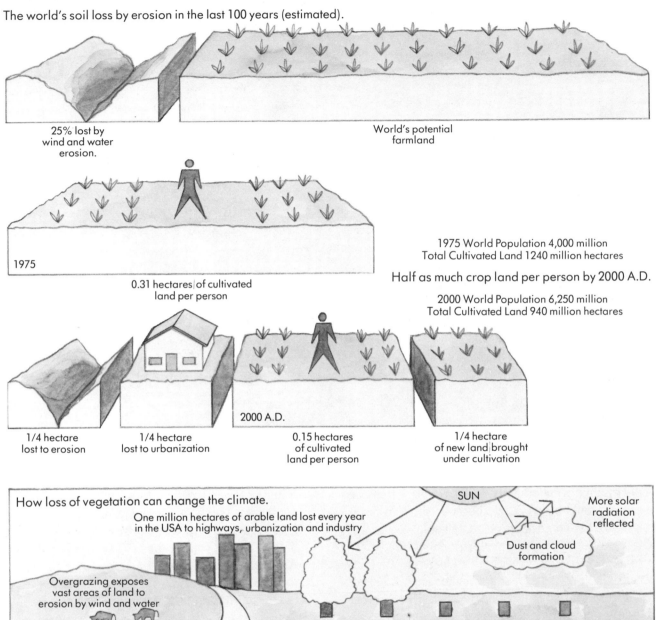

25% lost by
wind and water
erosion.

World's potential
farmland

1975

0.31 hectares of cultivated
land per person

1975 World Population 4,000 million
Total Cultivated Land 1240 million hectares

Half as much crop land per person by 2000 A.D.

2000 World Population 6,250 million
Total Cultivated Land 940 million hectares

1/4 hectare
lost to erosion

1/4 hectare
lost to urbanization

2000 A.D.

0.15 hectares
of cultivated
land per person

1/4 hectare
of new land brought
under cultivation

How loss of vegetation can change the climate.

One million hectares of arable land lost every year
in the USA to highways, urbanization and industry

SUN

More solar
radiation
reflected

Dust and cloud
formation

Overgrazing exposes
vast areas of land to
erosion by wind and water

Cutting down trees leaves soil
exposed to wind and water erosion

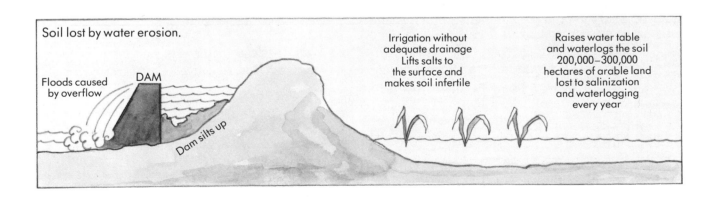

Soil lost by water erosion.

Floods caused
by overflow

DAM

Dam silts up

Irrigation without
adequate drainage
Lifts salts to
the surface and
makes soil infertile

Raises water table
and waterlogs the soil
200,000–300,000
hectares of arable land
lost to salinization
and waterlogging
every year

☐ Even if we could afford to maintain such high energy inputs indefinitely, it is doubtful that the results would be worth it, because modern farming methods do not appear sustainable. In the last 30 years, commercial *fertilizer* inputs have increased over tenfold without a corresponding increase in yield. The need for higher applications of fertilizers is probably connected with the fact that commercial farming techniques have a destructive effect on the condition of the soil. It is estimated that the farm soils in the United States are being depleted 8 times faster than they are being built up naturally, and that 34% of the U.S. croplands are declining in productivity from excessive topsoil loss. According to a state study, California farm soils are being depleted 20 to 80 times faster than the natural building process. In fact, the San Joaquin Valley, where 25% of the total food and 40% of the fruits and vegetables consumed in the United States are grown, is in the early stages of desertification.

☐ Farmland is being lost in another way — through *urbanization.* According to a recent government report,[1] the U.S. is losing prime farmland and other farmland to urbanization and non-agricultural conversion such as shopping malls, parking lots and roads at the rate of one square mile every two hours. As the report says, "Ten years from now, Americans could be as concerned over the loss of the nation's prime farmlands as they are today over the shortages of oil and gasoline." Ecology Action can attest to this fact. After over eight years of growing and testing, we lost the lease on our test garden site in Palo Alto in 1980, and we were forced into a temporary halt. The land was needed for a parking lot.

☐ *Water* — clean water — is becoming an increasingly precious resource. Commercial agricultural

---

[1] Shirley Foster Fields, *Where Have the Farm Lands Gone,* National Agricultural Lands Study, U.S. Govt. Printing Office, Washington D.C., 1979 (Fourth Printing: January, 1981), p. 8 and cover. Other non-governmental studies including all farm land loss including that due to suburbanization and poor agricultural practices put the figure as high as 3 square miles every 2 hours.

practices use large amounts—about 20 gallons per 100 square feet per day or double the average use under biointensive methods. In fact, agriculture in the U.S. consumes 80% of the nation's water. Heavy water use combined with increased use of chemical fertilizers and pesticides has often led to the harming of remaining fresh water supplies through polluted runoff. In some areas, water has been pumped out of underground reservoirs to the point of exhausting the supply. In other areas the pumping has actually caused the land to sink as much as 20 feet and sometimes crack. Some other examples of the water situation are:

- One part of the United States Midwestern Region rests on top of a great underground reservoir. Currently, this Ogallala Aquifer is being pumped out from western Nebraska to northern Texas at the rate of 48 inches annually, while rain is only replenishing it at the rate of one quarter inch per year.

- 50,000 pounds of water (6,250 gallons) are required to "grow" 1 pound of meat eaten in the U.S.

- In the Third World, women often spend much of their day just obtaining water.

☐ Another major problem that needs to be addressed is *deforestation*. In the last 25 years, 50% of the world's forests have been cut down. According to a study sponsored by the Rockefeller Foundation, if we continue cutting at this rate, the remaining 50% could disappear in the next 40 years.

These lost forests pose several problems. Nutriments brought up from the deep subsoils into the trees' leaves and then dropped to enrich the soils are no longer present. The soil micro-climate created by the trees' shade, leaf mulch, and roots is lost, resulting in erosion from wind and rain. Water tables drop without the trees' transpiration, and there is a subsequent loss of easy water access. Important reserves of fuel and building materials disappear. Lastly, one-third of the world's people experience a different kind of energy crisis—not enough firewood. (Half of the world's people still depend on wood for two of their most basic needs: cooking their food and heating their homes.) After spending 4 to 6 hours searching for wood and brush, children return home where their families must often burn animal manures (as well as the wood they have found) to cook food and, perhaps, heat their home. Manures would be better utilized as fertilizer to nourish crops and as a source of organic matter for the soil.

The Need for Small-Scale Biological Farming

The United States Department of Agriculture and other researchers recently issued reports on organic farming. Comparative studies have shown organic farming to be economically competitive and more energy conserving than similarly sized chemically oriented farms.

The U.S. Senate Subcommittee on Practice and Procedure, Committee on Judiciary, noted with in-

terest late in 1977 a memo written by the head of the Farmer's Home Administration (FHA) and endorsed by USDA's Assistant Secretary for Rural Development, Alex Mercure:

Because of an imminent scarcity and eventual exhaustion of our national resources, particularly fossil fuels, there is some concern for the heavy reliance by American agriculture on inorganic fertilizers and chemical pesticides, both largly petroleum based... We recognize the (1) low energy intensiveness, (2) low potential for environmental damage, and (3) the feasibility of the producer to shift to conventional methods, as advantages of organic farming.

There is a *paucity* of experimental results and economic studies related to organic farming versus conventional (sic!) farming. Recent experience in California in the use of natural methods of insect control has been *very successful.* A study of organic farming in the Cornbelt States, although somewhat limited and qualitative, indicates that further research is warranted into organic methods of crop production as well as alternatives that lie between the conventional and organic methods.

Based on the California experience and the Cornbelt studies we consider organic methods of farming to be *viable* where supported by experimental results, proven to be *practical* by a number of operators in the area, and where the *cost is competitive* with alternative methods. [Emphasis added.]

At the international farm level, it has long been recognized that small-scale farming is more productive per unit of area than large-scale agriculture. Sterling Wortman of the Rockefeller Foundation observed in 1976 that:

... most large-scale mechanized agriculture is less productive per unit area than small-scale farming can be. The farmer on a small holding can engage in intensive, high-yield "gardening" systems such as intercropping (planting more than one crop in the same field, perhaps in alternative rows), multiple cropping (planting several crops in succession, up to four a year in some places), relay planting (sowing a second crop between the rows of an earlier, maturing crop) or other techniques that require attention to individual plants...

In October 1976, the U.S. League for International Food Education (L.I.F.E.) held a workshop for biointensive practitioners, agronomists, and private overseas volunteer organizations, such as CARE. The topic was "Improving the Nutrition of the Most Economically Disadvantaged Families."

At the end of the workshop, key members of the American Society of Agronomy issued a statement supporting the applicability and dissemination of biointensive small garden technology and low resource agriculture. It also recommended that "members of the scientific disciplines become involved in these efforts" and that A.S.A. members in particular become more involved. Home gardeners have important applications for biointensive techniques as well. Sim Van der Ryn, former California Director for Alternative Technology, noted:

The prevalent suburban pattern in the United States could be easily adapted to save even more energy, by being converted to intensive garden production... The 19 million acres of suburban lawns in this country are major consumers of pesticides and fertilizers; if they were converted to mini-farms, they could... feed this country!

Working together, we can all make a difference.

Biointensive Mini-Farming

It is clear that the deterioration of the world's natural resources is becoming increasingly critical as the world populaton rises. Ecology Action strongly believes that biointensive farming, with its emphasis on small growing area, low resource consumption, and sustainability with higher yields than commercial agriculture can be a solution to the problems discussed here. It is a personalized approach to food-raising, a living system which works to give the plants an optimum environment in which to grow and prosper. Approaching farming as a living system of relationships (of which each of us is an integral part) is a nurturing experience rewarded through bountiful yields. Ecology Action does not purport that mini-farming will provide "instant" results. Experience is necessary for good results — experience, knowledge, and understanding.

Many, who have never had the opportunity to work with Nature and who live in a world of instant results, have difficulty comprehending the many years it takes to develop the sustainable mini-farming system presented in this book. The need for patience cannot be overemphasized, however. As a living system, it is different from an instant cereal or a computer kit. Any farmer takes years to feel competent with his or her farm. Although mini-farming, compared to traditional agriculture, is done on a small scale, is easier to master, and uses considerably fewer resources (per unit of food produced) it will still take 3 to 5 years to build up one's soil and skill (usually 4 to 5). Understanding that is of paramount importance when beginning.

Step-By-Step Mini-Farming

STEP 1. *Paper Research and Review.* The first thing to do is to make a preliminary assessment of potential cash crops. Use market reports (the address can be obtained through your county agriculture agent), survey your area for potential buyers (local restaurants, produce stands, markets, shops, and so on), check the data in *How to Grow More Vegetables,* and in other sections of this book, especially the planning calendars. In particular:

In examining potential crops for a basic mini-farm, Ecology Action looked at many things, including: the average wholesale prices per month per crop; marketing potential for a particular crop; getting a head-start (or extending a season) with the use of inexpensive mini-greenhouses; and specialty items, such as true Roman Camomile for seed, flowers, leeks, herb seedlings, dried herbs, Christmas plants, and the like. We suggest that the beginning mini-farmer grow the everyday vegetables with which we are all familiar.

The important questions in developing a mini-farm scenario are:

☐ How long does it take to prepare and maintain a bed?

☐ What is the cost of the bed in terms of purchased fertilizer, seeds and water?

☐ What is the harvesting and marketing time involved?

☐ How long is a particular crop in a bed before it starts producing?

☐ How soon will that bed be finished harvesting so another crop can be started?

☐ What is the yield of a particular crop?

☐ How much money will a crop bring in?

In addition, there is this question:

☐ How do you make the work you do interesting, varied and fun? (Radishes, for example, have the potential of bringing in $2,000 per month by using "the method." But who wants to be saddled with the boredom of growing, tending, harvesting, and marketing over 170,000 radishes every month!)

We believe that such crops as garlic, cucumbers, red-leaf lettuce, Romaine lettuce, zucchini, green bunching onions (scallions) and perhaps tomatoes will give a substantial return. Parsley returns a reasonable amount of money per square foot, but when the time is factored in for harvesting and bunching, it does not appear to be that profitable. Actually, the only way to determine profitability is to grow the crop, which is one reason why a 3 to 5 year learning period is important in mini-farming.

One thing we do *not* encourage is the growing of only one type of crop. This would then simply be a small-scale version of mono-cropping and you will encounter many of the problems which large-scale mono-cropping brings. Diversity is the key to a successful mini-farm.

The problem of mono-cropping dependence is underscored by the experience of a farmer who was having numerous difficulties with his 600-acre farm —not the least of which was a ketchup company's threat to not purchase his 300 acres of tomatoes. The farmer had reduced the number of pesticide sprays on the fields from 10 to 6. But a random sample by the company had found a few more worms in his tomatoes than was considered normal. At 20 tons per acre, the farmer was facing the nightmarish possibility of having to dispose of 12 million pounds of tomatoes! His income for the past 3 years had averaged only $8,000 per year and he was very much in debt. When it was suggested that he consider growing things other than tomatoes, he told the story which is repeated by many farmers — his investment in tomato production equipment was so big, that he was no longer free to do anything *but* grow tomatoes.

Growing several different crops on a mini-farm makes it more desirable for buyers to come pick up from you, since you can supply them with all or a large part of their needs. The data in Table 7 (beginning on page 30) show incomes which may be possible if an entire mini-farm is grown in one crop for comparative purposes only. A mix of vegetables will give you a more cost-effective mini-farm and the diversity can help balance out single-crop price fluctuations in the market place.

One workable combination might be 2 months of transplanted Romaine lettuce grown under mini-greenhouses in March and April; followed by 3 months of transplanted cucumbers — using mini-greenhouses in the last month or so, followed by 4 months of a cover crop when possible.

Even better would be a more diverse cropping during each month of the 8-month season. Forty beds of radishes or lettuce will probably be harder to market at one time than a mixture of crops — and single-cropping risks an insect or disease infestation which can destroy an entire crop.

STEP 2. *Make a Long Range Plan.* A 10-year plan for one farmer working a 40-hour week in an 8-month growing season is given in Table 4. (It would also apply to a family mini-farm operated by a couple working 20 hours a week each, or full time each in a 4-month growing season with twice the land.)

Using this table as a guideline, make your own plan based on your own situation, feelings and expectations. It is a good idea to put this down on paper, even though it may seem impossible at first to make meaningful projections. It will help you to see how mini-farming will fit into your life, to plan ahead, and to focus your efforts. It will also help you to measure your successes or failures so you can adjust your expectations more realistically and alter your plans as you progress.

As you can see in the chart, you might be earning $5,000 to $6,000 by the 5th year of running a mini-farm. (A diversified 1/8 acre vegetable mini-farm is capable, when fully developed and run by skilled people, of providing all the vegetables and soft fruits — about 322 pounds per person in a 6-month growing period — for 40 people for one year.) During the initial period, you should keep your present job. Do not plunge recklessly into a new career before finding out whether or not you will feel comfortable in this new pursuit. Working another job will make you no different from the typical farmer: 40% of the average commercial U.S. farmer's *total* income is derived from off-farm work.

Be sure to make an assessment of just how much

Table 4. Developmental plan for 1/8 acre mini-farm (5' x 20' beds plus path space, mixed vegetables).

Year	Number of Beds	Planting and Considerations	Possible Income Ranges
1	5	1 bed red-leaf lettuce; 1 bed garlic; and 3 beds spinach — to be followed by 1 bed each cherry tomatoes, zucchini, and cucumbers	Negligible
2	10	Best crops for you according to your experience	Negligible
3	20	Begin to think about mini-farming and marketing	$2,000
4	30	Plan a mini-farm and consider changing your regular job to part-time hours	up to $4,000
5	40	Become a full-time mini-farmer	$5,000–6,000
6	40	" " "	$6,000–7,500
7	40	" " "	$7,500–10,000
8	40	" " "	$7,500–15,000[1]
9	40	" " "	$10,000–17,500
10	40	" " "	$10,000–20,000

1. Over $10,000 will probably involve special direct marketing and/or a vegetable stand retail sales approach — and/or marketing crops in the best weeks/months for highest prices — and/or off-season crop growing when prices are high using mini-greenhouses and mini-shadehouses.

money you need to live on in a year's time. Your budget will enable you and your family to make realistic plans. A tentative breakdown for an annual $2,500 to $3,000 per person simple living budget is given in Table 5. This budget will seem low for many people, but can serve as a reference point for planning.

STEP 3. *Plant the crops your paper research shows to be profitable.* Order seeds, prepare the planting beds, and plant seeds in flats, or directly in beds. Keep accurate records of all that you do. (See sample data log and harvesting record on page 29.)

You will especially want to monitor:

☐ the time spent planting, watering, and harvesting each bed, as these factors vary from crop to crop. Digging and weeding time should also be included, but will be about the same for various crops.

☐ the yield of your bed compared to the yields in Table 7. Those crops particularly suited to your climate and soil may do better than Ecology Action's projections. On the other hand, you may have trouble with a particular class of crops, e.g. root crops in a very rocky soil or cabbage family members in a hot weather region.

☐ the harvesting schedule. Can you predict when crops will be most effectively and economically marketable and in what quantities? This will be important in contracting to sell your produce.

☐ any unforeseen problems or bonuses, such as insect damage, or an especially lucrative market for seedlings, potted Christmas plants, or dried herbs and flowers.

If you feel you want to continue, and the results warrant it, by the end of the third year you may consider working your present job only part-time. You will have enough to do developing relationships in marketing and tending 30 beds. Marketing is a skill in itself which you, as an independent agent, will have to develop for economic viability and survival once you begin to reduce the connection with your present job.

STEP 4. *Develop a good and workable marketing strategy.* Ecology Action's experience with the first year mini-farm was surprising to some. Digging the beds actually took less time than we expected. The most time-consuming garden chores were watering, harvesting, and marketing. Overall, about half the time was spent on marketing and we were quite frustrated with the time and gasoline it took to harvest, arrange (by bundling or packing in boxes), coordinate with buyers, deliver, collect payment and complete all the other marketing procedures. The growing often

Table 5. Four-Person Sophisticated, Low-Technology Budget. Expenses are in U.S. Dollars. Blanks have been provided for you to determine your own budget.

Category	Yearly Expense	Your Expense
Rent	$ 0[1]	_____
Land Taxes	300	_____
Utilities	150	_____
Phone	120	_____
Food	2400[2]	_____
Fodder	560	_____
Garden Supplies	550	_____
Car Repair Maintenance Insurance	210	_____
Gasoline	320	_____
Pocket Money Entertainment Home Improvement Vacations Birthdays Etcetera	1350	_____
Medical Insurance	1680	_____
Dental	400	_____
Life Insurance	520	_____
Clothing	300	_____
Memberships Subscriptions School Supplies Church Other	600	_____
Credit Card	0	_____
Total	$9460 Per Person $2365	_____

1. Assumes rural land already owned.
2. Assumes purchase of most food during the first years while the soil is being built up and while everyone is getting settled.

turned out to be the easier half of the job! The key is to sell *all* the produce and to sell it *fast* (since you do not have hydro-coolers and other expensive storage equipment). Certain vegetables, such as garlic and potatoes, will store better and require less frequent marketing, which can be a real advantage.

Also check into applicable marketing and packaging regulations. These are available through your county agriculture agent. Sorting and packaging regulations

Keeping Records

It is a good idea for all gardeners to keep records of what happens throughout the year in their gardens—what fertilizers have been added, when seeds were planted, what yields were, problems that have come up, and so on. For the mini-farmer, keeping good records is almost essential. To be economically successful, you cannot rely on memory or guesswork. You need to know what worked and what did not so you can plan ahead, and avoid misfortune.

Following are some samples of records Ecology Action kept when it tested cucumbers as a cash crop, and one type of "data log" which you may find useful. You will find many more data logs in Chapter Three, and at the end of the book are 12 planning calendars and monthly logs. We hope you will use these materials, or devise and use your own. A few moments taken to jot down a note or figure today may make a significant difference in what you experience and learn a year or two from now. Keeping records for several years in a row will allow you to monitor your progress and your soil's improvement.

CALCULATING TIME, EXPENSE, AND PROFIT

It is good to keep track of time and money spent in growing and marketing a crop, and of the income from its sale. This will help you decide whether it is worthwhile for you to keep that crop in your mini-farm scenario. The following shows Ecology Action's calculations for six beds of cucumbers grown in 1979. (Note: Average pounds for the six beds are based *only* on those cukes that were truly marketable. The beds actually produced more than the figures indicate.)

TIME:

BED PREPARATION (U-Bar, shape, adding compost and fertilizer)	2 hours
FLAT TIME (Sift compost, mix soil, plant, and water)	1/2 hour
TRANSPLANTING SEEDLINGS	1 hour
WATERING	5 hours
HARVESTING	3 hours
MARKETING	1/2 hours*
COMPOST MAKING	1 hour*
WEEDING	negligible (in established beds)
	13 hours

EXPENSE:

FERTILIZER COST $2.50

COST OF SEED 50

COST OF WATER 1.00

GAS FOR MARKETING/CAR MAINTENANCE 75*

$4.75

PROFIT:

355.8 lbs. average/bed

$\times$ 22¢ average wholesale price/lb.

$78.28 per bed

− 4.75 costs of production

$73.43 profit per bed for an average of *15-1/2 weeks* in-ground time

* Pro-rated with regard to 40 mini-farm beds

---

can be expensive and time-consuming, but a careful reading may suggest easier approaches. For example, in some areas, potatoes marketed in units above 100 pounds do not fall within special sorting and packaging requirements, so a 101-pound bag might be considered. Direct marketing can sometimes be done without undue sorting and the simple containers involved can be continuously recycled between you and the buyer. This will save considerable expense.

A few places to think about and explore further are:

☐ Organic wholesalers who can pick up produce at your site

☐ Groceries and restaurants

☐ Vegetable stands — including starting your own, although this requires more staff and can quickly use up the profit margin

☐ A 'Pick Your Own' farm

☐ Selling at a local Farmer's Market once or twice a week

☐ A local delivery route

☐ A cooperative with other mini-farmers and/or a direct marketing cooperative grocery store

Marketing strategies may often determine which crops are grown. The key factor to consider is which strategy requires the least amount of time. Direct marketing through farmer's markets, roadside stands, local delivery routes, or wholesale marketing through local restaurants, small grocers, and health food stores increases the price you receive for your produce. Try to minimize the time spent marketing, however, or the income you earn per hour may soon be cut in half.

STEP 5. *By the fifth year, you should be able to decide, once and for all, whether a commitment to mini-farming is your cup of tea.* It is at this time that you must decide whether the security of a regular job, a Nobel Prize, and so on, are more important to you than raising quality food for your immediate community.

You must remember that the amount of money you make as a full-time mini-farmer is entirely dependent on: whether your soil is in good shape, how skilled you have become, your yield histories, and whether you have thoroughly examined your marketing potential. The income ranges given in Table 1 are indicative of just how well you may do. But make sure by

Table 6. Cumulative Harvest Record for Cucumbers: An Example of Cumulative Record-keeping.

Year	Bed Name	Date Planted	Weeks to Harvest	Begin Harvest	Weeks of Harvest	Total Time in ground (Weeks)	(lbs.)	Weekly Yield During Harvest (average) (lbs.)	Weekly Yield In-Ground Time (average) (lbs.)
1973	Hummingbird 8	7/2/73	9	9/23/73	7	16	153	21.8	9.5
1973	River-Run 4	6/23/73	9	8/30/73	6	15	140	23.3	9.3
1974	Hummingbird 12	4/10/74	12	7/3/74	12	24	353	29.4	13.9
1975	Hummingbird 18	5/24/75	7	7/16/79	11	19	298	27.9	15.7
1979	Sun-Ray 14	4/21/79	11	7/7/79	7	18	382	54.6	21.2
1979	River-Run 3	4/27/79	10½	7/9/79	6	16½	268	44.7	16.2
1979	River-Run 6	5/5/79	9½	7/9/79	7	16½	297	42.4	18.0
1979	Hummingbird 5	5/21/79	7	7/10/79	7	14	404	57.7	28.9
1979	River-Run 9	5/21/79	7	7/10/79	7	14	391	55.9	27.9
1979	River-Run 16	5/21/79	7	7/9/79	7	14	393	56.1	28.0

analyzing your market prices and actual marketing agreements with people. Finally, determine whether or not the income you are going to make per year, month, week, and hour, plus the pace of the work involved meet your personal needs.

The vegetables given for Year One are those that Ecology Action has found to be some of the easier ones to grow and market with a good dollar return for hours worked once one is skilled and has good soil. You may, however, decide to grow others—perhaps your area has a market for bok choy, leeks, or parsley. This is all up to you, but for the first years, we suggest you grow things that you yourself like to eat and phase in other items as you become more experienced and your soil improves. (See Table 7 for more detailed marketing/income information.)

STEP 6. *Increase your income potential by developing new strategies.* Some possibilities to consider:

☐ Extend the season with greenhouses, shade-houses, and/or other tools. Crops grown during the off-season often command a higher price.

☐ Grow specialty crops such as shallots, sweet basil, dill, and luffa sponges.

☐ Grow for special markets such as gourmet restaurants or people especially allergic to pesticides.

☐ Process the crop into a higher-priced, value-added product, such as dried fruits and vegetables, home-made jams, flower garlands, or develop a catering service. As one example, three women in Santa Cruz, California have created an enviable livelihood growing and arranging flowers for weddings and other special occasions. They coordinate subtle colors, fragrances, and meanings into their homemade arrangements.

Off-season growing can increase your income markedly. Bringing an item to market one or two weeks before other growers and getting the jump on the season is something to consider after a few years of mini-farming. For this reason, you should keep records of your planting dates, the time crops are in the beds before harvest, and the number of weeks they are harvested—in addition to the yields and prices obtained.

Another way you may increase income is by growing more than one crop of a specific vegetable in an 8-month period when normally the climate would allow the growth of only one crop. This can be done with various kinds of miniature greenhouses, bird-netting houses, and shade-netting houses which protectively drop over the growing beds (see Resource Guide, page 190, for more information). For example, late spring cantaloupes might be grown under a mini-greenhouse, and summer spinach under a shade-netting house.

Crop Income Potential per 1/8 Acre

Table 7 will give you some idea of what crops will be most cost-effective to grow, and help you make long-range plans. The table gives projected yields per 1/8 acre for many commonly grown crops, and the

DATA LOG. You may want to use the chart on this page to organize the data from your own garden. Performed several years in a row, this will allow you to monitor your soil's improvement. You can enlarge this chart to include time spent per crop, costs, water use, and so on.

Bed No.	Year	Crop, Name, & Source	Fertilizers & Compost or Manure (Amt.)	Date Planted	Begin Harvest (Date)	End Harvest (Date)	Total In-ground Time	Yield

Daily Harvest Amounts. (**Lbs.** or **Kgs.** — circle one). The spaces are divided into weeklong segments. The first box should correspond to the date in the 'Begin Harvest' space above. Remember to put an X in a box if you did not harvest on that day.

Sun	Mon	Tues	Wed	Thurs	Fri	Sat	Total

Table 7. Crop income potential per 1/8 acre in mini-farming and in regular agriculture with selected yields.

	General Data (A–C)		Bio-Intensive Mini-Farming Figures for Beginning, Good, and Excellent					
A	B	C	D	E	F	G	H	I
Crop	Growth Period in months / No. of crops[1] per 8 months	1978[2] S.F. whsl. $/lb. average / $/lb. range	Beginning[9] mini-farming yield in lbs. per 1/8 acre / Approx. plant yield—averaged[z]	$ Income[10] per 1/8 acre per crop average / Range	$ Income[11] per 1/8 yield 8 months average / Range	Good[9] Mini-farmer acre per in lbs. per 1/8 acre / Approx. plant yield—averaged[z]	$ Income[12] per 1/8 yield crop average / Range	$ Income[13] per 1/8 acre per 8 months average / Range
Artichoke, Jerusalem	4-6 / 1	DNYA	4000 / 20.8 oz.	DNYA		8240 / 41.6 oz.	DNYA	
Artichoke, Globe	2 / 1	.516 / .244–.888	DNYA	DNYA				
Asparagus	2 / 1	.755 / .469–1.75	380 / 1.25 oz.	$286 / $178–665	$286 / $178–665	760 / 2.4 oz.	$572 / $356–1330	$572 / $356–1330
Beans, Broad (Dry)	3–6 / 1	DNYA	200 / 1/3 oz.	DNYA		360 / 1/2 oz.	DNYA	
Beans, Bush Lima	4–6 / 1	DNYA	460 / 1/3 oz.	DNYA		688 / 3/5 oz.	DNYA	
Beans, Pole Lima	4–6 / 1	DNYA	460 / 3/4 oz.	DNYA		688 / 3/5 oz.	DNYA	
Beans, Snap Bush	3–5 / 1	.443 / .18–.78	1200 / 2/5 oz.	$531 / $216–936	$531 / $216–936	2880 / 1 oz.	$1275 / $518–2246	$1275 / $518–2246
Beans, Snap Pole	3–5 / 1	.443 / .18–.78	1200 / 1 oz.	$531 / $216–936	$531 / $216–936	2880 / 2 oz.	$1275 / $518–2246	$1275 / $518–2246
Beets, Cylindra (with tops)	2 / 4	.132 / .116–.15	4400 / 1 oz.	$580 / $510–660	$2320 / NA	8800 / 2 oz.	$1160 / $1020–1320	$4640 / NA
Beets, Regular (with tops)	2 / 4	.132 / .116–.15	2200 / 1/2 oz.	$290 / $255–330	$1160 / NA	4400 / 1 oz.	$580 / $510–660	$2320 / NA
Broccoli	2–4 / 2	.339 / .255–.465	1040 / 5.33 oz.	$352 / $265–483	$704 / NA	1560 / 8 oz.	$528 / $397–725	$1056 / NA
Brussels Sprouts	3–6 / 1–2	.749 / .666–.80	2840 / 25.6 oz.	$2127 / $1891–2272	$4254 / NA	4240 / 38.4 oz.	$3175 / $2823–3392	$6350 / NA
Chinese Cabbage	2–3 / 3–4	DNYA	3840 / 8.8 oz.	DNYA		7640 / 17.6 oz.	DNYA	
Cabbage, Regular	2–4 / 2–4	.105 / .059–.218	3840 / 19.2 oz.	$403 / $226–837	$806 / NA	7640 / 38.4 oz.	$802 / $450–1665	$1604 / NA

J	K	L	M	N	O	P	Q	R
Excellent[9] mini-farmer yield in lbs. per 1/8 acre	$ Income[14] per 1/8 acre per crop average	$ Income[15] per 1/8 acre per 8 months average	1976[3] average U.S. yield per 1/8 acre	$ Income[4] per 1/8 acre per crop average	$ Income[5] per 1/8 acre per 8 months average	1976[6] 'good U.S. farmer' yield in lbs. per 1/8 acre	$ Income[7] per 1/8 acre per crop average	$ Income[8] per 1/8 acre per 8 months average
Approx. Plant Yield— Averaged[z]	Range	Range		Range	Range		Range	Range
16800	DNYA							
86.4 oz.								
DNYA			950	$490	$490	1900	$980	$980
				$231–843	$231–843		$462–843	$462–843
1520	$1147	$1147	312	$235	$235	624	$470	$470
4.8 oz.	$712–2660	$712–2660		$146–546	$146–546		$292–1092	$292–1092
720	DNYA							
1 oz.								
920	DNYA		312	DNYA		624	DNYA	
3/4 oz.								
920	DNYA		312	DNYA		624	DNYA	
1.33 oz.								
4320	$1913	$1913	462	$204	$204	924	$409	$409
1.6 oz.	$777–3369	$777–3369		$83–360	$83–360		$166–720	$166–720
4320	$1913	$1913	462	$204	$204	924	$409	$409
4 oz.	$777–3369	$777–3369		$83–360	$83–360		$166–720	$166–720
21600	$2851	$11404	3650	$481	$1924	7300	$962	$3848
4.5 oz.	$2505–3240	NA		$423–547	NA		$864–1095	NA
10800	$1425	$5700	1675	$221	$884	3350	$442	$1768
2.25 oz.	$1252–1620	NA		$194–251	NA		$388–502	NA
2120	$718	$1436	1012	$343	$686	2024	$686	$1372
10.9 oz.	$540–985	NA		$258–470	NA		$516–940	NA
5680	$4254	$8508	1500	$1123	$2246	3000	$2246	$4492
51.2 oz.	$3782–4544	NA		$999–1200	NA		$1998–2400	NA
15320	DNYA							
35.2 oz.								
15320	$1608	$3216	2370	$248	$496	4740	$496	$992
78.4 oz.	$903–3339	NA		$139–516	NA		$278–1032	NA

A	B	C	D	E	F	G	H	I
Crop	Growth Period in months	1978[2] S.F. whsl. $/lb. average	Beginning[9] mini-farming yield in lbs. per 1/8 acre	$ Income[10] per 1/8 acre per crop average	$ Income[11] per 1/8 acre per 8 months average	Good[9] Mini-farmer yield in lbs. per 1/8 acre	$ Income[12] per 1/8 acre per crop average	$ Income[13] per 1/8 acre per 8 months average
No. of crops[1] per 8 months		$/lb. range	Approx. plant yield— averaged[z]	Range	Range	Approx. plant yield— averaged[z]	Range	Range
Carrots (without tops)	2–3	.164	4000	$656	$1968	6000	$984	$2952
3		.112–.245	1/3 oz.	$448–980	NA	1/2 oz.	$672–1470	NA
Cauliflower	2–3	.43	1760	$756	$1512	4000	$1720	$3440
2		.30–.70	9 oz.	$528–1383	NA	21 oz.	$1200–2800	NA
Celery	4–5	.166	9600	$1593	$3187	19200	$3183	$6366
2		.112–.272	8 oz.	$1075–2611	NA	16 oz.	$2148–5216	NA
Chard	8	.215	8000	$1720	$1720	16200	$3483	$3483
1		.148–.296	12 oz.	$1184–2368	$1184–2368	24 oz.	$2397–4794	$2397–4794
Collards	3–4	DNYA	3840	DNYA		7640	DNYA	
2			13 oz.			25.6 oz.		
Corn	2–3	.672	680	$456	$1368	1360	$913	$2739
18″ centers)[16] (shelled wt) — 3		.468–.964	6.4 oz.	$318–655	NA	15.2 oz.	$636–1311	NA
Cucumbers	2–3	.23	6320	$1453	$4360	12640	$2906	$8720
3		.106–.545	20.8 oz.	$669–3444	NA	42 oz.	$1339–6888	NA
Eggplant	3–6	.34	2160	$734	$734	4320	$1468	$1468
1		.19–.476	19 oz.	$410–1028	$410–1028	38 oz.	$820–2056	$820–2056
Garlic	4–6	.82	2400	$1968	$1968	4800	$3936	$3936
1–2		.70–$1.00	1/2 oz.	$1680–2400	$1680–2400	1 oz.	$3360–4800	$3360–4800
Horseradish	6	DNYA		DNYA				
1								
Kale	4	DNYA	3040	DNYA		4560	DNYA	
2			16 oz.			24 oz.		
Kohlrabi	2	DNYA	2680	DNYA		5400	DNYA	
2			1 oz.			2 oz.		
Leeks	5	DNYA	9600	DNYA		19200	DNYA	
1			2 oz.			4 oz.		
Lettuce, Butter	2–3	.242	4040	$977	$3910	5400	$1306	$5227
3–4		.12–.46	6 oz.	$484–1858	NA	8 oz.	$648–2484	NA

J	K	L	M	N	O	P	Q	R
Excellent[9] mini-farmer yield in lbs. per 1/8 acre	$ Income[14] per 1/8 acre per crop average	$ Income[15] per 1/8 acre per 8 months average	1976[3] average U.S. yield per 1/8 acre	$ Income[4] per 1/8 acre per crop average	$ Income[5] per 1/8 acre per 8 months average	1976[6] 'good U.S. farmer' yield in lbs. per 1/8 acre	$ Income[7] per 1/8 acre per crop average	$ Income[8] per 1/8 acre per 8 months average
Approx. Plant Yield— Averaged[z]	Range	Range		Range	Range		Range	Range
43200	$7084	$21254	3275	$537	$1611	6550	$1074	$3222
4 oz.	$4838–10584	NA		$366–802	NA		$732–1604	NA
11640	$5005	$10010	1150	$494	$988	2300	$988	$1976
59 oz.	$3492–8148	NA		$345–805	NA		$690–1610	NA
38360	$6367	$12734	6275	$1041	$2082	12550	$2083	$4166
32 oz.	$4296–10433	NA		$702–1706	NA		$1405–3413	NA
32400	$6966	$6966	DNYA					
48 oz.	$4794–9588	$4794–9588						
15320	DNYA							
51 oz.								
2720	$1827	$5481	1000	$672	$2016	2000	$1344	$4032
24 oz.	$1272–2622	NA		$468–964	NA		$936–1928	NA
23240	$5345	$16035	1300	$299	$897	2600	$598	$1794
68.8 oz.	$2463–12665	NA		$137–708	NA		$274–1416	NA
6520	$2216	$2216	2537	$862	$862	5074	$1724	$1724
59 oz.	$1238–3103	$1238–3103		$482–1207	$482–1207		$964–2414	$964–2414
9600	$7872	$7872	1312	$1075	$1075	2624	$2150	$2150
2 oz.	$6720–9600	$6720–9600		$918–1312	$918–1312		$1836–2624	$1836–2624
6120	DNYA							
32 oz.								
10800	DNYA							
4 oz.								
38400	DNYA							
8 oz.								
8080	$1955	$7820	3000	$726	$2904	6000	$1452	$5808
12 oz.	$969–3716	NA		$360–1380	NA		$720–2760	NA

A	B	C	D	E	F	G	H	I
Crop	Growth Period in months	1978[2] S.F. whsl. $/lb. average	Beginning[9] mini-farming yield in lbs. per 1/8 acre	$ Income[10] per 1/8 acre per crop average	$ Income[11] per 1/8 acre per 8 months average	Good[9] Mini-farmer yield in lbs. per 1/8 acre	$ Income[12] per 1/8 acre per crop average	$ Income[13] per 1/8 acre per 8 months average
	No. of crops[1] per 8 months	$/lb. range	Approx. plant yield— averaged[z]	Range	Range	Approx. plant yield— averaged[z]	Range	Range
Lettuce, Head	2–3	.158	3000	$474	$1896	6000	$948	$3792
	3–4	.08–.529	10 oz.	$240–1587	NA	20 oz.	$480–3174	NA
Lettuce, Red Leaf	2–3	.25	5400	$1350	$5400	8100	$2025	$8100
	3–4	.12–.52	8 oz.	$648–2808	NA	12 oz.	$972–4212	NA
Lettuce, Romaine	2–3	.20	5400	$1080	$4320	8080	$1616	$6464
	3–4	.11–.45	8 oz.	$594–2430	NA	12 oz.	888–3636	NA
Melon, Cantaloupe	3–4	.166	2000	$332	$332	2880	$478	$478
	1	.07–.341	9.6 oz.	$140–682	$140–682	16 oz.	$201–982	$201–982
Melon, Crenshaw	4–6	.205	2000	$410	$410	2880	$590	$590
	1	.095–.349	9.6 oz.	$190–698	$190–698	15 oz.	$273–1005	$273–1005
Melon, Honeydew	4–6	.176	2000	$352	$352	2880	$506	$506
	1	.087–.317	9.6 oz.	$174–634	$174–634	15 oz.	$250–912	$250–912
Mustard	2–3	.274	7200	$1972	$3944	9000	$2466	$4932
	2	.181–.363	5.9 oz.	$1303–2613	NA	7.5 oz.	$1629–3267	NA
Okra	4–5	.665	1200	$798	$798	2400	$1596	$1596
	1	.40–$1.25	4 oz.	$480–1500	$480–1500	8 oz.	$960–3000	$960–3000
Onions, Bunching	4	.47	4000	$1880	$1880	8000	$3760	$3760
	1	.357–.714	1/10 oz.	$1428–2856	$1428–2856	1/5 oz.	$2856–5712	$2856–5712
Onions, regular, red	4	.158	4000	$632	$632	8000	$1264	$1263
	1	.11–.36	2/5 oz.	$440–1440	$440–1440	4/5 oz.	$880–2880	$880–2880
Onions, regular, white	4	.168	4000	$672	$672	8000	$1344	$1344
	1	.135–.30	2/5 oz.	$540–1200	$540–1200	4/5 oz.	$1080–2400	$1080–2400
Onion, regular, white boilers, 2" center	4	.36	4000	$1440	$1440	8000	$2880	$2880
	1	.26–.54	2/5 oz.	$1040–2160	$1040–2160	4/5 oz.	$2080–4320	$2080–4320
Onions, regular yellow	4	.09	4000	$362	$362	8000	$734	$734
	1	.05–.24	2/5 oz.	$200–960	$200–960	4/5 oz.	$400–1920	$400–1920
Onions, red torpedo	4	DNYA	8000	DNYA		16000	DNYA	
	1		2/5 oz.			2 oz.		

J	K	L	M	N	O	P	Q	R
Excellent[9] mini-farmer yield in lbs. per 1/8 acre	$ Income[14] per 1/8 acre per crop average	$ Income[15] per 1/8 acre per 8 months average	1976[3] average U.S. yield per 1/8 acre	$ Income[4] per 1/8 acre per crop average	$ Income[5] per 1/8 acre per 8 months average	1976[6] 'good U.S. farmer' yield in lbs. per 1/8 acre	$ Income[7] per 1/8 acre per crop average	$ Income[8] per 1/8 acre per 8 months average
Approx. Plant Yield—Averaged[z]	Range	Range		Range	Range		Range	Range
12000	$1896	$7584	3000	$474	$1896	6000	$948	$3792
40 oz.	$960–6348	NA		$240–1587	NA		$480–3174	NA
10800	$2700	$10800	3000	$750	$3000	6000	$1500	$6000
16 oz.	$1296–5616	NA		$360–1560	NA		$720–3120	NA
21600	$4320	$17280	3000	$600	$2400	6000	$1200	$4800
32 oz.	$2376–9720	NA		$330–1350	NA		$660–2700	NA
5800	$962	$962	1662	$276	$276	3324	$552	$552
30 oz.	$406–1977	$406–1977		$116–566	$116–566		$232–1132	$232–1132
5800	$1189	$1189	DNYA					
30.4 oz.	$273–2024	$273–2024						
5800	$1020	$1020	2100	$369	$369	4200	$739	$739
30.4 oz.	$504–1838	$504–1838		$182–665	$182–665		$364–1330	$364–1330
10800	$2959	$5918	DNYA					
8.9 oz.	1954–3920	NA						
4800	$3192	$3192	DNYA					
16 oz.	$1920–6000	1920–6000						
21600	$10152	$10152	4025	$1891	$1891	8050	$3782	$3782
1/2 oz.	$7711–15422	$7711–15422		$1436–2873	$1436–2873		$2872–5746	$2872–5746
21600	$3412	$3412	4025	$635	$635	8050	$1270	$1270
4 oz.	$2376–7776	$2376–7776		$442–1449	$442–1449		$884–2898	$884–2898
21600	$3628	$3628	4025	$676	$676	8050	$1352	$1352
4 oz.	$2916–6480	$2916–6480		$543–1207	$543–1207		$1086–2414	$1086–2414
21600	$7776	$7776	4025	$1449	$1449	8050	$2898	$2898
4 oz.	$5616–11664	$5616–11664		$1046–2173	$1046–2173		$2092–4346	$2092–4346
21600	$1944	$1944	4025	$362	$362	8050	$724	$724
4 oz.	$1080–5180	$1080–5180		$201–966	$201–966		$402–1932	$402–1932
43200	DNYA		8050	DNYA		16100	DNYA	
8 oz.								

A Crop	B Growth Period in months No. of crops[1] per 8 months	C 1978[2] S.F. whsl. $/lb. average $/lb. range	D Beginning[9] mini-farming yield in lbs. per 1/8 acre Approx. plant yield—averaged[z]	E $ Income[10] per 1/8 acre per crop average Range	F $ Income[11] per 1/8 acre per 8 months average Range	G Good[9] Mini-farmer yield in lbs. per 1/8 acre Approx. plant yield—averaged[z]	H $ Income[12] per 1/8 acre per crop average Range	I $ Income[13] per 1/8 acre per 8 months average Range
Parsley	5–8	.525	1040	$546	$546	2080	$1092	$1092
	1	.187–1.12	2/5 oz.	$194–1164	$194–1164	4/5 oz.	$328–2328	$328–2328
Parsnips	4	DNYA	4760	DNYA		9520	DNYA	
	2		1 oz.			2 oz.		
Peas, bush, regular, with pods	5–6	.378	1000	$378	$378	2120	$801	$801
	1	.272–.544	1/5 oz.	$272–544	$272–544	2/5 oz.	$576–1153	$576–1153
Peas, pole, regular, with pods	5–6	.378	1000	$378	$378	2120	$801	$801
	1	.272–.544	1/5 oz.	$272–544	$272–544	2/5 oz.	$576–1153	$576–1153
Peas, pole, sugar, with pods	5–6	1.64	500	$820	$820	1060	$1738	$1738
	1	.25–4.00	1/10 oz.	$125–2000	$125–2000	1/5 oz.	$265–4240	$265–4240
Peppers, cayenne	5–8	DNYA	400	DNYA		1000	DNYA	
	1		1.25 oz.			3.33 oz.		
Peppers, chili	5–8	.565	920	$519	$519	2160	$1220	$1220
	1	.35–.95	3 oz.	$322–874	$322–874	7.2 oz.	$756–2052	$756–2052
Peppers, green	5–8	.391	1440	$563	$536	3320	$1298	$1298
	1	.216–.933	4.8 oz.	$311–1343	$311–1343	11 oz.	$717–3097	$717–3097
Potatoes red	4	.14	4000	$560	$1120	8000	$1120	$2240
	2	.085–.165	7.5 oz.	$340–660	NA	15 oz.	$680–1320	NA
Potatoes, russet	4	.144	4000	$576	$1152	8000	$1152	$2304
	2	.125–.18	7.5 oz.	$500–720	NA	15 oz.	$1000–2880	NA
Potatoes, white	4	.152	4000	$608	$1216	8000	$1216	$2432
	2	.10–.19	7.5 oz.	$400–760	NA	15 oz.	$800–1520	NA
Potatoes, sweet, garnet	5–6	.26	3280	$852	$852	6560	$1705	$1705
	1	.18–.30	6 oz.	$590–984	$590–984	12 oz.	$1180–1968	$1180–1968
Potatoes, sweet, yellow Jersey	5–6	.309	3280	$1013	$1013	6560	$2027	$2027
	1	.268–.325	6 oz.	$879–1066	$879–1066	12 oz.	$1758–2132	$1758–2132

J	K	L	M	N	O	P	Q	R
Excellent[9] mini-farmer yield in lbs. per 1/8 acre	$ Income[14] per 1/8 acre per crop average	$ Income[15] per 1/8 acre per 8 months average	1976[3] average U.S. yield per 1/8 acre	$ Income[4] per 1/8 acre per crop average	$ Income[5] per 1/8 acre per 8 months average	1976[6] 'good U.S. farmer' yield in lbs. per 1/8 acre	$ Income[7] per 1/8 acre per crop average	$ Income[8] per 1/8 acre per 8 months average
Approx. Plant Yield— Averaged[z]	Range	Range		Range	Range		Range	Range
4240	$2226	$2226	DNYA					
1.6 oz.	$792–4748	$792–4748						
19160	DNYA							
4 oz.								
4240	$1602	$1602	375	$141	$141	750	$282	$282
9/10 oz.	1153–2306	1153–2306		$102–204	$102–204		$204–408	$204–408
4240	$1602	$1602	375	$141	$141	750	$282	$282
9/10 oz.	1153–2306	1153–2306		$102–204	$102–204		$204–408	$204–408
2120	$3476	$3476	187	$306	$306	375	$612	$612
9/20 oz.	$530–8480	$530–8480		$46–748	$46–748		$92–1496	$92–496
1600	DNYA							
5.25 oz.								
3420	$1932	$1932	DNYA					
11.4 oz.	$1197–3249	$1197–3249						
5240	$2048	$2048	1225	$478	$478	2450	$956	$956
17.6 oz.	$1131–4888	$1131–4888		$264–1142	$264–1142		$528–2284	$528–2284
24000	$3360	$6720	3250	$455	$910	6500	$910	$1820
44.8 oz.	$2040–3960	NA		$276–536	NA		$552–1072	NA
24000	$3456	$6912	3250	$468	$936	6500	$936	$1872
44.8 oz.	$3000–4320	NA		$406–585	NA		$812–1170	NA
24000	$3648	$7296	3250	$494	$988	6500	$988	$1976
44.8 oz.	$2400–4560	NA		$325–617	NA		$650–1234	NA
19680	$5116	$5116	1425	$370	$370	2850	$740	$740
36.8 oz.	$3542–5904	$3542–5904		$256–427	$256–427		$512–855	$512–855
19680	$6081	$6081	1425	$440	$440	2850	$880	$880
36.8 oz.	$5274–6396	$5274–6396		$381–463	$381–463		$762–926	$762–926

	A	B	C	D	E	F	G	H	I
	Crop	Growth Period in months	1978[2] S.F. whsl. $/lb. average	Beginning[9] mini-farming yield in lbs. per 1/8 acre	$ Income[10] per 1/8 acre per crop average	$ Income[11] per 1/8 acre per 8 months average	Good[9] Mini-farmer yield in lbs. per 1/8 acre	$ Income[12] per 1/8 acre per crop average	$ Income[13] per 1/8 acre per 8 months average
		No. of crops[1] per 8 months	$/lb. range	Approx. plant yield—averaged[z]	Range	Range	Approx. plant yield—averaged[z]	Range	Range
Pumpkin		4	DNYA	1920	DNYA		3840	DNYA	
		1		40 oz.			80 oz.		
Radishes with tops		3–9 wks.	.185	4000	$740	$4440	8000	$1480	$8880
		4–6–8	.133–.266	1/10 oz.	$532–1064	NA	1/5 oz.	$1064–2128	NA
Rhubarb		4–6	.317	DNYA					
		1	.276–.342						
Rutabagas		3	DNYA	8000	DNYA		1600	DNYA	
		2		6.4 oz.			12.8 oz.		
Salsify		4	DNYA	8000	DNYA		16000	DNYA	
		2		3/4 oz.			1.5 oz.		
Shallots (3", 4", 6" centers[16])		4–6	DNYA						
		1–2							
Spinach, New Zealand		4–8	DNYA	7200	DNYA		9000	DNYA	
		1		24 oz.			30 oz.		
Spinach, regular		2	.289	2000	$578	$1156	4000	$1156	$2312
		2	.159–.534	3/4 oz.	$318–1068	NA	1.5 oz.	$636–2136	NA
Squash, acorn		4–5	.204	2000	$408	$408	4000	$816	$816
		1	.141–.305	41.6 oz.	$282–610	$282–610	83.2 oz.	$564–1220	$564–1220
Squash, banana		4–5	.111	2000	$222	$222	4000	$444	$444
		1	.06–.17	41.6 oz.	$120–340	$120–340	83.2 oz.	$240–680	$240–680
Squash, crook neck		4–7	.349	1400	$448	$448	3000	$1047	$1047
		1	.142–.681	7.2 oz.	$198–953	$198–953	16 oz.	$426–2043	$426–2043
Squash, hubbard		4–5	.125	2000	$250	$250	4000	$500	$500
		1	.12–.13	41.6 oz.	$240–260	$240–260	83.2 oz.	$480–520	$480–520
Squash, patty pan		4–7	.343	3000	$1029	$1029	6000	$2058	$2058
		1	.142–.636	16 oz.	$426–1908	$426–1908	32 oz.	$852–3816	$852–3816
Squash, zucchini		4–8	.297	6400	$1900	$1900	12,760	$3800	$3800
		1	.125–.636	48 oz.	$800–4070	$800–4070	96 oz.	$1600–8140	$1600–8140

J	K	L	M	N	O	P	Q	R
Excellent[9] mini-farmer yield in lbs. per 1/8 acre	$ Income[14] per 1/8 acre per crop average	$ Income[15] per 1/8 acre per 8 months average	1976[3] average U.S. yield per 1/8 acre	$ Income[4] per 1/8 acre per crop average	$ Income[5] per 1/8 acre per 8 months average	1976[6] 'good U.S. farmer' yield in lbs. per 1/8 acre	$ Income[7] per 1/8 acre per crop average	$ Income[8] per 1/8 acre per 8 months average
Approx. Plant Yield— Averaged[z]	Range	Range		Range	Range		Range	Range
7640	DNYA							
160 oz.								
21600	$3996	$23976	DNYA					
1/2 oz.	$2872–5744	NA						
			DNYA					
38400	DNYA							
32 oz.								
43200	DNYA							
4 oz.								
DNYA								
10800	DNYA							
36 oz.								
9000	$2601	$5202	950	$274	$548	1900	$548	$1096
3.2 oz.	$1431–4806	NA		$151–507	NA		$302–1014	NA
7640	$1558	$1558	DNYA					
160 oz.	$1077–2330	$1077–2330						
7640	$848	$848	DNYA					
160 oz.	$458–1298	$458–1298						
6000	$2094	$2094	DNYA					
30.4 oz.	$852–4086	$852–4086						
7640	$955	$955	DNYA					
160 oz.	$916–993	$916–993						
12280	$4212	$4212	DNYA					
64 oz.	$1743–7810	$1743–7810						
19120	$5678	$5678	DNYA					
144 oz.	$2390–12160	$2390–12160						

A	B	C	D	E	F	G	H	I
Crop	Growth Period in months	1978[2] S.F. whsl. $/lb. average	Beginning[9] mini-farming yield in lbs. per 1/8 acre	$ Income[10] per 1/8 acre per crop average	$ Income[11] per 1/8 acre per 8 months average	Good[9] Mini-farmer yield in lbs. per 1/8 acre	$ Income[12] per 1/8 acre per crop average	$ Income[13] per 1/8 acre per 8 months average
	No. of crops[1] per 8 months	$/lb. range	Approx. plant yield— averaged[z]	Range	Range	Approx. plant yield— averaged[z]	Range	Range
Sunflowers	3	DNYA		DNYA				
	1							
Tomatoes, cherry (18″ ctr)[16]	4–7	.444	4000	$1776	$1776	7760	$3445	$3445
	1	.166–.866	30.2 oz.	$644–3464	$644–3464	58.5 oz.	$1288–6720	$1288–6720
Tomatoes, regular (24″ ctr)[16]	4–7	.335	4000	$1340	$1340	7760	$2599	$2599
	1	.09–.727	64 oz.	$360–2908	$360–2908	124 oz.	$698–5641	$698–5641
Turnips, with tops	2–3	.172	4000	$688	$1376	8000	$1376	$2752
	2	.125–.25	4/5 oz.	$500–1000	NA	1.6 oz.	$1000–2000	NA
Watermelon (24″ ctr)[16]	4–6	.126	2000	$252	$252	4000	$504	$504
	1	.035–.20	26.6 oz.	$70–400	$70–400	53.3 oz.	$140–800	$140–800

FOOTNOTES:

1. The number of crops of a particular vegetable which can be grown under more or less normal conditions in a more or less usual growing season. The number can sometimes be increased with mini-greenhouses, bird-netting houses, and/or shade-netting houses. houses, bird-netting houses, and/or shade-netting houses.

2. United States Department of Agriculture Marketing Service, Fruit and Vegetable Division, Market News Branch, Federal-State Market News Service, San Francisco, California, **San Francisco Fresh Fruit and Vegetable Wholesale Market Prices — 1978**, 23 pp.

3. United Nations Department of Agriculture, **Agricultural Statistics — 1978**, U.S. Governmental Printing Office, Washington, D.C., 605 pp. Yield per acre figure divided by 8 = column D.

4. Column C × column M.

5. Lower box in column B × column N.

6. Generally, the **good** farmers in the United States obtain a yield 2 times the **average** U.S. yield. Therefore column G = column M × 2.

7. Column C × column P.

8. Lower box in column B × column Q.

9. From yield column (E) in **How to Grow More Vegetables . . .**, John Jeavons, Ten Speed Press, Berkeley, California, pp. 68 and 72. Beginning, good, and excellent yields per 100 square feet × 40 used to determine 1/8 acre figure. Difference between the 4,000 square foot total and the 5,445 square feet in 1/8 acre is the path space involved (approximately 1 foot around each bed).

10. Column C × column D.

11. Lower box in column B × column E.

12. Column C × column G.

13. Lower box in column B × column H.

14. Column C × column J.

15. Lower box in column B × column K.

J	K	L	M	N	O	P	Q	R
Excellent[9] mini-farmer yield in lbs. per 1/8 acre	$ Income[14] per 1/8 acre per crop average	$ Income[15] per 1/8 acre per 8 months average	1976[3] average U.S. yield per 1/8 acre	$ Income[4] per 1/8 acre per crop average	$ Income[5] per 1/8 acre per 8 months average	1976[6] 'good U.S. farmer' yield in lbs. per 1/8 acre	$ Income[7] per 1/8 acre per crop average	$ Income[8] per 1/8 acre per 8 months average
Approx. Plant Yield— Averaged[z]	Range	Range		Range	Range		Range	Range
16720	$7423	$7423	2125	$943	$943	4250	$1886	$1886
127 oz.	$2775–14479	$2775–14479		$352–1840	$352–1840		$704–3680	$704–3680
16720	$5601	$5601	2125	$711	$711	4250	$1422	$1422
268 oz.	$1504–12155	$1504–12155		$191–1544	$191–1544		$382–3088	$382–3088
14400	$2476	$4952	DNYA					
3 oz.	$1800–3600	NA						
12800	$1612	$1612	1387	$174	$174	2774	$349	$349
170.6 oz.	$448–2560	$448–2560		$48–277	$48–277		$96–554	$96–554

16. Spacings used for all crops are those noted in column H of How to Grow More Vegetables . . . on pages 69 and 73, except for ones further clarified in column A of this table.

NA. The lower portion of the boxes in columns F, I, L, O, and R entries is "Not Applicable," when more than one crop can be grown in the 8-month growing period. This is because these columns are for the highest marketing price multiplied by the number of crops, and the highest price usually occurs in one short period during the year.

z. The Approximate Plant Yield Averages in the lower portion of the boxes in the column entries in some instances will be much lower than one would expect. For example, a beginning mini-farmer will get carrots much larger than the 1/3 oz. noted, but all of his or her carrots will probably not be as large. Therefore, it is estimated that the average weight of the carrots would be 1/3 oz. (based as if all 4320 seeds germinated).

projected incomes from those crops. The figures are for an 8-month growing season, and are based on 1978 average wholesale prices in San Francisco. Yields are given for beginning, good, and excellent mini-farmers (these yields are drawn from data presented in *How to Grow More Vegetables*), and, for purposes of comparison, for average and good yields under conventional farming methods.

If you are considering growing a cash crop of cherry tomatoes, according to Table 2 you might expect a first year yield of 4,000 pounds and an income of $1,776; in the third or fourth year a yield of roughly 7,760 pounds and an income of $3,445; and a high (perhaps in your sixth or seventh year) of 16,720 pounds and a projected income of $7,423.

In many cases, it is possible to grow more than one crop per season. (Column B of the tables gives the months to maturity and the number of crops that can be grown in an 8-month season.) For example, 3 to 4 crops of Romaine can be grown in 8 months. A good mini-farmer might expect to grow 8,080 pounds of lettuce on 1/8 acre (Column G), and earn $1,616 (Column H) in 2 to 3 months (Column B). If lettuce is transplanted out as seedlings, about 2 months are required in the ground and up to 4 crops can be grown in 8 months. The income for 4 crops for this kind of lettuce on 1/8 acre would be $6,464 (Column I).

A quick scan of Column L will highlight the most lucrative crops based on the highest projected replicable yields, and the greatest number of crops which can be grown in 8 months. One can easily see why mini-farming efforts might emphasize crops such as lettuce, cucumbers, and green onions.

There are also a number of factors outside of crop yields which can make a big difference in income. We had difficulty selling, even at reduced prices, the small potatoes which usually constituted 10% of the crop by weight. However, when we placed these potatoes in cherry tomato-type baskets, marked them 'soup and stew potatoes,' and doubled the price per pound, the demand was greater than we could supply. Also, when it is possible to sell lettuce by the individual piece rather than by the pound, one can usually do better.

It must be emphasized that the mini-farm yield levels in Table 7 are *estimates and projections* based on our experiences and research, and that your yields may be significantly higher or lower than those given.

Some of the figures are based on our own sample tests of small areas, others are based on reports gathered from other sources, and are based on both biointensive and regular "row" type growing techniques.

The 1978 vegetable prices used for calculating the possible income figures in Table 7 will no doubt need to be adjusted to reflect current prices. The prices you charge can be significantly higher, especially if you are marketing direct to a store or restaurant, food-buying club, or produce stand. As a local grower, your extra-fresh produce can be in high demand. If you are in the large urban areas outside of California, prices may be substantially higher: the cost to transport food from California to New York, Hawaii and other states is significant.

Some crops may experience special problems that will be reflected in your income. A good stand of lettuce, for instance, may be quickly ruined by snails — or, especially slugs. Another crop, radishes, has good income potential, but harvesting and bundling thousands of them every three to four weeks can become tedious and use up too much time.

Complete Diet Mini-Farming

This section is intended to acquaint large families or neighborhood groups with the idea that they can provide their own food in a balanced way and thereby eliminate the supposed dependence on a whole complex structure which has grown up around the food system in most developed nations. You might have to give up bananas if you live in North Dakota; but, perhaps, that would give farm workers in the Tropics a chance to become more self-reliant and begin to be less dependent on exports for their own food and income needs.

Complete diet mini-farming is not a simple matter. It takes skilled people working with soil that is already very good. It is based on a complete, balanced vegetarian diet (meat diets take 2 to 4 times the space), which requires that special attention be paid to nutrition, particularly if growing children are being fed. To be realistic, it will likely take at least three years and probably much more before you can be totally independent — and even then, only with great skill and care.

Begin with five beds the first year to see if you are really that interested in this kind of food raising. Keep your current job, and during this first year, try to record all the food that you and your family eat every day — from the toastie crunchies to the filet mignon and everything in between.

Weigh everyone, too. Write down any special illnesses which have occurred in the family. Just as it is important to keep your soil healthy, it is also important to keep yourself healthy. All this information will be useful to you later in determining just exactly what and how much food you will grow when you do a complete diet garden.

The eventual diet will be tailored to your likes and dislikes and to your own personal needs. Only you will be able to determine these aspects of your garden plan. We suggest that after the first year of observing your own personal diet, you go through it, item by item, and with the help of your doctor or nutritionist, and books like the U.S. Department of Agriculture's *Composition of Foods* (Handbook 8) and the National Academy of Science's *Recommended Daily Allowances*. In this way you can find out how much nutrition you have been putting into your body and how many 'empty' calories.

In doing this do not forget such things as the special need of young children for Vitamin A and Iron, and pregnant women for Calcium and Iron.

Complete diet mini-farming in a very small space is still experimental and, for the present, should only be attempted by people experienced with biointensive food-raising who have built up their soil. However, beginners may, after two or three years, wish to start growing one bed each of the "grains" to get the all important experience with protein producing plants.

Complete diet mini-farming is especially important over the long run, since it is more environmentally sound than vegetable farming:

- more crops are grown
- grains consume less organic matter from the soil than vegetables
- grains generally produce more straw and crop residues
- the waste products from your crops go back into your compost.

These compost residues, along with cover-cropping, will help insure the sustainability of biointensive mini-farming. In fact, at Ecology Action's Common Ground Research Site, one wheat test which produced a yield that was five times the U.S. average per unit of area also produced a straw yield that was twice the U.S. average per pound of dry grain yield — or 10 times the straw yield per unit of area!

Keeping in mind that it takes over 10,000 square feet to provide a basic balanced vegetarian diet using U.S.-type agriculture (feeding about four people per acre), one begins to see the potential that the biointensive method presents for alleviating hunger and promoting self-reliance throughout the world.

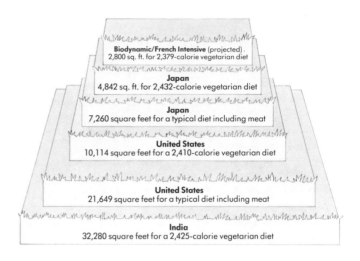

Figure 4. Amount of land required to support various daily diets.

Biodynamic/French Intensive (projected).
2,800 sq. ft. for 2,379-calorie vegetarian diet

Japan
4,842 sq. ft. for 2,432-calorie vegetarian diet

Japan
7,260 square feet for a typical diet including meat

United States
10,114 square feet for a 2,410-calorie vegetarian diet

United States
21,649 square feet for a typical diet including meat

India
32,280 square feet for a 2,425-calorie vegetarian diet

Figure 4 shows the different land areas required for different diets assuming the typical agricultural practices of the country involved are used. The potential small scale advantage of biointensive mini-farming is clear.

The half-acre complete diet scenario (see Table 8), feeding four people to thirty-one people will devote most of its area to the raising of grains (which requires less labor to maintain than vegetables do). (See Table 9 for general nutritional assumptions.) To aid in planning, Ecology Action eventually hopes to publish a complete diet guide and planning booklet.

A 5,600 square foot per person diet uses about 1/8 of an acre. Beginning yields of about *two* times the U.S. average (approximately what good U.S. farmers obtain) and a 4-month growing season are assumed in the beginning. Increased yields are assumed in subsequent years.

A 2,800 square foot per person diet and lower assumes an 8-month growing season with or without mini-greenhouses and shadehouses. Special skill is required for this kind of growing. The same result can be obtained in a 4 to 6 month growing season with yields *four* times the U.S. average. Good skill is required for this kind of growing.

A 1,400 square foot per person diet and lower

Table 8. Developmental plan for 1/2 acre complete diet mini-farm (4–6 month growing season — 5' × 20' beds plus path space).

Year	Number of Beds	Planting and Considerations	Number of people fed	Sq. ft. per person
1	5	1 bed each: Soybeans, wheat, rice, peanuts, and assorted vegetables	NA	NA
2	10	2 beds each of the above, but plant two dwarf fruit trees in one of the assorted vegetable beds.	NA	NA
3	20	Double the number of beds in year two	NA	NA
4	56	Complete diet for one person. As noted in the text, the diet will be determined by you.	NA	5600
5	At this point, most of the area will be put into a large double-dug production area without paths.	Complete diets	4	5600
6		Complete diets	4–5	5600–4200
7		Complete diets	5–8	4200–2800
8		Complete diets	8–10	2800–2100
9		Complete diets	10–15	2100–1400
10		Complete diets	15–31	1400–700

Table 9. General Yield, Nutriment. (Protein, Calories, Calcium), Growing Period and Area Characteristics for various one-person complete balanced vegetarian diets for a person weighing 145 pounds.[1]

Yield Assumed	Growing Period Involved	Daily Protein Assumed	Daily Calories Assumed	Daily Calcium Assumed	Area (Square Feet)
2× U.S. average	4–6 months	37–65 grams[2]	2500 calories[3]	800 mg.[4]	5600
2× U.S. average	8 months	" " "	" "	" "	2800
4× U.S. average	4–6 months	" " "	" "	" "	2800
4× U.S. average	8 months	" " "	" "	" "	1400
4× U.S. average	4–6 months	" " "	" "	400 mg.[5]	1400
4× U.S. average	8 months	" " "	" "	400 mg.[5]	700

1. Approximate average of U.S. men's (154 lbs.) and women's (128 lbs.) weights.

2. The first figure in the range reflects the recommendation of the United Nation's Food and Agriculture Organization (FAO) and the World Health Organization (WHO) — 1961–1972. The second figure reflects the Recommended Daily Dietary Allowances (RDA) of the National Research Council — 1974.

3. U.S. RDA range for weight involved is 2000–3000 calories. U.N. FAO/WHO range for the weight involved is 2200–3070 calories.

4. U.S. RDA range is 800–1200 mg. See: National Research Council, **Recommended Dietary Allowances**, National Academy of Sciences, 1974, 128 pp.

5. See: Food and Agriculture Organization and World Health Organization, **Calcium Requirements** (Technical Report Series No. 230), World Health Organization, Geneva, 1962, 54 pp.

Other related papers:

Alexander R. P. Walker, "The Human Requirements of Calcium: Should Low Intakes Be Supplemented?", **The American Journal of Chemical Nutrition**, May 1972, pp. 518-530.

B. A. McGance, et al, "The Effect of Protein Intake on the Absorption of Calcium and Magnesium," **Biochemical Journal**, 1942, pp. 686-691.

C. Frank Consolazio, et al, "Relationship Requirements," **Journal of Nutrition**, 1964, pp. 78-88.

Waste food from a restaurant becomes the foundation of a compost pile.

assumes special low calcium diets that meet United Nations World Health Organization calcium standards, but not National Academy of Sciences Recommended Daily Allowances calcium requirements and/or plants that produce much more oxalic free calcium and substantial protein per square foot, (such as collards).

Complete meat diet mini-farming will grow *one half* to *one quarter* the total number of diets per unit of area because of the large space needed for fodder.

Once you are very skilled, complete diet mini-farming may work for income also, but the income for a one farmer, 1/2 acre, complete diet mini-farm with an 8-month growing season, growing complete, balanced vegetarian diets will probably, at best only produce $10,000 — and then only if the food is directly marketed at full retail prices.

Compost and Cover Cropping

The soil is a very complex organism teeming with life. The constant ebb and flow of water through the soil and plants, the action and interaction of bacteria and other micro-organisms converting organic matter and minerals into food for plants, resident insects and invertebrates, makes for a delicate network of relationships and balances that easily can be disrupted through improper management. Improper treatment of the soil can damage it so that thousands of years are required for nature to fully repair it.

In recognition of these facts, the biointensive method focuses its attention as much on building up and maintaining a dynamically fertile soil as it does on high productivity. The importance of maintaining the soil's fertility cannot be overemphasized. The difference between farming for income and farming for one's own nutrition must be understood — and this is particularly true in tropical areas where the soil system is fragile. In Nature, plants are born, live, and die in their own immediate vicinity. In marketing, however, your precious plants go elsewhere to be consumed, reducing the organic matter and nutrients you have available to replenish the soil. One must recycle as much of this vegetation as possible and at all times. By developing a sensitivity to your soil's needs, mini-farming for marketing should be possible through recycling, composting, adequate cover cropping, and a minimum of purchased organic fertilizers.

3

Crop-Testing

How basic research methods can help you improve yields, consume less water and fertilizers, and select better varieties for your location

This chapter is written to explain the process of crop-testing, a process that is the backbone of Ecology Action's research into the biointensive method. It will give you the opportunity to examine the way we do things so you will understand a bit more about the work we have been doing over the years. We hope you will begin looking at "the method" with a keener eye, and that you will be inspired to initiate your own crop tests, perhaps to the extent of participating in our research program.

You do not have to participate in the research program, however. You can simply grow some of the crops we have described here and enjoy them as additions to your garden. By following the tests in this chapter, you can determine for yourself what the optimal spacing is (if you continue to test over a period of years) and see for yourself how the yields increase over a period of time.

It is important for all of us to record what we are putting into the soil, what we are removing, and to monitor and learn from the results. So even if you do not participate in the full testing program, we urge you to use the data logs contained in this chapter.

Keeping records, measuring yields, and comparing results annually is one of the best ways for you to learn about yourself and your garden. The data logs have been designed to help the backyard gardener or regional organization do just that. The forms will allow you to watch your progress as both the soil and your skills improve, and to share your findings with others over the years as successive tests are performed.

If you do decide to participate in Ecology Action's research program, we recommend that you read this chapter completely through before beginning. Plant the test beds according to the instructions given, and forward your data to us. You will need to keep accurate records of all that happens in the test beds — measuring yields, water use, and the effects of the biointensive method upon your soil.

Your input can help us immeasurably in our research, because one group, in one location, cannot possibly discover all the best approaches for different parts of the world. The more information we all gather, the better we can determine the nuances of biointensive food raising which occur in different soils, climates, altitudes, and weather conditions. People in areas such as the Tropics will need to modify composting techniques and develop more sensitivity to ground cover and sustainability. People in cooler climates will need to utilize mini-greenhouses or to plant faster maturing varieties in their shorter growing season. In hotter, dry climates, growers will need the aid of trees or shadenetting to preserve precious moisture. But most of the easy to learn biointensive principles will continue to be reference points. These basics are: double-digging and soil aeration; the close spacing of the plants to create a *living mulch* and mini-climate; composting for sustainable soil fertility, and overhead watering by hand or rainfall with most crops.

We wish you all the best and hope, after reading this chapter and running a learning test, you will begin to understand the research process. Together we can, as the former president of the Bank of China remarked after visiting with Ecology Action, "mix theory with practice" and perhaps one day — practice will make perfect.

Crop-testing is done in three stages. The 10 crops chosen for these tests were selected for particular reasons — especially for value and growing ease. They are to be grown in specific sequences.

STAGE ONE: The first stage is a 100 square foot test bed planted with *beets, lettuce, tomatoes, soybeans,* and *wheat.*

The reason we have chosen these 5 crops is to enable people to begin to observe the general growth characteristics of *leaf, root,* and *fruiting vegetable plants* and different *protein producing plants.* Cherry tomatoes, Romaine lettuce, and cylindra beets have been chosen for their ease of growth, nutritive content, and economic return in relation to time invested. The protein crops will allow you to learn to grow more of your own, and your soil's, food needs. The soybean, a legume, takes nitrogen from the air and concentrates it into the soil, while wheat stalks provide carbon and organic matter for continued soil fertility.

We suggest that you concentrate your first year's work in performing the Stage One one-bed, five-crop plan only. It will be a significant responsibility to gather the materials needed, start and water seedling flats, dig and prepare the bed, plant seeds and seedlings, water daily, observe, harvest, weigh crops, and keep data sheet records.

The plants are your responsibility. In return, they will teach you about your area, their growth, and how

Common Ground Garden, Willits, California, in late October, 1982 (started June 2, 1982).

to feed youself. Alan Chadwick observed this relationship when he observed that "it is the garden makes the gardener."

STAGE TWO: After the first year, think about adding two more test beds. In one, plant *cucumbers* (a good income crop), *collards* (which are high in protein and oxalic acid-free calcium); *alfalfa* (a leguminous fodder crop); and two more sections of *soybeans* (to introduce the idea of comparative testing). The other test bed will have three varieties of *potatoes.* (Potatoes are an important food crop which provide a significant percentage of the world's protein, calcium and caloric needs in a relatively small area.)

STAGE THREE: At this time, a more permanent form of food production can be initiated — trees. We recommend you plant at least one growing bed with two dwarf trees. If your situation permits, you can plant many more. We recommend dwarf trees since they can be grown in smaller areas, yet are highly productive. We suggest you start with apples in cold regions, and oranges in warm areas where apples will not grow well. Or you can choose another fruit that you especially enjoy. Your local agricultural extension agent can help you select an appropriate variety. He or she will have lists of trees that are suited to your specific area and will know publications that can be valuable to you. Remember, your trees will be with you for a long time, so it is wise to do research before planting one.

In the sections that follow, you will find information on each of these 10 crops, planning calendars, and bed plans, and data logs on which to record information and make notes. You can keep records in this book, but may find it more convenient to duplicate or copy the charts and logs and keep them in a separate notebook. Whatever method you find easiest, it is important that your records be as complete and accurate as possible. Record everything you do and date each entry.

The data logs have been designed to help you keep track of the resources used in your garden and the resulting harvests from the different kinds of plants. If your yields for any of the crops are substantially lower than the U.S. average yields given at the end of each crop data log, *or* if your yields are 5 times greater (or more), you can help by sending us a note with copies of your crop data log and climate information sheets.

Modify the data logs if you can devise forms better suited to your own purposes.

Stage One: Getting Started

All good gardening and farming begins with proper planning and preparation, and so does crop-testing. So much of the dissatisfaction that gardeners (especially beginning gardeners) experience can be minimized or eliminated if only a small amount of effort is spent planning beforehand and studying one's particular situation. Keep this in mind as you take the preliminary steps outlined below.

1. *Read or re-read How to Grow More Vegetables...* A working knowledge of the biodynamic/French intensive method is essential, so you should review this basic manual to be sure you understand all the principles and techniques.

2. *Test your soil, using the LaMotte Soil Test Kit.* This will give you an accurate analysis of the pH of the soil, and of the levels of phosphorus, nitrogen, and potassium. Then consult chapter 3 of *How to Grow More Vegetables...* to find out exactly what fertilizers to add to your soil, and how much of each

type. If you do not use this kit to test your soil, we suggest you take a representative soil sample (see page 20 of *HTGMV*) and save it for a reference test at a later date, should this become desirable.

Ideally, you will test any compost and/or aged manure used, too. Note the results of these tests, and of the soil tests, in the data log on page 84. For information on ordering the LaMotte kit, see the Resource Guide, page 192.

3. *Gather seeds from your favorite suppliers.* Or you may find it simpler to order seeds from the Redwood City Seed Company. They have put together a seed packet specifically for this 5-crop test. It contains the varieties of lettuce, tomato, soybean, and wheat seeds called for, with two times the seed needed to perform the test. If you prefer to get your seeds this way, use the order form on page 197.

4. *Gather all the tools and equipment you will need during the season using the following checklist.* Please note that you will need a scale so that you can accurately weigh your crops in pounds and ounces at harvest.

- ☐ 1. 3 flats
- ☐ 2. 1-inch mesh chickenwire piece large enough to fit over flats for spacing when planting seeds
- ☐ 3. watering can for flats (optional)
- ☐ 4. spade
- ☐ 5. spading fork
- ☐ 6. bow rake to level bed after digging
- ☐ 7. planting board, 5/8″ plywood, about 3′ × 4′
- ☐ 8. trowel or hand fork
- ☐ 9. spacing sticks
- ☐ 10. measuring tape

11. soil test kit
12. fertilizers
13. compost/manure
14. hose
15. fan nozzle or watering wand for hose
16. wheelbarrow (optional)
17. scale
18. pen or pencil
19. cookie sheets for drying seeds
20. seed storage jars
21. water meter (optional)
22. minimum/maximum thermometer (optional)

5. *Get climate information.* At the very least, you need to know: 1) the last spring frost date (this determines when you should begin planting flats and beds); and 2) when the night temperature generally reaches 60 degrees and stays at that level or higher (this is critical information for growing soybeans). However, the more you know about your growing season and your local conditions, the better you will be able to make plans.

If winters are severe in your area, you may have to delay planting. If saturating rains are a problem, for instance, you may have to wait 2 or 3 weeks more for the ground to dry sufficiently for double-digging. Deep frost penetration will also affect you. Mini-greenhouses can be used to help you shelter the ground from rains and to warm up the soil in early spring. They can also be used to help you extend your growing season. If planting is delayed too far into the warmer part of spring, mini-shadehouses may be needed to keep crops like lettuce from bolting. (See Chapter Five for details on the construction of a multi-use mini-greenhouse.)

The best sources for weather information are your county agricultural agent or local weather station. Neighborhood gardeners can also supply you with a wealth of information.

Enter the last frost date and the date the night temperatures start to be 60 degrees or more on the planning calendar on page 50, then determine when to plant the various seeds in flats. You can also fill in the background data sheet on page 80. This is not essential if you are running this test for your own information, but if you plan to send your test results in to Ecology Action, please do send in the background data sheet filled in as completely and accurately as possible.

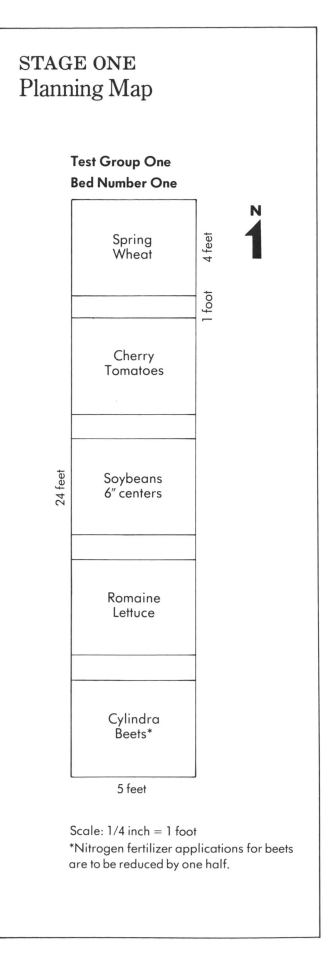

STAGE ONE
Planning Map

Test Group One
Bed Number One

N 1

Spring Wheat

4 feet

1 foot

Cherry Tomatoes

Soybeans 6" centers

24 feet

Romaine Lettuce

Cylindra Beets*

5 feet

Scale: 1/4 inch = 1 foot
*Nitrogen fertilizer applications for beets are to be reduced by one half.

STAGE ONE
Planning Calendar

Enter the week of the last spring frost date in your area, then working forward and backward in time, enter the rest of the dates. This will give you the approximate times to plant or transplant the crops in the first stage of crop-testing.

Week of:	
	WHEAT: Plant 1.4 flats on 1" centers.
	TOMATOES: Plant 28 seeds on 1" centers in 0.1 flat.
	WHEAT: Transplant on 5" centers when 3" tall.
	LETTUCE: Plant 0.5 flat on 1" centers.
	✿ **LAST FROST DATE**
	LETTUCE: Transplant on 8" centers when 3" tall.
	SOYBEANS*: Plant 1 flat on 1" centers.
	TOMATOES: Transplant on 18" centers. BEETS: Sow in bed on 3" centers.
	SOYBEANS: Transplant on 6" centers.

*Ideally, plant soybeans in flats 2 weeks before the night temperature begins to average 60 degrees.

STAGE ONE
Tests

Soil	Result	Recommendations per 100 sq. ft.*
Nitrogen		
Phosphorus		
Potash		
ph		

Compost	Result
Nitrogen	
Phosphorus	
Potash	
ph	

Aged Manure	Result
Nitrogen	
Phosphorus	
Potash	
ph	

(Note type of manure, how long it has aged, and percentage and type of other materials in the manure — straw, sawdust, and so on.)

*Refer to *HTGMV,* page 22 for recommended fertilizer applications.

Table 10. Planning Data for Stage One, Crop-Testing.

Variety	Crop	Flats	Ounces of Seeds	Spacing in Flat	Weeks in Flat	Weeks to Maturity
Wheat	Hard Red Spring #906R	1.4	.66	1"	1–2	16–18
Cherry Tomatoes	Large Red	0.1	.003	1"	6–8	8–13
Lettuce	Paris Green	0.5	.006	1"	2–3	6–13
Soybeans	Altona	1.0	2.5	1"	2	16–17
Beets	Cylindra	—	.3	—	—	8–9

6. Raise seedlings. All the crops, with the exception of beets, are started in flats, and later transplanted into the growing bed. Beet seeds are actually little pods containing more than one seed, and as a root crop, perform better when planted directly in the ground. You will need three flats, and will be planting twice the number of seedlings needed. Select the best seedlings for transplanting. Table 10 indicates for each crop the number of flats needed, number of seeds, spacing in the flats, time in flats, and weeks to maturity. For more detail on seed propagation, refer to chapter 5 of *How to Grow More Vegetables . . .*

The idea of beginning seeds in flats has often brought rumblings from those who feel it takes too much time to transplant seedlings into beds. However, by starting seeds in flats, you can compensate for varying germination rates, and can choose the healthiest seedlings. Time and water are saved, and weeding time is eliminated in the flats and greatly reduced after the seedlings have been transplanted into freshly dug, uncompacted beds (because the plants have a head start on weeds and crowd out many of them). Once you are skilled, you will be able to stagger the growth of plants in flats and beds so that no space will be wasted. This allows you to grow more food in smaller spaces.

Remember that if you start your seedlings in a greenhouse, or mini-greenhouse, you should take the flats outside or remove the mini-greenhouse at least 1 week before transplanting in order to "harden-off" the seedlings. This allows the seedlings to get used to the more diverse outdoor environment. The optimum way to "harden-off" seedlings is to place the flats in a partially sheltered area. If frost threatens, place them back in a completely sheltered area temporarily.

7. Prepare the planting bed. The planning map (page 49) shows the optimal positioning of the test bed: running on a north-south axis, wheat would be planted at the northern end, tomato seedlings in the next secton, then soybeans, lettuce, and finally, beets at the southernmost end. Placed this way, the plants will each get maximum sunlight during their respective growing periods, as no one section will shade out another to its detriment.

You will notice that, while the bed makes best use of sunlight, it is *not* set up in the most efficient manner in terms of sequential planting or harvesting. For this reason, we recommend a 1-foot section be left undug between crops so as to minimize disturbing the sections to either side as you prepare the soil, transplant, and harvest. The bed will actually be 24 feet long by 5 feet wide, but the space used to grow crops will total 100 square feet, and not 120.

If you do not have an area measuring 24 feet by 5 feet, you can still perform this 5-crop test! If there are 5 areas in your garden that get adequate sun, each measuring 4 feet by 5 feet, dig and plant each section when the time comes, and grow the crops in separate areas.

You can either double-dig the whole bed at one time, or section by section as your seedlings are ready to be transplanted. Whichever way you do it, there are two important things to remember. 1) Add fertilizers and compost the same day you transplant. 2) *Apply only 1/5 the fertilizers and compost recommended for a 100-square foot bed, as each section is equal to only 1/5 the area.*

If you double-dig the whole bed in the beginning, remember to lightly water the unplanted areas to maintain the microbial activity in the soil. Then, when it is time to plant, incorporate air into the upper 12

WATER MONITORING (Optional)

The retention of soil moisture is affected by a number of things: the soil type—its structure and texture; climate—including air temperature, humidity, and wind characteristics; and the plants themselves (or lack of plants).

The biointensive method's emphasis on building a healthy soil from the very beginning should not be overlooked when examining the system's capacity to absorb and retain moisture to the benefit of the plants. The deep soil preparation and the addition of good coarse compost allows the soil to hold this moisture longer. (Compost holds 6 times its weight in water, and the addition of compost to the soil can cut water consumption by as much as 75% per pound of food produced.) Not only does organic matter help in the retention of moisture, it also encourages the breakup of heavy clay soils and the aggregation (or binding) of loose, sandy soils. This benefits the plants considerably by allowing the tiny root hairs (not the big roots we usually see) to take up the nutrients the plants need with far less stress and with greater efficiency.

Other aspects of the biointensive method further increase water use efficiency. Due to the *living mulch* of intensive spacing, evaporation can be reduced by 13%–63%. And because a high level of soil fertility is maintained, transpiration by a plant can be reduced by 10%–75%. (It is well known that plants lacking nutrients use more water to try to get the necessary elements.) Finally, the biointensive method calls for watering to be done approximately 2 hours before sunset when it is less subject to evaporation, and the water has over half a day to sink down to the root zone before the hot sun appears again. This saves considerable water.

While it may not be possible for all who will be conducting these tests to monitor the water used on each particular crop, we do want to encourage the consideration of this all-important aspect. Those of you who live in areas with metered water may use the water company's meter. Hersey Products, Inc., makes a relatively inexpensive water meter ($50 a few years ago) that measures in tenths of a gallon, is relatively lightweight, and is easily mounted at the spigot. (If you cannot buy one locally, contact Hersey Products, Inc., Water Meter and Controls Division, 250 Elm Street, Dedham, MA 02026 for information. The order number for the one we have had good results with is: QOHO201-MVR-COMPACT-10-SCG-B-LCONN-RZ-BOTTOM.)

It is also possible to *estimate* water use without a meter. Measure the time it takes for your hose to fill up a gallon bucket while spraying at a constant rate (the flow at which you will be watering your crop). Then simply count the minutes and seconds you water and note it on the water monitoring log. While this is not exact, it will give you an idea of how much water you are using.

inches of soil by "fluffing" it with a spading fork. (Compaction of the soil begins immediately after double-digging, but it has been our experience that the lower 12 inches tend to compact far less quickly than the upper 12 inches which are more affected by the elements.) Finally, apply the compost and fertilizers to the section, and sift them into the top 2 to 3 inches of soil.

WHEAT

In the children's story, *The Little Red Hen,* the hen sowed wheat seed in a small patch; harvested, threshed and milled it; took the flour and shaped loaves, and finally baked bread. Every step of the way, she attempted to get help from others. Every time she asked, "Would you help me?" the replies were always the same: "Not I!" But when the aroma of freshly baked bread drifted out and the Little Red Hen asked, "And who will help me eat the bread?" everyone lined up at her back door saying, "I will! I will!" But, of course, she and her little chicks ate it all themselves.

If the Little Red Hen had been Italian, she might have made pasta; if she had been Indian, it might have been chappatis; if from the Baltic, she might also have grown rye and added it in equal proportions to create a very hearty, filling bread. But whatever way wheat is used, it should be remembered that many an empire has been won or lost over this particular crop. Some have even credited wheat with the formation of our present day western urban cultures.

Whether you plant wheat to bake into bread or to sprout, wheat can be one of the most satisfying crops in the garden. It is not so much because any of the other crops are less exciting or easier to grow, but because a stand of wheat is not usually part of the backyard gardener's cropping plan — and watching a breeze ripple through wheat, gently swaying the stand, causes the hardest of hearts to swell with primeval and unutterable feelings of peace and prosperity.

Wheat will be an important crop in complete diet mini-farming where, eventually, one may not transplant each wheat seedling, but may broadcast the seed by hand over a much larger growing area. The organic matter from the wheat stalks will also be important in enabling the soil to remain sustainable over time. (See page 43 for more information on this.)

Wheat should be sown in flats (1.4 flats on 1-inch centers) about 6 weeks before the last frost date in your area, and transplanted into the growing bed on 5-inch centers, 2 weeks later. Remember that you will only be planting a 20 square foot area, and fertilize accordingly (1/5 the recommended amount for a

100 square foot bed). Keep this in mind for all the tests in this stage.

Harvest the wheat heads when the plants have lost their green-ness and are golden. Clip the heads off with pruning shears, catching them in a paper bag. Then dry them further on a high kitchen shelf for 2 weeks or so.

Clip off the stalks as close to the ground as possible. Weigh these stalks and record their weight.

After the wheat heads have dried for 2 weeks, weigh them, too. Then separate the seeds from the chaff and stems by placing them on the plywood digging board and shuffling thoroughly across them wearing a pair of shoes with smooth or slightly corrugated soles (or use whatever method you are used to); separate the seeds from the rest by tossing the materials into the air in a light breeze. And then pick out any stems that remain with the seeds. Weigh the seeds and record the weight; subtract the weight of these seeds from the weight of the dried heads and record this weight in the space provided for the dried chaff and stems. Finally, count out 100 seeds at random, weigh these seeds, and record the weight in the space provided.

You may want to tag those individual wheat plants that do exceptionally well and keep those seeds separate from the others for future plantings.

Whatever happens, you should have at least enough wheat for a loaf of bread and you will gain a new appreciation of what goes into "our daily bread."

Note: Should the wheat be nearing the golden color and rainy weather threatens to ruin the crop, try harvesting it, stalk and head together, and hanging the whole bunch upside down in a dry place until it all turns completely golden. Record this procedure in the data log, then follow the directions for weighing stalks, seeds, and chaff.

TOMATOES

In 1980, California produced over 11.5 billion pounds of tomatoes for the fresh crop market. This was almost 80% of all fresh tomatoes grown in the entire United States! Because of this, tomatoes grown commercially are bred not so much for taste, but for "shipping qualities." They are sprayed 10 to 15 times with pesticides, picked unripe, and often gassed with ethylene to speed the ripening process. So the only way to be assured of a tomato worthy of the name "love apple," is to grow them yourself.

Cherry tomatoes have been chosen for this test section for a number of reasons. Alan Chadwick, the man who combined aspects of biodynamic gardening with the French intensive method, loved cherry tomatoes for their delicate flavor and ease of eating. It is impossible to walk by a stand of cherry tomatoes without picking one and popping it into your mouth.

(For this test, do not forget to weigh the harvest before eating!) It is also one of those crops whose growing season can be extended into the early winter with the aid of a mini-greenhouse. Finally, the market value of cherry tomatoes is much higher than that of regular tomatoes. (Even without using the biointensive method, an income of $10,000 an acre is not uncommon.)

For this test, plant 28 seeds on 1-inch centers in a container or flat, 5 weeks before the last frost. About 4 weeks after the last frost, transplant the tomatoes to the growing bed on 18-inch centers. Depending on your local conditions, harvesting can begin anywhere from 2 to 3 months after the seedlings are planted, and can last for up to 4 months.

The tomato is one of the few crops Ecology Action stakes and ties in the garden, and is also one crop that is optimally watered at the base of the plants, and not on the leaves. We do suggest that you get 7- to 8-foot lengths of 1" × 1" wood, sink them about 1-1/2 to 2 feet into the ground next to each plant, tie twine (or strips of cloth) to the stake, and loop it loosely around the stem as needed.

Tomatoes can be harvested ripe or green — green tomatoes can be used for making chutney or other dishes — just make sure they are all harvested before the first major frost of winter comes around.

SOYBEANS

Soybeans produce an upright bush, about waist high, attractive enough to grow with flowers. The beans are an excellent source of protein. They are super-concentrated, and will swell to 3 times their size when cooked. Cooked or sprouted beans make a great addition to soups and stir-fried dishes.

Soybeans are particularly sensitive to the length of the days and nights (especially the nights) and to the night temperatures. There is a built-in "clock" that signals each plant when it is time to begin flowering and producing the seeds with which to continue the next generation of soybeans. As the nights get longer and warmer, the timer sets this process in motion.

Some people will find soybeans a little harder to document than other crops in this chapter. In addition to basic planting and harvesting data, you will need to take note of sunrise and sunset times, and of temperature ranges. (Your local newspaper or radio station may help you gather this information.)

For this test we have selected Altona soybeans, which are available from Johnny's Selected Seeds. They are a 105-day variety that should be ready to harvest 16 to 17 weeks after planting. Ideally, soybeans would be planted in flats 2 weeks before the average night-time temperature reaches 60 degrees. Lacking that information, you would plant them about 3 weeks after the last frost date. However you establish the time, plant 1 flat on 1-inch centers, and 2 weeks later, transplant the seedlings on 6-inch centers. Set the seedlings in so that the first set of true leaves is 1/2 to 3/4 inches above ground.

You will notice that, as the plants reach maturity, the pods will be green and full, with three, four, or five beans, and will begin drying on the bushes. The plants will not all mature at the same time, so continue watering normally, as needed.

As the pods begin to dry out, they will turn a light brown color, and the leaves will dry out. When about 70% of the plants reach this stage, stop watering, and let them dry out even more. When most of the pods have become brittle, the leaves withered and dropping, and the stems brown, it is time to begin harvesting. You do not want the pods to reach the shattering point — when the pods split open and spill their seeds — so keep a close watch.

Harvest either by pulling the whole plant out of the ground, or by cutting each one off at the base. Pick off the pods by hand, or shake the plant against the sides of a clean garbage can or barrel. Most of the pods should split open or fall off the plant, but check to make sure. Shell those pods that have not opened, and separate the beans from the rest of the plant residue.

Place the beans on a cookie sheet, and put them up high on a kitchen shelf for about 2 weeks to dry even more. (Since heat rises, they will dry much better there, but make sure they do not get eaten by any mice!) After 2 weeks, take them down and place them, uncovered, somewhere else with a more even, normal "room" temperature. In this way, they will take on some moisture again and arrive at their "true air dry weight." Take 100 seeds at random, weigh them, and record their weight in the space provided on the data log.

You can now pick out those seeds that are larger and save them for planting next year. Be sure to store them in a cool, dry place. You could also note any particular plants that are doing exceptionally well during the growing season and keep those seeds separate from the others during the harvesting, shelling, and drying processes.

Some researchers have found a correlation between yield levels and the height of the soybean plant at flowering and the height at maturity. We have included a space to record this information on the soybean data log. Simply measure the height of the plants when you transplant, when the first flowers appear, when most of the plants are flowering, and at maturity. You may want to single out and tag those plants that are considerably taller than the others at the flowering stages and at maturity, and note the yields from these plants on the log form.

For further information on soybeans, refer to Ecology Action's Self-Teaching Mini-Series #2, *One Crop Test Booklet: Soybeans.*

LETTUCE

Lettuce is another crop that reflects the overcentralization of modern agriculture. Two states provide almost 90% of all the lettuce consumed in the United States (California, 74%; Arizona, 15%), and because the lettuce is shipped all over the U.S., the primary variety grown is the hard-headed iceberg variety — a lettuce with far less taste and fewer vitamins and minerals than Cos (or Romaine) and loose-leaf varieties.

Cos lettuce (named after the Greek island 60 miles northwest of Rhodes, just off the coast of Turkey) took on the name of Romaine lettuce after it was introduced to Italy. Not only is Romaine lettuce tastier than the iceberg variety, but it contains 50% more potassium and protein, 3 times the iron, calcium, and ascorbic acid (Vitamin C), and 6 times the amount of Vitamin A.

Romaine and loose-leaf lettuce are easy to grow, almost as easy as radishes — and with a little planning (and a sunny window), can be grown all year long almost anywhere in the world. By growing your own lettuce, you can provide vitamins and minerals for your family, and save quite a few dollars as well. Additional advantages of Romaine and loose-leaf varieties are: the outer leaves can be picked as they mature, leaving at least two-thirds of the plant to continue growing; they reach maturity much quicker than head lettuce and many other vegetables; and they are generally more tolerant. Heat tolerance can be helped along by providing shade for lettuce growing in mid-summer, perhaps with the use of a mini-shadehouse (see page 135).

About 2 weeks before the last frost date, plant .5 flat of lettuce on 1-inch centers. Transplant the seedlings 3 weeks later, setting them out on 8-inch centers. Make sure that you water your lettuce plants every day — twice a day if the weather gets very dry. Lettuce needs an adequate and even supply of water to maintain good growth.

Romaine lettuce normally matures in 10 to 12 weeks. While it is frequently advisable to harvest vegetables in the early morning, it is almost imperative to do so with lettuce because it will last longer and taste better. (It will taste better because during the night, much of the salt contained within the leaves returns to the roots. As the day gets warmer, these salts return to the leaves.)

BEETS

There are few meals as refreshing and satisfying on hot summer days as a bowl of Lithuanian *saltbarsciai* (pronounced shalt-barsht-shay) — also called borscht, or cold beet soup. Served with a baked potato on the side, this chilled soup, which contains beets, beet greens, cucumbers, a little vinegar, dill, green onions, and some sour cream or yogurt, fills you up without weighing you down.

Beets are one of those vegetables that are rather underused these days, even though they are packed with nutrition and are very tasty. Not only are the beet roots edible, but the tops are, too, and eaten fresh or steamed, contain many essential vitamins and minerals. In fact 3-1/2 ounces of steamed beets and 3-1/2 ounces of steamed beet tops provide the U.S. Recommended Daily Allowance for Vitamin A, almost one-half the Vitamin C, and about one-fifth the Iron.

Beets are very easy to grow, and are the only crop in Stage One to be planted directly in the bed as a seed rather than as a seedling. Each seed is actually a seed pod containing anywhere from 2 to 6 seeds — though on the average, only 1.5 seeds germinate per seed pod. Apply only *one-half* the general nitrogen fertilizer indicated to be added to 1/5 of a bed by the soil tests. (This is generally true for all root crops.) Then, about 4 weeks after the last frost date, plant the beet seeds on 3-inch centers. Believe it or not, the 20 square foot section you will be planting can provide you with up to 500 cylindra beets! Some people advise that thinning should be done so that beets will have room on the 3-inch centers. It has been Ecology Action's experience that much thinning is not really necessary, but if you do thin, remember that these tender seedlings can be eaten, too. Keep the patch weeded—beets especially do not like weeds.

In 8 to 9 weeks, the cylindra beets should be ready for harvest. Weight them with the tops first. Then cut the tops off about 1/2 inch from the root crown— to avoid cutting into the beet root and having it bleed—and then weigh the roots again. Record the weights on the data log.

Beets can be stored in a cool dark place. Put them on a bed of sand, side by side (try not to let them touch each other). Cover the first layer of beets with more sand, and continue building your pile until finished. The sand should be slightly moist to keep the beets from drying out.

Stage Two: Continuing the Process

This second stage of the testing program calls for the addition of *two more 100 square foot beds*. The crops chosen for this section will allow you to compare yields within your own garden, and will help you develop a better understanding of the possibilities that exist in your backyard mini-farm.

In the *first bed*, continue to plant wheat, beets, tomatoes, soybeans and lettuce. In the *second bed*, you will be planting alfalfa, collards, cucumbers, and more soybeans. *Alfalfa* has been included because it is an important fodder crop and is a good cover crop which fixes nitrogen in the soil. *Collards* are an excellent source of vitamins and minerals and are easily grown in many climates. (Cup for cup, steamed collards contain up to twice as much calcium as milk; as a source of calcium, they are much more space efficient.) Besides their welcome taste in salads and as pickles, *cucumbers* can also be a reasonable source of income. Two more sections of *soybeans* are to be added (one section planted on 9-inch centers, and one planted on 12-inch centers) so that a test for optimum spacing can be performed. Eventually, you may wish to try other spacings.

In the *third bed*, you will be planting three types of *potatoes:* Red Lasoda, which is good for frying and boiling; White Rose, which is good for baking and boiling, and Russet, which is good for boiling. This will enable you to make comparisons, while providing you with easily storable nutrition at the same time.

Since this is your second year of crop-testing, you should have a fairly good understanding now of the basic routines involved. Follow the preliminary steps described for Stage One (pages 48–53)... review pertinent chapters of *How to Grow More Vegetables* ... check to see that you have all the tools and equipment you need... order seeds, and so on.

You can write to the Redwood City Seed Company for the second year seeds (use the order form on page 197) or get them from your local nursery. You will have to get seed potatoes from your local nursery, or from one of the mail-order sources listed in the Resource Guide. Tell them what varieties you want (Red Lasoda, White Rose, and Russet). You will need about 6.2 pounds of each, or about 50 2-ounce potatoes pieces for each section.

You will need 5 flats to start seedlings. In addition to wheat, tomatoes, lettuce, and soybeans, you will also be starting collards and cucumbers in flats this year. Table 11 indicates for each crop the number of flats needed, number of seeds, spacing and time in flats, and weeks to maturity.

Use the Stage Two planning map to help you lay out your garden areas, and fill in the dates on the planning calendar so you can begin to schedule your time. It would be a good idea, too, to review your notes from last year's data logs. It may help you head off problems, or indicate the need for alterations in planting schedules.

STAGE TWO
Planning Map

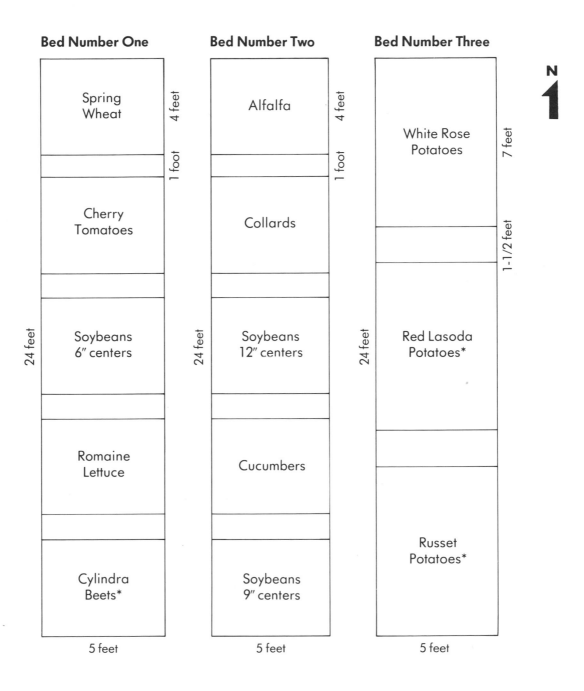

Bed Number One

Spring Wheat	4 feet
	1 foot
Cherry Tomatoes	
Soybeans 6" centers	24 feet
Romaine Lettuce	
Cylindra Beets*	

5 feet

Bed Number Two

Alfalfa	4 feet
	1 foot
Collards	
Soybeans 12" centers	24 feet
Cucumbers	
Soybeans 9" centers	

5 feet

Bed Number Three

White Rose Potatoes	7 feet
	1-1/2 feet
Red Lasoda Potatoes*	24 feet
Russet Potatoes*	

5 feet

N
1

Scale: 1/4 inch = 1 foot

*Nitrogen fertilizer applications for potatoes and beets to be reduced by one half.

STAGE TWO
Planning Calendar

Enter the week of the last spring frost date in your area, then working forward and backward in time, enter the rest of the dates. This will give you the approximate times to plant or transplant the crops in the first stage of crop-testing.

Week of:	
	COLLARDS: Plant 0.3 flats on 1" centers.
	WHEAT: Plant 1.4 flats on 1" centers.
	TOMATOES: Plant 28 seeds on 1" centers in 0.1 flat.
	WHEAT: Transplant on 5" centers when 3" tall.
	LETTUCE: Plant 0.5 flat on 1" centers.
	CUCUMBERS: Plant 1 flat on 2" centers.
	❁ LAST FROST DATE COLLARDS: Transplant on 12" centers when 3-4" tall.
	ALFALFA: Sow 1 heaping tablespoon (.3 oz) in bed. LETTUCE: Transplant on 8" centers when 3" tall.
	POTATOES: Plant on 9" centers 9" deep in all 3 test sections. CUCUMBERS: Transplant on 12" centers when 2-3" tall.
	SOYBEANS*: Plant 1.4 flats on 1" centers (for all 3 test sections).
	TOMATOES: Transplant on 18" centers. BEETS: Sow in bed on 3" centers.
	SOYBEANS: Transplant 3 test sections, on 6", 9", and 12" centers.

*Ideally, plant cucumbers 6 weeks before the average night temperature reaches 60 degrees; plant soybeans 2 weeks before it averages 60 degrees. In any case, it should be noted that all times are approximate. Local circumstances may necessitate adjustments.

STAGE TWO
Tests

Bed Number One

Soil	Result	Recommendations per 100 sq. ft.*
Nitrogen		
Phosphorus		
Potash		
ph		

Bed Number Two

Soil	Result	Recommendations per 100 sq. ft.*
Nitrogen		
Phosphorus		
Potash		
ph		

Bed Number Three

Soil	Result	Recommendations per 100 sq. ft.*
Nitrogen		
Phosphorus		
Potash		
ph		

Compost	Result
Nitrogen	
Phosphorus	
Potash	
ph	

Aged Manure	Result
Nitrogen	
Phosphorus	
Potash	
ph	

*Refer to *HTGMV,* page 22 for recommended fertilizer applications.

Table 11. Planning Data for Stage Two, Crop-Testing.

	Crop	Variety	Flats	Ounces of Seeds	Spacing in Flat	Weeks in Flat	Weeks to Maturity
STAGE ONE	Wheat	Hard Red Spring #906R	1.4	.66	1″	1–2	16–18
	Cherry Tomatoes	Large Red	0.1	.003	1″	6–8	8–13
	Lettuce	Paris Green	0.5	.006	1″	2–3	6–13
	Beets	Cylindra	—	.3	—	—	8–9
	Soybeans	Altona	2	4.0	1″	2	16–17
STAGE TWO	Collards	Georgia	0.3	.008	1″	8–10	12
	Cucumbers	Sunnybrook	1.0	.064	2″	3–4	7–10
	Potatoes	Red Lasoda	—	5.1 lbs.	—	—	17
		White Rose	—	5.1 lbs.			
		Russet	—	5.1 lbs.			
	Alfalfa	Cody Certified	—	.33	—	—	17

ALFALFA

"The name 'Alfalfa' is from an Arabic word meaning 'the best fodder,' which honor it can certainly still claim," wrote F. D. Coburn in his 1906 treatise, *The Book of Alfalfa*. In this book, he quotes a man named George L. Clothier, M.S., who had studied alfalfa for many years—in the field, feed lot, and laboratory. Mr. Clothier's "word picture" of this particular plant is not only a pleasing one, but also forces us to re-examine our own attitudes and views and compare them to ones of 75 years ago:

The cultivation and feeding of alfalfa mark the highest development of our modern agriculture. Alfalfa is one of nature's choicest gifts to man. It is the preserver and the conserver of the homestead. It is peculiarly adapted to a country with a republican government, for it smiles alike on the rich and the poor. It does not fail from old age. It loves the sunshine, converting the sunbeams into gold coin in the pockets of the thrifty husbandman. It is the greatest mortgage lifter yet discovered.

The alfalfa plant furnishes the protein to construct and repair the brains of statesmen. It builds up the muscles and bones of the war-horse, and gives his rider sinews of iron. Alfalfa makes the hens cackle and the turkeys gobble. It induces the pigs to squeal and grunt with satisfaction. It causes the contented cow to give pailfuls of creamy milk, and the Shorthorn and whitefaced steer to bawl for the feed rack. Alfalfa softens the disposition of the colt and hardens his bones and muscles. It fattens lambs as no other feed, and promotes a wool clip that is a veritable golden fleece. It compels skim-milk calves to make gains of two pounds per day... Alfalfa transforms the upland farm from a sometime waste of gullied clay banks into an undulating meadow fecund with plant-food. It drills for water, working 365 days in the year without any recompense from man. The labor it performs in penetrating the subsoil is enormous. No other agricultural plant leaves the soil in such good condition as alfalfa. It prospects beneath the surface of the earth and brings her hidden treasures to the light of day. It takes the earth, air, moisture, and sunshine, and transmutes them into nourishing feed stuffs and into tints of green and purple, and into nectar and sweet perfumes, alluring the busy bees to visits of reciprocity, whereon they caress the alfalfa blossoms, which, in their turn, pour out secretions of nectar fit for Jupiter to sip. It forms a partnership with the micro-organisms of the earth by which it is enabled to enrich the soil upon which it feeds. It brings gold into the farmer's purse by processes more mysterious than the alchemy of old. The farmer with a fifty-acre meadow of alfalfa will have steady, enjoyable employment from June to October; for as soon as he has finished gathering the hay at one end of the field it will be again ready for the mower at the other. The homes surrounded by fields of alfalfa have an esthetic advantage unknown to those where the plant is not grown. The alfalfa meadow is clothed with purple and green and exhales fragrant, balmy odors throughout the growing season to be wafted by the breezes into the adjacent farmhouses.

Alfalfa is an excellent fodder crop. Properly cared for, it can be harvested year after year without having to be reseeded. It also has great value as a cover crop because it is a "nitrogen-fixing" plant. It can take nitrogen from the air, and with the help of certain bacteria, attach the nitrogen to its roots. The nitrogen is concentrated in nodules (little lumps the size of a small match-head) on the roots which can be seen if one pulls the plant out, roots and all. If the plants are allowed to die, the roots decompose, and this nitrogen combines with other elements in the soil and becomes available as plant food for future crops.

Gardening under the biodynamic method makes alfalfa even more effective as a nitrogen-fixing plant. The double-dig and the final sifting of fertilizers to the upper layers of the soil increase the amount of air incorporated in the soil; and the more air, the more nitrogen available to the alfalfa roots. Few people realize that air is 78% nitrogen, by volume.

One week after the last frost, sow 1 heaping tablespoonful (.3 ounce) on lightly raked soil. Cover the seed with a thin layer of soil and water well. This is a heavy sowing for such a small area, but the weaker plants will die back to provide a good plant spacing. After sowing, keep the bed watered and weeded. Alfalfa, like beets, takes time to become established, and weeds will inhibit it from doing so.

When 10% of the plants are flowering, harvest half of the 20 square foot section, leaving the other half standing. Cut from 1/2 to 1 inch above the growing crown. (Since the area is so small, a pair of hand clippers will suffice for harvesting.) Weigh the harvested alfalfa; then put it in a warm, partially shaded place to dry. Turn it daily until it is dry, but still has a greenish tint to it (usually about 2 or 3 days). You do not want it to become bleached and bone dry. Weigh it and record the weight. (If you want to feed it fresh to animals, weigh the whole harvest after cutting, put aside 10% to dry and re-weigh later, and feed the remainder to your animals.)

When the other 10 square foot section has 80%-90% of its flowers in bloom, cut, dry, and weigh the harvest just as you did the first section. Afterwards, it will simply be a matter of *cutting every other section as each reaches approximately 50% of the flowering.*

Cutting half the stand at a time affords beneficial insect populations a place to live, as they can move from cut to uncut section each time. Cutting the alfalfa 1/2 to 1 inch above the crown should strengthen the stand further. When the alfalfa plant is cut back, the crown reacts by sending out new stems. A stand of alfalfa will thicken after each cut until it finally attains a "steady state" and cannot multiply any further. Proper management of alfalfa stands has made it possible to keep fields in production for 25 years or more. (In fact, there have been fields which have produced for 50, 100, and even 200 years! Currently, though, due to soil depletion and overgrazing, stands often last only 3 to 4 years before requiring replanting.)

Bees have a very positive effect on the productivity of alfalfa. Some reports indicate a 1300% increase in clover seed yields for bee-pollinated plants. It has also been noted that beehives located near fields of alfalfa produce much more honey than those not near alfalfa fields.

Harvested alfalfa that is not used for fodder should be composted and returned to your soil as organic matter.

COLLARDS

Collards are remarkable plants. Lightly steamed or stir-fried, gram for gram collards have up to twice the amount of oxalic acid-free calcium as milk, over 8 times the amount of Vitamin A as tomatoes, 1-1/2 times the amount of ascorbic acid (Vitamin C) as orange juice, 70% of the potassium found in bananas, as much iron and phosphorus as potatoes, and almost twice the protein as oatmeal or white rice! Eaten raw, collards have even higher nutritional value. As a calcium-producer, collards are highly space-efficient, producing 6 to 16 times more per unit of area than a milk-producing animal would.

Collards are also remarkable because they can be grown in both cool and warm but not hot climates. They are frost-hardy plants that become tastier after a light frost.

About 8 weeks before the last frost, plant .3 flat with seeds on 1-inch centers. Transplant them on 12-inch centers 1 day after the last frost. (In mild winter areas, they can be planted out about a month before the last frost.) The plants will take anywhere from 8 to 12 weeks in the bed before you can begin harvesting.

Start the harvest when the bottom set of leaves have just begun to take on a yellow tint. Afterwards, pick them when you notice a slight change in the greenness of the bottom leaves in comparison to those higher up. You will only be picking the outer leaves, as the plant will continue to produce. After picking, weigh each set of leaves and record the weight on the data log. In a mild climate, harvesting can continue for up to 6 months if you snip the top off whenever it begins to go to seed. (Collards have a tendency to begin seeding long before their useful life is over, and "pinching" them back will help keep the leaves from getting bitter with time and will extend the leaf-producing period.)

SOYBEANS

In this second stage of crop-testing, you will be planting 3 test sections of soybeans. Plant 2 flats of seed on 1-inch centers 2 weeks before the average night temperature reaches 60 degrees (or 3 weeks after the last frost date). When the seedlings are approximately 3 inches tall (about 2 weeks after planting) they can be transplanted to the test beds. In Bed One, you will again set them out on 6-inch centers. In Bed Two, one section will be planted on 9-inch centers, and another on 12-inch centers. After you have recorded the harvest yields, you can then make comparisons to see what effect spacing has on productivity. Refer to page 56 for details on the proper method for harvesting soybeans.

CUCUMBERS

He had been eight years upon a project for extracting sunbeams out of cucumbers which were to be put in phials and hermetically sealed, and let out to warm the air in raw inclement summers.

When Jonathan Swift wrote these words in *Gulliver's Travels* in 1727, the cucumber had already been cultivated for almost 9500 years according to carbon dating of seeds found near the borders of Thailand and Burma. While it may be that the Thai people raised them for "warming the air" (cucumbers are warmth-loving plants that also like shade and concentrate water in their fruit), it would seem that the nature of cucumbers would be to offer respite from the heat rather than add to it. The phrase "as cool as a cucumber" comes immediately to mind. Perhaps what Swift's character was really looking for was a way to pickle cucumbers in those "hermetically sealed phials" in order to retrieve them at a later date. Regardless of that, cucumbers are a welcome addition to any garden and have been included in the second year bed as another fruiting vegetable crop that has good marketing potential.

The first booklet in Ecology Action's Self-Teaching Mini-Series was *Cucumber Bonanza*. It explains our work with this crop, how through time, patience, and observation, we increased the marketable cucumber yield from 140 pounds to over 400 pounds per 100 square foot bed. We encourage you to read that booklet for more information.

Plant 1 flat of cucumber seed on 2-inch centers about

6 weeks before the average night temperature reaches 60 degrees. If you cannot establish that date, plant them 1 week before the last frost date. Transplant the seedlings 2 to 3 weeks later. Set them out on 12-inch centers.

Cucumbers love heat, but also enjoy some shade during the day. This is one reason why we do not advocate trellising them. Letting them sprawl also helps keep the ground moist, and cucumbers like moisture, too.

Depending on your climate, cucumbers should reach the harvestable stage between the 7th and 10th weeks after transplanting and, also depending on your climate, can be harvested continuously for up to 26 weeks. (A more realistic span is 7 to 12 weeks.) You can tell when they are ready for harvest by observation: as they ripen, cucumbers will enlarge somewhat, turn from a dark green color to a lighter green, and the spines will fall off easily when touched. Continual picking encourages the plants to produce more. Remember to record the daily yield in the data log.

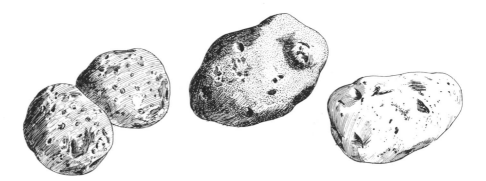

POTATOES

Potatoes and sweet potatoes are two of the most important food crops world-wide. Together, they account for 12% of all the calories, 8% of all the protein, and 18% of all the calcium consumed in the world today, and are produced on only 2.4% of the world's farmland. They are an excellent food source, especially if eaten with the skin. They are loaded with vitamins and minerals and, contrary to popular belief are not fattening as their fat content is only .1% of their composition. (It is this lack of fat that results in our adding mounds of butter or sour cream to the potato and these fat-rich substances are the real sources behind the "fattening potato" myth.) The starch of the potato is more easily digested than cereal starches, and is more quickly converted into energy, too. Meat and many cereals have excess acid-forming elements which can acidify the blood. In contrast, potatoes have an abundance of alkaline salts that help maintain the alkalinity of healthy blood. (This could be the reason why meat and potatoes evolved as complementary foods — eaten together, potatoes may help neutralize the meat's acidity.)

The reason it takes such an amount of land and resources to meet America's demand for animal products is again the fact that the conversion of plant foods (feeds) to flesh and dairy products is very inefficient. It takes 11 pounds of corn to put one pound on a steer, and only about half the steer's carcass is used for meat so it takes about 22 pounds of corn to produce a pound of meat. However, the pound of meat contains a third fewer calories than a pound of corn so it takes over 33 pounds of corn to produce the caloric equivalent of a pound of corn as beef. Putting land into tubers yields about 50 times as much food energy as would be derived from meat.

Normally when authors and reporters call attention to the inefficiency of meat-eating, they base their comparison on available protein. A pound of meat protein requires about ten pounds of corn protein, but this is a poor comparison for when land is devoted to say tubers and greens, it yields up to 50 times as many calories as when the land is used for animal feeds, and when an individual derives adequate energy from tubers and leaf vegetables he obtains an abundant supply of protein...

ROBIN HUR
Food Reform: Our Desperate Need

Several special precautions need to be taken in order to grow potatoes successfully.

1. As a member of the *Solanaceae* family, potatoes should not be planted where potatoes, tomatoes, eggplant, green peppers, chilies, tobacco, petunias, or deadly nightshade (all members of the same family) were grown the year before. It is also recommended that smokers wash their hands before

handling any solanaceous plants as they can transmit plant virus diseases from the tobacco to the plants.

2. As the potato removes a great deal of nitrogen, phosphorus, potassium, and calcium from the soil, care must be taken not to exhaust the soil of these materials. Legumes, cover crops, and compost should eventually be able to provide these nutriments on a continuous basis. Periodic soil tests should be done to assure that the soil has not become depleted of any element.

3. We do not encourage the use of fresh manure in the biointensive system, and it can be a special problem when introduced to soil where potatoes will be grown, since it is reported to invite scab virus. While this is not harmful to people, it does make potatoes unpleasant in appearance.

Potatoes need a reasonably loose, well-aerated soil if they are to thrive. The biointensive method — with its emphasis on the incorporation of air into the soil — lends itself to the growing of this crop and can increase yields significantly. (One woman in England obtained a yield of 192 pounds in a 25 square foot area — or about 15 times the U.S. average commercial yield!)

If you live in an area where spring is very wet, you will have to wait until the ground dries out a bit before digging and planting potatoes. Working the soil when it is wet can damage the soil structure, resulting in soil compaction. You could place a mini-greenhouse over the bed to protect it from rain and to help the soil dry out. Then you can begin to work the soil earlier than usual.

Potatoes should be planted 1 to 2 weeks after the last frost. Plant slightly sprouted 2-ounce seed potato pieces (about the size of a large egg) on 9-inch centers, 9 inches deep. The time from planting to maturity is about 17 weeks. They are ready to be harvested after most of the tops have died down. They can also be left in the ground for about a month if the weather is not too cold, too wet, or too warm — until you find the time to harvest them. Cure the dug potatoes by keeping them outside for a day or two — but keep them out of the sun as they will turn green, making them poisonous to eat. After they have been cured, weigh each section, record the data, and store the potatoes in a cool, dark place — preferably at about 40 degrees Fahrenheit.

Stage Three: Trees

As we look at the world to-day, we see many parts that have been denuded of tree cover. During this past century we have bitten deeper into the natural resources of the earth than all former generations of mankind. We have upset the water cycle by removing the tree cover.

The ancients believed that the earth was a sentient being and felt the behavior of mankind upon it. As we have no proof to the contrary, it might be as well to accept this point of view and act accordingly.

Modern techniques have speeded up the process of destruction. It took about fifteen hundred years for the Arabs to make the Sahara desert. In the United States it [took] only about forty-four years to form the Dust Bowl which [spread] very rapidly. The "improved" ploughs driven by tractors at high speed have accelerated erosion...

The time has surely come to win back the areas that have been lost. The weapon in this great work of reclamation is the tree. The tree not only protects the soil and keeps the water in circulation but itself provides shelter, food and fuel.

RICHARD ST. BARBE BAKER
Dance of the Trees:
The Adventures of a Forester
Oldbourne Press, London, 1956

The tree is man's best friend... How dependent we are upon trees has yet to be fully realized. Only in a vague sort of way can we assess the real contribution that trees make to human existence on this planet. Their functions are legion and their life is interwoven with earth... To the trees we owe the quality of our food, the quantity of our water, and the purity of the very air we breathe.

RICHARD ST. BARBE BAKER
Green Glory: The Forests of the World
A. A. Wyn, Inc., New York, 1949

You have probably sat on a hillside and·the air has been clear; you look out over a valley of woods with a breeze coming towards you from the sea. Cumulus clouds begin to form over the forest—you see them building up as you watch—and later they may come down as rain. If there was no transpired moisture from the land surface, the water droplet with its millions of companions that had been lifted from the sea would have gone on indefinitely until it reached the ocean again, where moisture was still coming up. It might then have come down in the form of rain over the sea.

Trees are the essential link where we want to bring back rain to the land. In an island like Britain there are other forces at work. You cannot say that only trees bring rain; we have the advantage of the Gulf Stream and the fact that we are never very far away from the sea along all our boundaries. In this island we get moisture brought to us from large water areas. It precipitates in the form of rain or dew, but even so, we could not exist without trees.

The roots of trees tap subterranean supplies of water and bring them up to the surface in the stream flow to the leaves. The leaves having fulfilled their function of transpiration and wood formation, fall to the ground and keep it cool. ... This and the shade of the trees maintain a normal ground temperature... If the ground is bared and the canopy of trees is opened up too much, the sun gets into the surface of the forest floor, the temperature is raised and the water is dissipated. The water cycle is broken and growth is reduced.

There is not only a vertical movement of water from the forest through the transpired moisture but there is a horizontal movement as well. Whenever there is a clearing in a forest, the moist air comes out of the forest from all sides on to the clearing and condenses in the form of dew. This is the dew pond principle and in the morning there may be as much as the equivalent of a quarter of an inch of rain which has been condensed on to this patch, which during the night was cooler than the surrounding area.

There is another kind of horizontal precipitation such as that along the coasts on a hot summer's day in places like California in the realm of the Redwoods. Within ten miles of the Pacific Coast heavy mists come inland and the tall trees, three hundred feet high, trap the coast mists and form what is called horizontal precipitation. This mist condenses on the leaves of the trees and falls down just as if it were a gentle rain. There is a continual drip from the higher branches and that is how these Coast Redwoods get their moisture. The hotter the summer, the more water they get through horizontally precipitated coast mists. Thus it is when trees need more water in the heat of a dry summer nature provides it.

But what happens in a forest when there is a rainstorm? First of all the fall is broken by the leaf surface of the trees and the water comes gently down to the ground which is protected firstly by a layer of leaves or needles and then by the humus which has been formed by decayed leaves —a sort of compost. Next the water is held up by millions of hair roots of the trees—the feeder roots. The intricate network of support roots and channels formed by old roots that have died in the ground, also trap the water. It percolates slowly down and forms springs which may come up later, perhaps in the dry season even months afterwards.

When rain falls upon a bare hillside the water runs off, finding the quickest way to the rivers or the sea, and in doing so it probably takes with it valuable soil covering from the hill. So trees not only conserve water but they also conserve the soil and in this way tend to prevent floods and droughts.

RICHARD ST. BARBE BAKER
Dance of the Trees:
The Adventures of a Forester
Oldbourne Press, London, 1956

———There is probably no one on earth who knew more about trees and their importance than Richard St. Barbe Baker. Some claim that he was responsible for the planting of over 26 *trillion* trees throughout the world. It was through his intervention in the 1930s and again in the late 1970s that the United States still has its coast redwoods. And it was his personal meeting with the newly elected Franklin D. Roosevelt and Roosevelt's right-hand man, Henry Morgenthau, Jr., that initiated the formation of the Civilian Conservation Corps. In the 9 years of its existence, the Civilian Conservation Corps contributed some 730,000 man-*years* of work in forest protection, construction and maintenance of improvements in public forests, in tree planting, and in timber-stand improvements! Mr. Baker died recently at the age of 93. He was the author of 12 books on his experience with trees. (Many of them are now out of print, but may still be found in libraries. See Resource Guide for some of the titles.)

In reconstructing the history of humanity on earth, there are many traditional references which point to trees as the primary source for our survival. Some anthropologists have even advanced theories saying that the fate of civilizations is interwoven inextricably with the fate of the trees in their regions. While there are many theories as to what exactly happened in prehistoric times in different regions of the earth, there is ample evidence to suggest that man's hand in deforestation and overcultivation of vast areas of the globe has contributed to the destruction of soils, and hence, his own environment.

One of the biggest tragedies, the effects of which are still being felt today, took place in Northern China—its history coming to us only through folk tales from the people there.

In another land, a great distance from our own, and in other times, going back to the dim past, there flowed a mighty river through long and twisting valleys and vast plains.

That land was China, the time was more than four thousand years ago, and the river, not unlike our own Mississippi, was the Hwang Ho—the Yellow River, the River of Destiny.

In those far-off days all the land along the Yellow River, and deep inland both north and south, was covered with trees. From the Kunlun Mountains in the far west, through Kansu and Shawan, Shansi and Shensi, across Honan, and all the way to the Gulf of Pohai in the Yellow Sea, the banks of the Yellow River were bordered with trees. The forests were full of singing birds and wild animals; nuts and berries grew in abundance; and in the spring wildflowers covered the ground.

For many centuries the people on either side of the Yellow River had little to complain about to their ancestors, whom they worshiped... Life flowed happily in the part of the Flowery Kingdom that lay along the wooded banks of the Yellow River.

Then, about four thousand years ago, the land came under the rule of an emperor of the Hsia dynasty, named Shun. Emperor Shun carefully observed the rich forests on either side of the twenty-five-hundred-mile river, and decided that the soil was good for cultivation.

If the trees were cleared from the land, he reasoned, crops could be grown upon it. If the soil cultivated produced good crops, the farmers would be rich. If the farmers grew rich, the emperor would be able to levy new taxes upon them.

New sources of income were always welcomed by the royal head. And so it happened that Shun, after the manner of emperors, issued an order. It was dated nearly two thousand years before the days of the philosopher Kung. This order stated that the land along the Yellow River must be cleared for farming, and the Emperor appointed a forester by the name of Yih to destroy by fire all the forests along that section.

What Forester Yih thought about the emperor's order no one has ever recorded. But that he carried out the royal command thoroughly there can be no doubt, for soon after receiving his commission [he] started many fires. Long stretches of forest were turned into ashes. Most of the wild life was destroyed with the trees; some escaped into the southern provinces of China.

For a while there was rejoicing over the land plowed and seeded. For the land, rich in humus, grew crops plentiful beyond all expectation. Emperor Shun's name entered into grateful prayers.

But this happy state of affairs did not last. The topsoil of the cleared land, in rapidly melting snows and heavy rains, began to slide down into the Yellow River. Erosion crept across the farms. Hot winds of summer dried the fine soil; more hot winds that followed carried the rich topsoil away in storms of dust. The streams emptying into the rivers swelled with silt. Higher and higher rose the Yellow River. It broke through the barrier of banks and dikes. Water flooded the land.

When this happened the first time, people said it was unheard of, that it had not happened in ten generations or more. And when the flood subsided they returned to their farms, hoping it would not happen again for another ten generations or more.

But the Yellow River, which resembles our own Mississippi, began to show its power of destruction when no longer restrained by forests, until finally, each year during the heavy rainfalls, people began to dread the invasion of their homes by the waters of the river.

With the passing of time the floods became more frequent, the land grew poorer, and the misery of the people became greater.

Close to two thousand years passed from the days of

Emperor Shun to the days of Emperor Chin Shih Huang Ti. Emperor Chin gave much thought to the impoverished land. The suffering of the people along the Yellow River, he realized, was due to their poverty. And their poverty was due to the land's having been denuded of its forests.

The happiness and security of a people is the responsibility of its government, thought Chin. He therefore issued an order that the mistakes of Emperor Shun should be rectified, and the land along the Yellow River again be restored to the forests. "He who fails to grow a tree," the order read, "shall go coffinless to the grave."

The people were willing enough to follow the Emperor's order. But they were helpless. The land did not belong to them. The land was owned by the feudal lords.

When the order became public, the feudal lords assembled in great secrecy. They indignantly decided that the Emperor had no right to interfere with their manner of handling their own property. The governors of the provinces agreed with the feudal lords. They all shook their sage heads: the sovereign rights of the provinces must be upheld.

Many men went to their graves without coffins. But the land was not reforested.

In the four thousand years following Emperor Shun's decree the Yellow River has destroyed millions of lives and caused untold misery... (pp. 9 & 10)

As you move into Stage Three of the crop-testing program, you will involve yourself in a much more permanent type of food production. At the same time, in your own small way, you will be joining energies with those reforesting the earth's surface. Much needs to be done, and this will be your beginning step in learning more about tree cultivation.

In Stage Three, you will maintain the three beds that you started in Stages One and Two. In addition, you will be planting fruit trees — two, at least, more if you have room. At this point, it is important to begin a crop rotation pattern: grow Bed One crops in Bed Two; Bed Two crops in Bed Three; and Bed Three crops in Bed One. If you plant potatoes each year, it is important to keep up this crop rotation annually. The crop trees, of course, stay permanently in Bed Four.

We recommend the planting of *dwarf* fruit trees for the simple reason that they take up very little space. Because of this, most people can find space to grow a few of them on their property. Dwarf fruit trees also usually begin to bear earlier than the standard varieties (about 2 to 3 years after setting out). Their fruit — which is about as large as that from standard-sized trees — is more easily harvested, and the yield per square foot is almost as high.

There are many books on the subject of dwarf fruit trees. A few are recommended in the Resource

Guide. The Dave Wilson Nursery (see Resource Guide) has a very good catalog that not only explains the requirements for planting fruit trees, but also contains an in-depth evaluation of the particular climate zones throughout the United States — dividing U.S. into 31 regions and 149 sub-regions. These evaluations for the many fruit and nut trees they carry take some of the guesswork out of selecting varieties that will do well in a specific area. Consulting with local nurseries, the agricultural extension service in your area, and with neighbors experienced with fruit tree growing can also be very helpful to those people just starting out.

For this test, we suggest *apple* trees in cold winter climates, and *orange* trees in warmer ones. Check your nursery and local extension agents for varieties suitable to your area. It is also possible to order stock by mail: Tree Crops Nursery, for example, has excellent common and rare fruit tree stock. See the Resource Guide for their address.

A few necessary things to look for before choosing and planting trees are:

1. *Proper Soil Drainage.* No fruit tree will do well if its roots are sitting in water most of the time. One way to test the drainage of your soil is to dig a 2-foot hole where you will be planting your tree, completely fill the hole with water, and cover it. Check it 24

Figure 5. Planting patterns for fruit trees.

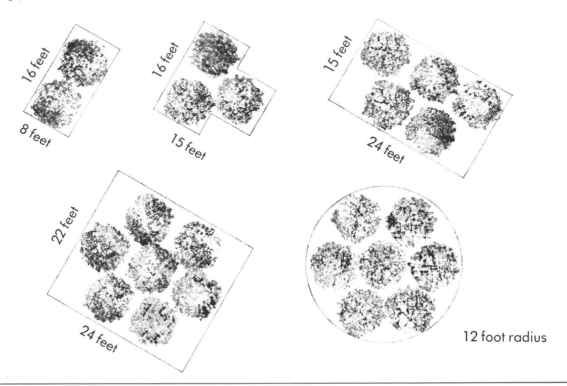

hours later and see how much water is still in the hole. If after 24 hours you still have water in the hole, there is a significant drainage problem, and you may have to triple-dig (dig 3 feet below the path depth). Hopefully, this will break up whatever hard-pan exists. If there is no problem, just double-dig.

2. *Frost Pockets or "Air Drainage."* Cold air, like water, flows downhill. This cold air can get trapped by barriers on a downslope or can sit at the bottom of a plain and harm the fruit-producing capacity of trees. Conversely, in areas that do not receive much cold weather during the winter, it may be necessary to plant *near* such barriers if the trees you have selected to grow need a period of cold in order to maintain their health and their capacity to fruit.

3. *Available Sunshine.* Without at least 11 hours of sunshine throughout the day, fruit trees will generally not bear fruit or ripen. Note the position of the sun from spring to fall in your yard during your first years of gardening so that you will not make a mistake when planting your trees.

4. *Pollination.* Some trees need to be planted in pairs in order to set fruit. Others are self-pollinating. When you purchase your trees, find out whether they are self-pollinating or not.

5. *Planting Time.* Many people recommend planting trees in the fall in order to let the roots grow a bit before winter sets in. Cold weather inhibits the movement of sap in trees, and trees become dormant and less subject to shock and disease. Other people recommend planting in the spring, saying that the tree does not have enough time to get firmly established before winter sets in. There are many factors that can be considered. Ask your nursery and your agricultural agent for the best planting time in your area.

BED PREPARATION

Whether you decide to plant 2, 3, 5, 7, or more trees, double-dig the areas that will receive the trees, just as you do for the planting of your vegetables. (The only exception is that if you have a drainage problem as we discussed earlier, you will need to triple-dig.) Prepare the bed at least a month before you plan to plant the trees.

Optimally, a bed holding 2 trees should be dug 8 feet wide by 16 feet long. However, if you are only planting 2 trees and are pressed for space, dig it 5 feet by 16 feet (5 feet being the width of a regular bed). Figure 5 shows planting patterns for different numbers of trees. In each pattern, the trees are planted in clusters to make better use of the trees' mini-climate potential. Each tree is set 8 feet away from its neighbors, and 4 feet away from the soil not double-dug. If you would like to do something special, you can double-dig a circular area as shown in Figure 5. (Seven trees will fit a circle with a radius of 12 feet.) Circular designs require less area (and therefore less digging) and lend themselves to interesting landscaping ideas.

After double-digging the area to be planted, tamp the soil heavily by walking on the digging board over the entire surface. Then water the bed lightly daily to keep the soil alive and to encourage micro-organism multiplication. After a month, again tamp the soil. This will minimize the possibility of the trees uprooting as the bed subsides.

Mark the locations where you will be planting the trees. Note how deep a hole you will need in order to keep the graft union of your dwarf varieties 3 to 4 inches above ground level. (It is important to make sure the graft union is kept above ground level as trees have been known to begin rooting above the union if it is in contact with the soil—turning the dwarf tree back into a normal-sized tree!) Dig the holes 2 feet wider than the width of the root ball.

After the holes are dug, gently spread out the roots of the tree as they would be spread naturally, place each tree in its hole, and fill the soil in around the root system—tamping the soil firmly as you go. When the hole is about 3/4 full, water the soil well and let it leach down to settle the soil and encourage the all-important good contact between soil and tree roots.

Afterwards, fill the hole to within 3 inches of the ground level—again, tamping it firmly as you go. Then fill the last 3 inches around the tree—leaving it fairly loose. Water thoroughly, and keep the area well watered to establish the tree in its new environment.

COVER CROPPING UNDER FRUIT TREES

While much can be said about the benefits of "dust mulching," "rock mulching," and mulching with straw, grass clippings, and other organic material, Ecology Action has been experimenting with cover cropping the area underneath dwarf fruit trees as a viable way to protect the soil beneath the trees while adding to its fertility and friability. In terms of the water needed to satisfy the requirements of both the cover crop and the tree, the unique biointensive soil preparation techniques better utilize the available water than commercial agricultural practices.

In the spring, broadcast 1/2 ounce of Medium Red Clover per 100 square feet after the trees have been planted. Sow the seed approximately one week after the last frost date. Do *not* sow seeds closer than 1 foot from the trees in the first year. The soil should be lightly fluffed (8 to 12 inches deep, depending on the depth of the tree roots). Then rake lightly, making very shallow furrows, sow the seeds, and cover with a thin layer of soil. Water well and keep the soil moist until the clover establishes itself.

When 10 per cent of the clover is flowering, cut half the area to within 1/2 inch of the growing crown. Weigh the harvest and record the weight on the data log, then compost the cuttings. When the clover in the remaining area reaches the 80–90 per cent flowering point harvest it. At the first frost of winter, dig all the new clover growth into the soil. Make sure that when you dig the clover in, you do not disturb the roots of the trees. As dwarf trees usually have rather shallow root systems, we would advise you not to dig the cover crop in deeper than 8 to 12 inches—less as you get nearer the trunk of the tree.

In following years, sow again, but only to within a 2-foot radius of the trunk. Follow the procedures for cutting and digging in as outlined above.

STAGE THREE
Planning Map

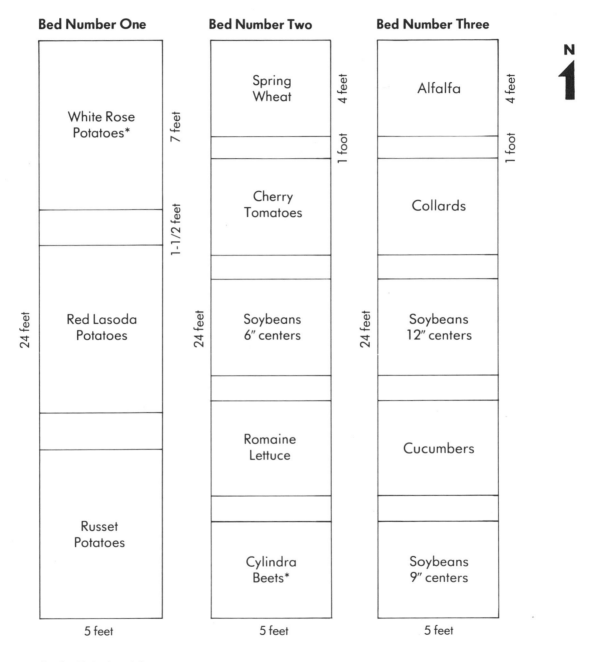

Bed Number One

White Rose Potatoes*

7 feet

1-1/2 feet

24 feet

Red Lasoda Potatoes

Russet Potatoes

5 feet

Bed Number Two

Spring Wheat

4 feet

1 foot

Cherry Tomatoes

24 feet

Soybeans 6" centers

Romaine Lettuce

Cylindra Beets*

5 feet

Bed Number Three

Alfalfa

4 feet

1 foot

Collards

24 feet

Soybeans 12" centers

Cucumbers

Soybeans 9" centers

5 feet

N

Scale: ¼ inch = 1 foot
* Nitrogen fertilizer applications for potatoes and beets to be reduced by one half.

STAGE THREE
Planning Calendar

Enter the week of the last spring frost date in your area, then working forward and backward in time, enter the rest of the dates. This will give you the approximate times to plant or transplant the crops in the first stage of crop-testing.

Week of:	
	COLLARDS: Plant 0.3 flats on 1″ centers.
	WHEAT: Plant 1.4 flats on 1″ centers.
	TOMATOES: Plant 28 seeds on 1″ centers in 0.1 flat.
	WHEAT: Transplant on 5″ centers when 3″ tall.
	LETTUCE: Plant 0.5 flat on 1″ centers.
	CUCUMBERS: Plant 1 flat on 2″ centers.
	❀ **LAST FROST DATE** COLLARDS: Transplant on 12″ centers when 3-4″ tall.
	ALFALFA: Sow 1 heaping tablespoon (.3 oz) in bed. LETTUCE: Transplant on 8″ centers when 3″ tall.
	POTATOES: Plant on 9″ centers 9″ deep in all 3 test sections. CUCUMBERS: Transplant on 12″ centers when 2-3″ tall.
	SOYBEANS*: Plant 1.4 flats on 1″ centers (for all 3 test sections).
	TOMATOES: Transplant on 18″ centers. BEETS: Sow in bed on 3″ centers.
	SOYBEANS: Transplant 3 test sections, on 6″, 9″, and 12″ centers.

*Ideally, plant cucumbers 6 weeks before the average night temperature reaches 60 degrees; plant soybeans 2 weeks before it averages 60 degrees. In any case, it should be noted that all times are approximate. Local circumstances may necessitate adjustments.

Dwarf fruit trees, which are to be planted at this stage of crop-testing, can be planted in fall or spring, and have not been included in the calendar. Consult your local nursery or agricultural agent for the best planting time in your area.

STAGE THREE
Tests

VEGETABLE BEDS

Bed Number One

Soil	Result	Recommendations per 100 sq. ft.*
Nitrogen		
Phosphorus		
Potash		
ph		

Bed Number Two

Soil	Result	Recommendations per 100 sq. ft.*
Nitrogen		
Phosphorus		
Potash		
ph		

Bed Number Three

Soil	Result	Recommendations per 100 sq. ft.*
Nitrogen		
Phosphorus		
Potash		
ph		

STAGE THREE
Tests

TREE BED(S)

Bed Number Four

Soil	Result	Recommendations per 100 sq. ft.*
Nitrogen		
Phosphorus		
Potash		
ph		

Compost	Result
Nitrogen	
Phosphorus	
Potash	
ph	

Aged Manure	Result
Nitrogen	
Phosphorus	
Potash	
ph	

*Refer to *HTGMV*, page 22 for recommended fertilizer applications.

Alternatives for Non-Temperate Climates

While most of the plants suggested for testing in this chapter can be grown anywhere in the world, it has been suggested that not all are suitable to tropical and semi-tropical climates. We have included some substitutes here, given seed sources, and some directions on how to plant and harvest each one. We invite you to write to us with other suggestions for inclusion in future revisions of this book.

Substituting Maize for Wheat

In Waverly Root's book, *Food* (see Resource Guide), he speaks of the importance of maize in the growth and maintenance of the ancient Incan Empire: "Corn was so plentiful that it was planted along the roadsides so that those in want might help themselves; nobody in Mexico could die of hunger at a time when Europeans could and did. In Peru, the Spaniards found an Inca Empire whose prosperity was built on maize... The Spaniards reversed the Inca priorities, which put corn first and gold second, and gave Peru the gift of malnutrition."

Many seed companies carry maize, but we suggest that you obtain seeds from a local supplier as they will probably have the varieties best adapted to your local conditions. We do encourage you to purchase non-hybrid seed. Mr. Root states: "The hybridization of maize has been called one of the agricultural triumphs of the 20th century, but it may be a triumph limited in its applications. One of the reasons why maize has spread so rapidly in certain areas, like Africa, has been its uncomplicated rustic sturdiness, which has given large yields under primitive conditions for the undernourished and usually overpopulated poorer regions of the world. But some of the new strains are being priced out of the reach of poor countries because their cultivation demands modern techniques and modern chemicals which [they] cannot afford."

Plant maize directly in the bed, one month before night temperatures reach 60°. Plant it on 15 inch centers, 2 seeds per center, and then thin to one plant if both seeds germinate. Approximately 40 seeds will be needed to do this. Keep the section weeded. The U.S. average yield per 20 square feet is about 3 pounds, shelled wet weight.

Substituting Mustard Greens for Romaine Lettuce

You could hardly find a better substitute for lettuce than mustard greens. Besides having more nutritive value overall, mustard greens contain about 40% more potassium, 2 times the phosphorus and iron, 3 times the calcium, 3-1/2 times the Vitamin A (7,000 International Units per 3-1/2 ounces!), and over 5 times the Vitamin C as Romaine lettuce. This can be a very important crop where many people suffer from Vitamin A and iron deficiency-related problems.

Start 1 flat (250 seeds) on 1-inch centers about one week after the last frost date. Transplant the best 1/2 of them 3 to 4 weeks later on 6-inch centers (when they are about 3 inches tall). Harvesting can begin 5 to 6 weeks later. Pick the lower/outer leaves of the plant, leaving 2/3 of the leaves unpicked. Picking can continue for up to 8 weeks or longer — until the plant goes to seed. (You can then harvest the seed to make fresh mustard.) Weigh the leaves as they are picked and record the amounts on the lettuce data log. The average U.S. yield per 20 square feet is probably about 18 pounds of fresh greens. You should be able to get much more!

Seeds can be ordered from the Redwood City Seed Company.

Substituting Pinto Beans or Winged Beans for Soybeans

Ecology Action is anxious to gather as much information as possible on soybean culture, but many people prefer the more tasy dry field beans or specialized beans to soybeans. For this reason, we also encourage the growing of local bean varieties. Two suggestions are the pinto bean and the winged bean.

The *pinto bean* has been grown with maize in Mexico for hundreds of years. They complement each other nutritionally. Pinto beans should be planted directly in the bed, when night temperatures reach 60°. Plant 1 seed on each 6-inch center; approximately 125 seeds will be needed to do this. Use new seeds for the best results. Replant 2 weeks later at those points where seeds did not germinate. If you choose to stake the beans, place 6-foot poles about 1-1/2 feet deep on 1-foot centers (in the center of the hexagon planting pattern). Then let the center plants climb up the poles and the other plants will hold on to the center ones and to each other.

Pinto beans take about 12 weeks to mature. Harvest and record data as for soybeans. The average U.S. yield for pinto beans is about 8-1/2 ounces dry weight per 20 square feet.

Seeds can be obtained from a local source or from Johnny's Selected Seeds (see Resource Guide).

The *winged bean* has only recently come to the attention of a large number of people throughout the world. It is grown in the humid tropics of Papua New Guinea, Indonesia, Malaysia, Philippines, Vietnam, Thailand, and Sri Lanka, so it should be adaptable to similar climactic regions of Central and South America, the Caribbean, Africa, Oceania, and West Asia. It seems that areas experiencing difficulties in growing high protein content foodstuffs would benefit by looking at the winged bean—especially areas where protein deficiencies exist. The winged bean averages 34% protein and 17% oil. Their tuberous roots contain 20% protein (compared to 1%–2% for other edible roots and tubers). As a nitrogen-fixing legume, it can also act as a soil-improving plant as well.

For more information, and for seed sources for the 40 seeds you will need to perform this test, write to one of the following:

Commission on International Relations (JH 215)
National Academy of Sciences–National Research Council
2101 Constitution Avenue
Washington, D.C. 20418, U.S.A.

Mrs. Joan Levy, Ed.
Winged Bean Flyer
Dept. of Agronomy
University of Illinois
Urbana, IL 61801, U.S.A.

Agricultural Information Bank for Asia
Southeast Asian Regional Center for Agriculture
College, Laguna 3720, Philippines

Plant 2 seeds on each 15-inch center directly in the bed, and thin to 1 plant if both germinate. The seeds germinate and grow slowly during the first 3 to 5 weeks after planting. The plants begin flowering as early as 2 months after planting (3 to 4 months at higher elevations) and although the green pods can be used as a fresh vegetable at the 10 to 13 week point, you should definitely determine the total amount of mature seeds that can be grown. Maturation can occur about 6 weeks after flowering/pollination takes place. Follow the procedure for drying as indicated for soybeans, and record the information on the soybean data log. Afterwards, harvest the tubers, weigh and record them also. The yield range for seeds and tubers under normal cultivation practices appears to be 1 to 4 pounds per 20 square feet.

We suggest you stake the winged bean plants to obtain the best seed yields. Keep the areas well weeded—especially during the beginning growth. Not doing so will result in a tangled mass and will make it very hard to harvest.

Like soybeans, the winged bean has trypsin inhibitors which obstruct the digestion of protein. Cooking both the fresh bean and dried bean deactivates this inhibitor.

Note: If you decide to grow an alternative to soybeans, in the first stage of testing, plant the beans in the wheat section (see the planning map on page 49), and move the wheat and tomato crops one section down. In the second year of testing, again plant the beans in the Bed One group as before, and in the Bed Two group, plant them in place of soybeans, but plant them on 7-inch and 9-inch centers (for pinto beans), and 12-inch and 18-inch centers (for winged beans).

Substituting Sweet Potatoes for "Irish" Potatoes

In tropical areas, sweet potatoes do much better than "Irish" potatoes. We encourage people who live in tropical climates to find three types of sweet potato to substitute for the White Rose, Red Lasoda, and Russet varieties suggested for Bed 3.

Plant sweet potatoes on 9-inch centers, 3 to 9 inches deep when the night-time temperatures reach 60 degrees Fahrenheit. They can also be planted in flats on 3-inch centers 4 weeks before this date. If so, they are transplanted 3 to 4 weeks after flat planting.

Sweet potatoes should be ready for harvesting from 4 to 7 months after planting. You can tell if they are mature when the leaves of the plant turn yellow and there is no visible new growth. In Hand and Cocerham's book, *The Sweet Potato* (Macmillan Publishing Co., New York, 1921), the authors write: "Another means which many growers find very reliable [for determining if the sweet potatoes are ready for harvest] is to break a tuber in two: if ripe, the broken part dries after a few minutes' exposure; if still green and in a growing state, the broken part remains milky and sticky." The average U.S. yield per 35 square feet is 8.2 pounds.

On the following pages, you will find all the data logs for this crop-testing chapter. How you use these logs is up to you: You may want to use them to keep records, to run your own crop tests, as a basis for a regional testing program, or to send in your results to Ecology Action.

Ecology Action would be pleased to hear about all your experiences with crop-testing, but we are particularly interested in your soybean and wheat test results, in any exceptional crop yields (yields that are exceptionally low, compared to the U.S. average yields, and yields 5 times greater or more than those averages). Data on crop-testing will probably not be significant until you have collected 3 to 5 years' worth of figures.

Whatever you have chosen to do with the information in this chapter, we hope you will continue "crop-testing" in some form or other as long as you continue to garden. It is an excellent way to keep learning and growing.

If you give a man a fish, he will have a meal.
If you teach him to fish, he will have a living.
If you are thinking a year ahead, sow seed.
If you are thinking ten years ahead, plant a tree.
If you are thinking one hundred years ahead, educate the
    people.
By sowing seed once, you will harvest once.
By planting a tree, you will harvest tenfold.
By educating the people, you will harvest one hundredfold.

ANONYMOUS CHINESE POET, 420 B.C.

Background Data Log

If you plan to send in your test results to Ecology Action, please fill out this form and enclose it with your soil test results (if you test your soil) and the data on crop yields. Weather information should be obtainable from your local weather station, airport, and/or radio station. Please give the source(s) of your information. If you do not test your soil, please give as complete a description of it as is possible. Please note your past experience with the soil, vegetation on it now, how long it has been in use (or not in use), what type of fertilizers have been used, and any other pertinent information.

1. **Location of your testing site.** (If you are not in a city or township, give points of reference so that we can locate it on a map — for instance, 30 miles south of San Francisco, 25 miles northeast of Santa Cruz, and 6 miles due east of the Pacific Ocean.)

_____

_____

_____

2. **Approximate altitude:** _____

3. **Monthly averages**

	Jan	Feb	Mar	Apr	May	Jun	Jul	Aug	Sep	Oct	Nov	Dec
Rainfall												
Minimum temperatures												
Maximum temperatures												

4. **First frost date (average):** _____

   Last frost date (average): _____

5. **Source(s) for weather information:** _____

_____

_____

6. **General terrain (include slope, direction it faces, and vegetation):** _____

_____

_____

7. **General soil type texture, and nutritive levels:** _____

_____

_____

8. **Source of water (well, lake, city water, etc.) and, if possible, the pH of the water:**

_____

_____

9. **Problems you or your neighbors have had with growing food in the past:** _____

_____

_____

Notes and Observations:

DATA LOG
Water Monitoring (optional)

Because it would be too time consuming to monitor each crop's water needs, we would like you to choose one crop. Since one crop only occupies a 20 square foot area, it will not take very long to water and monitor. Water the crop you have chosen either at the beginning or the end of the watering period. This will make it easier for you to record the information each day. (*Note:* Be sure to read the watering section in chapter 5 of *How to Grow More Vegetables* . . . to acquaint yourself with the proper watering technique.)

Number of days watered: _____

Total gallons: _____

Average water use per day: _____

Crop Chosen: _____

Meter Used: _____

If estimated, number of seconds per gallon: _____

Date watering begins: _____

Sun	Mon	Tues	Wed	Thurs	Fri	Sat	TOTAL

DATA LOG
Compost (optional)

Chapter 4 of *How To Grow More Vegetables* . . . describes compost making and the importance of compost in maintaining soil health. We have included this data log for those who wish to monitor the composition of their compost pile. Although it is not an exact measurement of the items, it will give you an indication of what the make-up of your compost is in general and help you to modify it in the future (if necessary).

Simply weigh one spadeful (or other unit) each of the general types of materials you are adding and record that weight in the spaces provided. Then, record the number of units of each material added to the pile each time you build it and total the quantities after completion. When the compost is finished "cooking" and is ready to use, weigh three separate samplings, enter these weights in the "Finished Compost" spaces, and find the average weight of the finished compost.

Material	Weight per Unit _____ lbs./shovelful	Date Added
SOIL		
FRESH GRASS CLIPPINGS		
DRY LEAVES		
KITCHEN WASTE (Gen'l)		
DRY WEEDS		
Other		
TOTAL NUMBER OF UNITS		

Finished Compost: _____   Average Sampling Weight _____

Notes and Observations:

DATA LOG
Wheat on 5″ centers

Variety and Source: *Hard Red Spring #906R (untreated)* _____

Flat planted: _____

Bed dug: _____

Sand/Compost/Manure/Fertilizer added:

DATE	TYPE	AMOUNT
_____	_____	_____
_____	_____	_____
_____	_____	_____
_____	_____	_____
_____	_____	_____
_____	_____	_____
_____	_____	_____
_____	_____	_____
_____	_____	_____

Transplanted: _____

Number of seedlings: _____

Harvested: _____

Dry weight of stalks _____

Weight of dried seeds _____

Weight of chaff and stems _____

Weight of 100 seeds _____

(U.S. average yield: wheat 0.7 lbs./20 sq. ft.; straw 1 lb./20 sq. ft.)

Notes and Observations:

DATA LOG
Cherry Tomatoes on 18″ centers

Variety and Source: *Large Red* _____

Flat planted: _____

Bed dug: _____

Sand/Compost/Manure/Fertilizer added:

DATE	TYPE	AMOUNT
_____	_____	_____
_____	_____	_____
_____	_____	_____
_____	_____	_____
_____	_____	_____
_____	_____	_____
_____	_____	_____
_____	_____	_____
_____	_____	_____
_____	_____	_____

Transplanted: _____

Number of seedlings: _____

Harvest begins: _____

Harvest ends: _____

Weight of total harvest: _____

(U.S. average yield: 6.1 lbs./20 sq. ft.)

Weight of each day's harvest:

Sun	Mon	Tues	Wed	Thurs	Fri	Sat	TOTAL

Notes and Observations:

DATA LOG
Soybeans on 6″ centers

Variety and Source: *Altona* _____

Flat planted: _____

Bed dug: _____

Sand/Compost/Manure/Fertilizer added:

DATE	TYPE	AMOUNT
_____	_____	_____
_____	_____	_____
_____	_____	_____
_____	_____	_____
_____	_____	_____
_____	_____	_____
_____	_____	_____
_____	_____	_____
_____	_____	_____

Transplanted: _____

Number of seedlings: _____

Harvested: _____

Dry weight of shelled seed: _____

Weight of 100 seeds _____

(U.S. average yield: 0.7 lbs./20 sq. ft.)

	At Planting	First Flowers	Full Flowering	Final Harvest
Date				
Sunrise				
Sunset				
High Temp				
Low Temp				
Height				

Notes and Observations:

DATA LOG
Romaine Lettuce on 8″ centers

Variety and Source: *Paris Green* _____

Flat planted: _____

Bed dug: _____

Sand/Compost/Manure/Fertilizer added:

DATE	TYPE	AMOUNT
_____	_____	_____
_____	_____	_____
_____	_____	_____
_____	_____	_____
_____	_____	_____
_____	_____	_____
_____	_____	_____
_____	_____	_____
_____	_____	_____

Transplanted: _____

Number of seedlings: _____

Harvested: _____

Weight and number of plants: _____

(U.S. average yield: 9.7 lbs./20 sq. ft.)

Notes and observations:

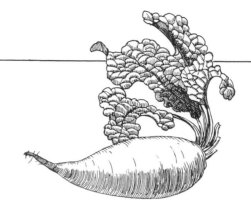

DATA LOG
Beets on 3″ centers

Variety and Source: *Cylindra* _____

Bed dug: _____

Sand/Compost/Manure/Fertilizer* added:

DATE	TYPE	AMOUNT
_____	_____	_____
_____	_____	_____
_____	_____	_____
_____	_____	_____
_____	_____	_____
_____	_____	_____
_____	_____	_____
_____	_____	_____
_____	_____	_____
_____	_____	_____

Bed planted: _____

Number of seeds planted: _____

Harvested: _____

Weight and number of plants: _____

Weight of beets without tops: _____

(U.S. average yield: 12 lbs./20 sq. ft.)

*For root crops, *use one-half* (1/2) the general nitrogen amount indicated to be added by the soil test.

Notes and Observations:

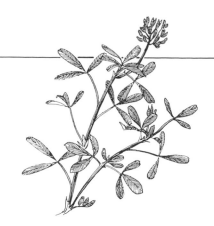

DATA LOG
Alfalfa — broadcast directly

Variety and Source: *Cody Certified* _____

Bed dug: _____

Sand/Compost/Manure/Fertilizer added:

DATE	TYPE	AMOUNT

Bed planted: _____

Weight of seeds planted: _____

Harvest begins*: _____

(U.S. average yield: 1.35 lbs./10 sq. ft. annually or about 0.45 lbs. per cutting.)

*At each cutting, only half the stand is harvested. If the bed lies on a north-south axis, harvest the *east* section (4′ × 2-1/2′) at the first cutting, and the *west* section at the second cutting, and so on. First cutting comes at 10% flowering, second cutting at 80–90% flowering, successive cuttings at 50% flowering.

Weight of harvest:

	Date	Fresh Weight	Dry Weight
1st cutting			
2nd cutting			
3rd cutting			
4th cutting			
5th cutting			
6th cutting			
Total			

Notes and Observations:

DATA LOG
Collards on 12″ centers

Variety and Source: *Georgia* _____

Flat planted: _____

Bed dug: _____

Sand/Compost/Manure/Fertilizer added:

DATE	TYPE	AMOUNT

Transplanted: _____

Number of seedlings: _____

Harvest begins: _____

Harvest ends: _____

Weight of total harvest: _____

(Possible U.S. average yield: 19 lbs./20 sq. ft.)

Weight of each day's harvest:

Sun	Mon	Tues	Wed	Thurs	Fri	Sat	TOTAL

Notes and Observations:

DATA LOG
Soybeans on 9″ centers

Variety and Source: *Altona* _____

Flat planted: _____

Bed dug: _____

Sand/Compost/Manure/Fertilizer added:

DATE	TYPE	AMOUNT
_____	_____	_____
_____	_____	_____
_____	_____	_____
_____	_____	_____
_____	_____	_____
_____	_____	_____
_____	_____	_____
_____	_____	_____
_____	_____	_____

Transplanted: _____

Number of seedlings: _____

Harvested: _____

Dry weight of shelled seed: _____

Weight of 100 seeds _____

(U.S. average yield: 0.7 lbs./20 sq. ft.)

	At Planting	First Flowers	Full Flowering	Final Harvest
Date				
Sunrise				
Sunset				
High Temp				
Low Temp				
Height				

Notes and Observations:

DATA LOG
Soybeans on 12″ centers

Variety and Source: *Altona* _____

Flat planted: _____

Bed dug: _____

Sand/Compost/Manure/Fertilizer added:

DATE	TYPE	AMOUNT
_____	_____	_____
_____	_____	_____
_____	_____	_____
_____	_____	_____
_____	_____	_____
_____	_____	_____
_____	_____	_____
_____	_____	_____
_____	_____	_____
_____	_____	_____

Transplanted: _____

Number of seedlings: _____

Harvested: _____

Dry weight of shelled seed: _____

Weight of 100 seeds _____

(U.S. average yield: 0.7 lbs./20 sq. ft.)

	At Planting	First Flowers	Full Flowering	Final Harvest
Date				
Sunrise				
Sunset				
High Temp				
Low Temp				
Height				

Notes and Observations:

DATA LOG
Cucumbers on 12″ centers

Variety and Source: *Sunnybrook* _____

Flat planted: _____

Bed dug: _____

Sand/Compost/Manure/Fertilizer added:

DATE	TYPE	AMOUNT
_____	_____	_____
_____	_____	_____
_____	_____	_____
_____	_____	_____
_____	_____	_____
_____	_____	_____
_____	_____	_____
_____	_____	_____
_____	_____	_____
_____	_____	_____

Transplanted: _____

Number of seedlings: _____

Harvest begins: _____

Harvest ends: _____

Weight of total harvest: _____

(U.S. average yield: 4.1 lbs./20 sq. ft.)

Weight of each day's harvest and number picked:

Sun	Mon	Tues	Wed	Thurs	Fri	Sat	TOTAL
Wt./No.	Wt./No.	Wt./No.	Wt./No.	Wt./No.	Wt./No.	Wt./No.	Wt./No.

Notes and Observations:

DATA LOG
Potatoes on 9" centers

Variety and Source: *Red Lasoda* _____

Bed dug: _____

Sand/Compost/Manure/Fertilizer added*:

DATE	TYPE	AMOUNT
_____	_____	_____
_____	_____	_____
_____	_____	_____
_____	_____	_____
_____	_____	_____
_____	_____	_____
_____	_____	_____
_____	_____	_____
_____	_____	_____
_____	_____	_____

Bed planted: _____

Pounds of seed potatoes planted: _____

Harvested: _____

Weight of harvest: _____

(U.S. average yield: 18.4 lbs./35 sq. ft.)

* For root crops, *use one-half* (1/2) the general nitrogen amount indicated to be added by the soil test.

Notes and Observations:

DATA LOG
Potatoes on 9″ centers

Variety and Source: *Russet* _____

Bed dug: _____

Sand/Compost/Manure/Fertilizer added*:

DATE	TYPE	AMOUNT

Bed planted: _____

Pounds of seed potatoes planted: _____

Harvested: _____

Weight of harvest: _____

(U.S. average yield: 18.4 lbs./35 sq. ft.)

* For root crops, *use one-half* (1/2) the amount of nitrogen fertilizers indicated to be added by the soil test.

Notes and Observations:

DATA LOG
Potatoes on 9″ centers

Variety and Source: *White Rose* _____

Bed dug: _____

Sand/Compost/Manure/Fertilizer added*:

DATE	TYPE	AMOUNT
_____	_____	_____
_____	_____	_____
_____	_____	_____
_____	_____	_____
_____	_____	_____
_____	_____	_____
_____	_____	_____
_____	_____	_____
_____	_____	_____
_____	_____	_____

Bed planted: _____

Pounds of seed potatoes planted: _____

Harvested: _____

Weight of harvest: _____

(U.S. average yield: 18.4 lbs./35 sq. ft.)

* For root crops, *use one-half* (1/2) the general nitrogen amount indicated to be added by the soil test.

Notes and Observations:

DATA LOG
Dwarf Fruit Trees on 8″ centers

Variety or Varieties and Source(s): _____

Bed dug: _____

Area of bed: _____

Sand/Compost/Manure/Fertilizer added:

DATE	TYPE	AMOUNT
_____	_____	_____
_____	_____	_____
_____	_____	_____
_____	_____	_____
_____	_____	_____
_____	_____	_____
_____	_____	_____
_____	_____	_____
_____	_____	_____

Bed planted: _____

Number of trees planted: _____

(Approximate U.S. average yield: apples — 18.3 lbs./64 sq. ft.; navel oranges — 10.2 lbs./64 sq. ft.)

Note: First year harvest will be minimal. Maximum yield point is reached in about 10 years and will continue at that level for about 20 additional years.

	Year	Harvest Begun	Harvest Completed	Yield
1				
2				
3				
4				
5				
6				
7				
8				
9				
10				

Notes and Observations:

DATA LOG
Medium Red Clover sown under dwarf fruit trees

Variety and Source: _____

Seed sown: _____

Amount sown: _____

Weight of harvest*: _____

Year	Cutting	Date	Fresh Weight
1	1		
	2		
	3		
	4		
2	1		
	2		
	3		
	4		
3	1		
	2		
	3		
	4		
4	1		
	2		
	3		
	4		
5	1		
	2		
	3		
	4		

(U.S. average yield: 5 lbs./60 sq. ft.

* At each cutting, only half the stand is harvested. If the bed lies on a north-south axis, harvest the east section at the first cutting, the west section at the second cutting, and so on. First cutting comes at 10% flowering, second cutting at 80–90% flowering, and successive cuttings at 50% flowering.

Notes and Observations:

Table 12. Nutriments per 100 gram portion (or a little more than 3-1/2 ounces). From **Composition of Foods**, USDA (see Resource Guide, p. 190)

Food	Water Percent	Food Energy Calories	Protein gm	Fat gm	Carbohydrate Total gm	Fiber gm	Ash gm	Calcium mg
Beets, raw	87.3%	43	1.6	.1	9.9	.8	1.1	16
boiled, drained	90.9%	32	1.1	.1	7.2	.8	.7	14
Beet greens, raw	90.9%	24	2.2	.3	4.6	1.3	2.0	119
steamed	93.6%	18	1.7	.2	3.3	1.1	1.2	99
Collards, raw leaves								
without stems	85.3%	45	4.8	.8	7.5	1.2	1.6	250
Collards, steamed	89.6%	33	3.6	.7	5.1	1.0	1.0	188
Cucumbers, raw	95.1%	15	.9	.1	3.4	.6	.5	25
dill pickles	93.3%	11	.7	.2	2.2	.5	3.6	26
Lettuce, Romaine raw	94.0%	18	1.3	.3	3.5	.7	.9	68
Potatoes, baked in								
skin	75.1%	93	2.6	.1	21.1	.6	1.1	9
boiled in skin	79.8%	76	2.1	.1	17.1	.5	.9	7
fried from raw	46.9%	268	4.0	14.2	32.6	1.0	2.3	15
Potato chips	1.8%	568	5.3	39.8	50.0	(1.6)	3.1	40
Soybeans, immature seeds, cooked, boiled, drained	73.8%	118	9.8	5.1	10.1	1.4	1.2	60
Soybeans, mature seeds, cooked	71.0%	130	11.0	5.7	10.8	1.6	1.5	73
Soybean curd (tofu)	84.8%	72	7.8	4.2	2.4	.1	.8	128
Soybean sprouts, dry weight, uncooked[d]	Data	varies						
Tomatoes, raw	93.0%	22	1.1	.2	4.7	.5	.5	13
canned	93.7%	21	1.0	.2	4.3	.4	.8	6
Wheat, whole-grain, hard red spring	13.0%	330	14.0	2.2	69.1	2.3	1.7	36
Whole wheat bread made with water	36.4%	241	9.1	2.6	49.3	1.5	2.6	84
Wheat sprouts, dry weight	Data	varies						
Apples, freshly harvested, with peel	84.8%	56	.2	.6	14.1	1.0	.3	7
Oranges, peeled fruit, raw	86.0%	49	1.0	.2	12.2	.5	.6	41

[a] Year round average. Recently dug potatoes contain about 26 mg. ascorbic acid per 100 grams. After 3 months' storage the value is only half as high; after 6 months', about one-third as high.

[b] Applies to product without added salt. If salt is added, the estimated average value for sodium is 236 mg/100 gms.

[c] Sodium content is variable and may be as high as 1,000 mg/100 gms.

[d] . . . unlike most other grains and pulses, soybeans contain substances called "soybean trypsin inhibitors (SBTI), which obstruct the functioning of the pancreas-secreted stypsin enzyme essential for the digestion of protein and the maintenance of proper growth. SBTI can—and must—be inactivated by cooking." (pp. 76–77) " . . . To deactivate soybean trypsin inhibitors, they (**soybean sprouts**) are always parboiled for 6 to 8 minutes, or lightly sauteed, before serving." **The Book of Tofu**, William Shurtleff and Akiko Aoyagi, Ten Speed Press, Berkeley.

Phosphorus mg	Iron mg	Sodium mg	Potassium mg	Vitamin A Value International Units (I.U.)	Thiamine mg	Riboflavin mg	Niacin mg	Ascorbic Acid (Vitamin C) mg
33	.7	60	335	20	.03	.05	.4	10
23	.5	43	208	20	.03	.04	.3	6
40	3.3	130	570	6100	.10	.22	.4	30
25	1.9	76	332	5100	.07	.15	.3	15
82	1.5	—	450	9300	.16	.31	1.7	152
52	.8	—	262	7800	.11	.20	1.2	76
27	1.1	6	160	250	.03	.04	.2	11
21	1.0	1428	200	100	Trace	.02	Trace	6
25	1.4	9	264	1900	.05	.08	.4	18
65	.7	4[b]	503	Trace	.10	.04	1.7	20[a]
53	.6	3[b]	407	Trace	.09	.04	1.5	16
101	1.1	223	775	Trace	.12	.07	2.8	19
139	1.8	1000[c]	1130	Trace	.21	.07	4.8	16
191	2.5	—	—	660	.31	.13	1.2	17
179	2.7	2	540	30	.21	.09	.6	0
126	1.9	7	42	0	.06	.03	.1	0
27	.5	3	244	900	.06	.04	.7	23[e]
19	.5	130	217	900	.05	.03	.7	17
383	3.1	(3)	370	(0)	.57	.12	4.3	(0)
254	2.3	530	256	Trace	.30	.10	2.8	Trace
10	.3	1	110	90	.03	.02	.1	7[f]
20	.4	1	200	200	.10	.04	.4	(50)[g]

[e] Year round average. Samples marketed from November through May average around 10 mgs/100 gms; from June through October, the average of fresh tomatoes is about 26 mgs/100 gms.

[f] Average value of a wide variety of commercially grown apples marketed through the year.

[g] Value weighed by monthly and total season shipments for marketing as fresh fruit. Figure is based on all commercial varieties: Navels, Valencias, etc. from different areas may vary.

( ): denotes values imputed from another form or similar food.

The Herbal Lawn

A *self-fertilizing alternative for the grass lawn*

Picture a natural meadow, a rolling carpet of green — lush, and fragrant, with tiny flowers adding occasional splashes of color to the rich background. Further imagine that this vision is *your lawn*. If this idea is appealing, why not give serious thought to removing your grass lawn, and putting in an herbal one? An herbal lawn is a delightful alternative to the traditional grass — not only is it pleasing to the senses, on the more practical side, it will require little care, little water, and no fertilizer at all once it is well-established.

The concept is not a new one. Self-fertilizing herbal lawns were developed in sixteenth century medieval England when landowners tired of monotonous lawns like those we have today. They wanted a more "natural" meadow.

Hardy bulbs were sometimes hidden underneath the lush green carpet of clovers and herbs so that colorful flowers would appear at different times of the year. English, Scotch, and Irish daffodils, winter aconite, wood hyacinths (*Scillas*), grape hyacinths, star narcissi, wood anemone, dog's-tooth violet, snake's-head (*Fritillaria*), tulips, stars of Bethlehem (*Ornithogalum*), and snowflakes (*Leucolium*) were used.

Our Experience

Ecology Action's experience with the herbal lawn has been a series of fortuitous misunderstandings. We first read about lawn alternatives in a charming little paperback book, *How to Enjoy Your Weeds,* by Audrey Hatfield. Less than two pages were devoted to a description of a thick and fragrant turf composed of so-called "weeds": white Dutch clover (*Trifolium repens*), suckling clover or lesser yellow trefoil (*T. dubium*), yarrow (*Achillea millefolium*), creeping thyme (*Thymus serphyllum*), and Roman chamomile (*Anthemis nobilis*).

With this sympathetic mixture we gain a richly colored lawn that is permanently and perfectly fertilized. The clovers, besides being a source of sodium, encourage and store the nitrogen-fixing bacteria in their root nodules. The yarrow provides copper, nitrates, phosphates, and potash. The camomile gives calcium and the thyme has other gifts... It is interesting that this "weed" mixture, which has produced many fine lawns, was evolved after the 1914–18 War for the Imperial War Graves Commission. They used it all over Europe to make the wonderful, fragrant turf of their huge cemeteries, where it has withstood the varying climatic and soil conditions and the treading of many thousands of visitors. (Hatfield, p. 31)

Further research and correspondence turned up only one additional short piece on *Clover Lawns* that appeared in the Journal of the Royal Horticultural Society, nearly 30 years ago. This article, probably the inspiration for what Hatfield wrote, talks about

An unmowed natural herbal lawn.

An herbal lawn that has been mowed.

reversing the trend towards all-grass lawns and using the chamomile, clovers, yarrow, and other "weeds" that creep in to advantage, since they are the most resistant to weed killers anyway. The article recommended sowing in seeds of these "weeds" and cited the successful experience of the English War Graves Commission and the resulting sturdy lawns that stayed green even in drought.

Somehow, in ordering seeds, locating the various herbs, and preparing the soil for our lawn, we forgot that these herbs were meant to be added to a primarily grass lawn. We took the idea back to the original lawn, or "natural meadow" idea and left the grass out entirely.

The resulting "herbal lawn" was beautiful. A thick lush turf resulted with delightful modulations of color, texture, and scent. This precious 200 square foot "meadow" was springy to walk on and a delight for garden meetings, lunch-times, and workbreaks.

As we were writing this chapter, another discrepancy came to light. Lesser yellow trefoil (*Trifolium dubium*) had been suggested, but the seed we

obtained was a birdsfoot trefoil (*Lotus corniculatus*). It turned out to be a fortunate error. *Lotus corniculatus* is easily available, hardy, and often recommended as a lawn substitute.

Our herbal lawn lasted for over a year, but during the second year, thatch built up underneath and eventually showed as much brown as green. Plans were begun to try to revitalize the lawn and identify the problem. We divided the lawn into two areas and began experimenting with each section, but the research was thwarted when the entire demonstration and community garden had to be closed due to the landowner's building program. We tend to think that perhaps the soil was not yet good enough to support any kind of lawn well, but we did not have time to verify this theory. Tests had shown it consisted of about 1/5 rock and 1/3 clay—not very conducive to lawn growing. Ecology Action has just obtained a new garden site and is eager to put in a new herbal lawn, trying ones both with and without grasses.

An herbal lawn is a dynamic working mixture of compatible plants. Each herbal lawn will be different, and each will reach its own state of equilibrium. Under adverse soil conditions, chamomile will try to dominate; but in shady spots, the thyme will try to fill in more for the straggly sun-lovers. As W.F.W. Harding described it in *Clover Lawns*:

One may say that this is the lazy man's method of making a lawn and in one sense this is true. It is true in so far as one is choosing to work with Nature rather than against her, and thus Nature herself does half the work and bears half the cost... It must, however, be emphasized here that any seed mixture will reach a different equilibrium in different soils, and as the conditions alter from year to year so the equilibrium will not remain static.

In other words, working with an herbal lawn gives one the opportunity to live with and learn from a dynamic, ever-changing, living system.

We suggest that you start with the five plants listed below, and add grasses if you wish. But leave room in your plans for the unforeseen — the unique "weeds" that may appear, spring bulbs that you want to tuck in here and there for a surprise, or that pretty ground cover plant you may find at a special nursery.

Five Basic Ground Covers

The white Dutch clover (*Trifolium repens*) and yellow narrowleafed trefoil (*Lotus corniculatus*) used in the lawn are legumes which take nitrogen from the air and fix it in the soil. This free nitrogen-fixing capacity is important because 1/2 the chemical nitrogen fertilizer currently consumed in the United States is used on lawns, golf courses, and cemeteries. The prime source for manufacturing this chemical fertilizer is natural gas.

Mixed with the legumes are dwarf yarrow (such as *Achillea nana* or *Achillea millefolium*), creeping thyme (*Thymus serphyllum*), and Roman chamomile or a petal-less creeping Roman chamomile (sold in some nurseries but apparently not yet identified botanically). It is similar to true Roman chamomile (*Anthemis nobilis*) in smell and appearance, but is slower-growing and without petals. The chamomile smells like crushed apples or tutti-fruiti when walked upon or mowed and concentrates the important nutriment calcium. The yarrow concentrates copper, nitrogen, phosphorus, and potash.

White clover is drought resistant — a good characteristic for green summer lawns when grasses pale, burn, or require large amounts of water. The lawn

requires only 1/2 to 1/3 the water to maintain — important since the United States may reach a point of insufficient water supplies during the 1980's. The lawn grows less rapidly which means about 1/2 the mowing. Ease of maintenance, plus reduced water and fertilizer consumption, led the English Imperial War Graves Commission to use the lawn in cemeteries after World War One. The mixture used was developed by the well-known British seed firm, Sutton and Sons.

The result is a luxuriant mixture of deep greens with a rich, spongy texture underfoot that smells delightful. Inhaling the scent of chamomile after a hard day of work is exhilarating and the thyme can even be used in cooking. Once it is established, you can sit or lie on the herbal lawn. It will be one of those simple pleasures to be enjoyed and remembered, like watching a sunset or sunrise, looking at the stars, or experiencing an electrifying thunderstorm.

The lawn holds up well under normal traffic, but not active sports, and does poorly in shady areas. It should be mowed regularly before the legume and herbal flowers appear and a little higher than most lawns. Too short a trim can kill off the plants; long growth, on the other hand, promotes leggy plants rather than a thick, green springy mat or pile. Clippings must be caught in a grass catcher and composted. Hand mowing is easy, aromatic and keeps one more in touch with the plants — try this pleasurable form of exercise at least once! The cured compost is spread evenly on the lawn in spring and fall to provide nutriments and rich humic acids and materials that feed the microbiotic life so essential to good healthy soil and plant growth. Sometimes small amounts of an organic nitrogen fertilizer (such as 1 pound of blood meal, fish meal, or hoof and horn meal) and of an organic calcium/phosphorus fertilizer (such as 2 pounds of bone meal) are added annually per 100 square feet.

Some people prefer to include grass seed with the clover and herbs. If you do, you might try a 1/4 (by weight) grass seed mixture, with a 3/4 (by weight) clover and trefoil combination. Be sure to sow each of the three components separately for the best results. A broad-bladed, tough grass combination of Red Fescue, Kentucky Bluegrass and Rye Grass has been suggested. In our area, Ferry Morse's Golden Gate lawn mixture is one good blend. The grasses do not fix nitrogen, however, and so the additional fertilizers mentioned above may have to be used.

For more ideas, and for a complete listing of various ground covers, see *Lawns and Ground Covers* by the editors of Sunset Books.

Common Ground's Recipe

Ecology Action's Common Ground Garden had been experimenting with the following recipe and procedure. It is best to begin with an *experimental*, 1 square yard (3' x 3') the first year. If this is successful, you can then expand the area the second year, perhaps modifying the mixture, and even add hidden bulbs according to your own imagination!

The herbal lawn should be planted in *early spring*. The clover and trefoil will grow and establish more rapidly at this cooler time of the year, enabling them to catch up with the herbal seedling starts. (In the fall, the legumes grow faster and will get an inappropriate edge on the herbs whose growth is slowing down.)

Herbal seedlings of Roman chamomile, creeping thyme, and dwarf yarrow can be purchased from a nursery in the spring. You can also start your own seedlings in flats, or, even better, plant divisions in flats. However, if you do this, you will have to plan far in advance, as much as a year ahead of time. Herbs can take 4 to 6 months more before they can be planted out in the garden.

If you are starting seeds in flats, use a soil mixture of 1/3 compost, 1/3 good soil, and 1/3 sharp sand. Initially, plant 60 seeds (all will not germinate) of each herb on 1-inch centers for each 100 square foot area to be planted. (A plan for standard flat construction is given in the chapter on Tools. The flat shown contains at least 250 1-inch centers.) Germination will take several weeks. After the herbal seedlings are 1-1/2 inches high, transplant them into another flat on 2-inch centers, where they will continue to grow until spring transplanting. If 25 good plants of each herb have not grown in the first flat, replant three times the additional number of seeds you need for the remaining plants. During the winter, the protection of a greenhouse or mini-greenhouse will be needed in many areas. (See chapter on Tools.)

Procedure

SOIL PREPARATION is most important for deep roots and a lush healthy look. Remove weeds and old grass, and add a 2-inch layer of cured compost or aged manure. *Double-dig* the area (or at least thoroughly loosen it to a depth of 12 inches.) See *How to Grow More Vegetables* for details. *Fertilize,* this time only, with:

2 pounds hoof and horn meal

2 pounds bone meal per 100 square feet

1 pound kelp meal

If the area to be planted is smaller, adjust the quantities accordingly.

SEEDING comes next. First tamp down the area thoroughly, using a 4' x 5' x 5/8" plywood board. Rake the area to create furrows and, using *new* seed, broadcast by hand 1/2 to 1 ounce each of clover and trefoil per 100 square feet. (An additional 1/8 to 1/4 ounce of lawn seed mixture is optional.) Gently smooth the earth with the flat back edge of a rake to fill in the furrows, and tamp again.

TRANSPLANT HERB SEEDLINGS of chamomile, thyme and yarrow on 18-inch centers. Distribute your weight to avoid unnecessary compaction by using your plywood board to walk and sit on when transplanting. Approximately 19 plants of each will be needed to cover 100 square feet. Plant herbs sequentially using offset or diagonal spacing.
spacing.

THE PLANTS take about 3 months to establish ground cover—about twice the time required for normal lawns. Several additional months will be needed before the lawn is mature. It can then be fully enjoyed. In the meantime, keep the lawn *weeded* and *watered* until it is well-established. Weeding is especially important during the early stages so the lawn plants will not be choked out before they have a chance to establish. Weeding should also be done, as necessary, later on.

Reseed clover and trefoil where needed using a handfork to loosen the soil.

Retamp as necessary until surface can be easily walked upon. Mow periodically (with blades set somewhat higher than normal) to encourage a dense spreading habit. Clippings should be caught and composted. It is important that they be returned to the lawn as compost since the lawn, once established, is meant to be self-fertilizing. Not catching clippings can increase thatch build-up and cause a choked-out lawn. In extremely cold or hot areas, freezing or burning of some of the plants—especially the chamomile—may be a problem. Experiment first with a small area to determine their suitability in your own climate. You may need to try substituting other plants. The herbal lawn does not do well in shady areas.

Plant Types

WHITE
DUTCH
CLOVER

WHITE DUTCH CLOVER (*Trifolium repens*)
This well-known little plant hardly needs an introduction. 95% of the white Dutch clover in this country is already used in lawn grass mixtures. It is low-growing with the typical shamrock leaves and a white flowerhead very attractive to bees — this may be its only drawback. For a 1 to 2 month period each year when the clover is flowering, going barefoot on an herbal lawn carries some risk of stepping on a bee. In spite of this, most schoolyards and parks add clover to the lawn to maintain a lush green look; clovers do not brown as rapidly as grasses in drought and supply steady doses of nitrogen to the plants around. Clover seed is available in some lawn and garden supply stores or may be ordered with trefoil seeds.

ROMAN CHAMOMILE (*Anthemis nobilis*)
Roman chamomile is a low-growing dense and hardy ground cover commonly sold in lawn and garden supply centers. Chamomile belongs in the compositae family, the hardest to identify and classify botanically. Thus one chamomile may vary from the next slightly. The flowers can look like small daisies with white petals and yellow centers and one other variety you can use has petal-less small yellow heads. The odor is very clean and pleasant, like crushed apples. Rubbing your hand or fingers lightly over the plant will release the scent.

Roman chamomile has traditionally been used for garden "couches," soft resting places formed of earth and planted with a covering of chamomile where the gardener can go to ease aches and pains and come back refreshed and revitalized. Chamomile is also placed near it. It has been used for lawns for hundreds of years. It can look rangy if not sheared periodically.

The German chamomile (*Matricaria camomila*) is a 1 to 2 foot plant that grows each summer and reseeds next year, often appearing in fields and waste places, even sidewalk cracks. Foliage, flowers and scent are very close to Roman chamomile although some closely related species can have disagreeable smells. It is not really suitable for an herbal lawn because of its height and short life.

ROMAN
CHAMOMILE

Chamomile tea is probably the best known and most popular worldwide, being mild and naturally sweet with a wonderful, relaxing effect. The tea is made from the dried flower heads of German chamomile. These can be collected in the morning as soon as they are dry and dried further in the sun or on a screen or paper placed in a dry warm place. For tea, pour 1 cup boiling water over 1 full teaspoon of dried flowers, let steep 4 to 5 minutes before drinking.

Chamomile grows best in full sun, and does poorly in shade. It is susceptible to freezing and burning in extremely cold or hot areas. Already started plants are recommended and these can easily be divided further.

DWARF
YARROW

DWARF YARROW

Of all the herbs, this has been the hardest to locate. Approximately 100 achillea species exist, many of them wild and native plants. The best for the herbal lawn is dwarf yarrow (*Achillea tomentosa*). *A. tomentosa* grows in a mat about 6 to 10 inches tall and must be searched for in the nurseries in spring when the selection is most varied.

The Sunset Western Garden Book lists several other short ground cover type achilleas: *A. ageratifolia* 4 to 10 inches, *A. argentea* 5 to 10 inches and *A.*

nana 2 to 8 inches. If these are available in your area they are certainly worth trying and we have even used the common yarrow (*A. millefolium*). The flower heads of *A. millefolium* form 1 to 3 feet from the ground but the fernlike foliage only grows 6 to 10 inches and can be kept trimmed to a lower suitable ground cover height.

Achilleas have graceful and very finely divided foliage. The flowers are borne in flat-topped clusters of striking grace and beauty. The blossoms are usually white, sometimes pink or reddish, though the dwarf yarrow has golden flowers. Blossoms of common yarrow make excellent cut flowers.

Yarrows do not need much water. They will form quite a dense clump and you may want to space them rather farther apart than other herbs in the lawn mix and divide them periodically, especially if the dwarf yarrow cannot be found and the more aggressive common yarrow is used.

Seeds are very tiny and difficult to obtain. Starts are easily divided off of already growing clumps.

Yarrow has many medicinal uses, dating back thousands of years, for which we suggest you consult *How to Enjoy Your Weeds* or *The Rodale Herb Book*.

CREEPING THYME

There are 50 different kinds of thyme, though most of them are too tall and woody to be used for the herbal lawns. The best ground cover is *Thymus serphyllum*, called creeping thyme or mother of thyme. It forms a low growing mat and an abundance of pale violet flowers loved by bees. If bees are going to present a problem, mow the lawn more frequently to keep flower heads from forming, OR plant the wooly thyme (*Thymus languinosus*) which does not flower as profusely. *How To Grow Herbs* also suggests caraway, profusely scented thyme (*T. herba-barona*), or silver thyme (*T. s. "Argentus"*) as ground covers so these and others can be experimented with as part of the herbal lawn mix. Just avoid woody stemmed thymes and stick to the soft creeping types.

Thyme will grow well even in poor soil, needs a minimum of water and will take to partially shaded areas better than other herbs. If starting thyme from

CREEPING
THYME

seed, plant in a flat and transplant out when well established. Small plants from a nursery are recommended.

The leaves are wonderful dried or fresh and have a number of uses in the kitchen and in potpourri. We are especially fond of a mixture of dried thyme, basil and parsley leaves to flavor many dishes.

BIRDSFOOT
TREFOIL

BIRDSFOOT TREFOIL (*Lotus corniculatus*)

Birdsfoot trefoil is a crop of major importance as a forage for cattle and also useful on a smaller scale for rabbits and chickens. It is high in protein and often will grow on soil too poor for alfalfa. It is a legume, like clover, which fixes nitrogen in the soil. There is a broadleaf or erect birdsfoot trefoil used with meadow grass, but the one for herbal lawns is called "narrow-leaf" and is a prostrate birdsfoot trefoil that spreads along the ground in a lacy pattern. Trefoils are also used for erosion control and work best in combination with other plants. Trefoil seeds mature unevenly making harvest difficult. Therefore, seeds may be hard to obtain, expensive, and germinate unevenly. If you experience trouble with the seed try again. We have usually had good results. Once started it re-seeds prolifically year after year, even in adverse conditions.

Trefoil has pretty yellow flowers similar to sweet peas and narrow leaves. An inoculant is recommended but not required to insure the nitrogen-fixing bacteria.

BULBS

For the crowning touch, try hiding some hardy bulbs underneath your herbal lawn. The spring flowers will look pretty and unexpected against the green lawn and during most of the year when the bulbs are not seen above ground the garden will not be left with a bare spot. Listed here are descriptions of the most suitable bulbs to try, based on suggestions from *The Wild Garden* and some discoveries of our own.

Keep these two things in mind:

1. Choose bulbs that flower early in the spring. January through April is best, May is acceptable in some cases. Flowers and foliage should be allowed to die back naturally before you need to mow.

2. Bulbs listed as "for naturalizing" are the best bets. They will come up year after year with little care.

For the most natural effect, simply scatter a handful of bulbs and dig holes where they fall. Many will spread and send up more flowers each year. Some planning will need to be done for sun/shade and for height and color for best effect.

Bulbs will bloom later in cold winter areas and earlier where winters are mild.

BULBS FOR ALL CLIMATES

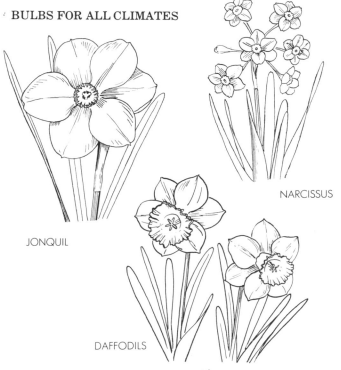

JONQUIL

NARCISSUS

DAFFODILS

Daffodils, Narcissus and Jonquils
> Bloom: February, March and April
> Height: generally 18″, 6-10″ for jonquils
> Colors: mostly yellow, also cream, pink and apricot

All kinds are splendid, especially mixtures sold for naturalizing and "species" narcissus and *Poeticus narcissus.*

TULIPS

GRAPE
HYACINTH

Tulips

    Bloom: March, April and May

    Height: *Greigii* — 10″ (early flowering)

            Kaufmanniana — 4–6″ (earliest)

            Fosteriana — 10–15″

            Others — check catalog

    Colors: Mainly reds and yellows but also pink
    orange, white and variegated

Tulips need a bit more care than other bulbs and the bold drama of most kinds is better for showy borders than naturalizing in lawns. For herbal lawn planting the botanical tulips such as (but not limited to) *greigii,- kaufmanniana,* and *fosteriana,* are best. Also worth trying might be the new Perrennial Tulips from White Flower Farm. Tulips usually need good sun.

Grape Hyacinth (Muscari)

    Bloom: April

    Height: 6–9″

    Color: blues and white

These endearing bulbs spread easily and bloom eagerly. They produce an abundance of long spaghetti-shaped leaves so you may want to try them around borders first.

HYACINTH

SNOWFLAKE

Wood Hyacinth (Scilla campanulata or *S. hispanica)*

    Bloom: May

    Height: 12–15″

    Color: pastel shades of violet, pink and white

These woodsy flowers love the shade. If May blooming will be a problem, plant along edges. Another scilla, *S. tubergeniana* blooms earlier with silvery-blue flowers.

Snowflake (Leucojum aestivum)

    Bloom: March and April; November, December
    and January in mild winter areas

    Height: 6–9″

    Color: white with pale green tips

Snowflakes look like snowdrops but will do better in southern areas.

FRITILLARIA

CROCUS

Snakeshead Fritillaria or Guinea-Hen Flower (*Fritillaria meleagris*)

Bloom: April

Height: 6″

Colors: white, maroon and variations

These unusual flowers are perfect for naturalizing in a lawn.

Crocus

Bloom: February

Height: 4″

Colors: yellow, white, purple, blue and striped

Crocus are low-growing and quick to bloom. They will do well in sun or shade. Grow in all areas but do best where winters are cold.

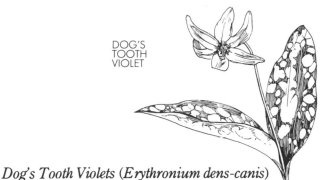

DOG'S TOOTH VIOLET

PUSCHKINIA

Dog's Tooth Violets (*Erythronium dens-canis*)

Bloom: April

Height: 6″

Colors: white, maroon and variations

These unusual flowers are perfect for naturalizing in a lawn.

Puschkinia (*Puschkinia libanotica*)

Bloom: April

Height: 6″

Color: blue/white

Offered by a few catalogs. Lovely.

STAR OF BETHLEHEM

DUTCH IRIS

Stars of Bethlehem (*Ornithogalum umbellatum*)

Bloom: May

Height: 8″

Color: white

These lovely flowers can be pesky as they spread rapidly. Well suited to the poorest soil.

Dutch Iris

Bloom: April-June

Height: 18–24″

Colors: white, yellow, violet, purple, blue

Most iris would not be suitable for an herbal lawn because of the year-round foliage, but the Dutch iris perform well, though in cold-winter areas they may bloom in June.

BULBOUS
IRIS

WINDFLOWER

Early or Bulbous Iris (*Iris reticulata,* also *Iris danfordiae*)

    Bloom: February and March

    Height: 4″

    Color: violet with yellow markings (*I. reticulata*) bright yellow (*I. danfordiae*)

Windflower (*Anemone blanda*)

    Bloom: March

    Height: 6″

    Color: pink

We tried these one year from K. Van Bourgondien's catalog and were delighted by the delicate pink flowers and lacy foliage. The experience has encouraged us to try other little-known flowers for natural gardens.

BULBS FOR MILD WINTER AREAS

BRODIAEA

SPARAXIS

Sparaxis

    Bloom: April

    Height: 8″

    Colors: mixed colors, orange through white

Gay little flowers do well under lawns.

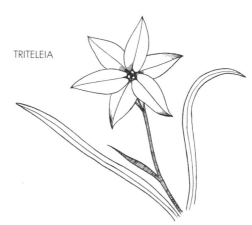

TRITELEIA

Brodiaea

    Bloom: *B. laxa* April to June

           B. pulchella March to May

    Height: 1–2 feet

    Color: violet-blue

These two brodiaeas are popular in California. *Sunset Western Garden Book* lists them as being adapted to clay soils.

Triteleia uniflora or Brodiaea uniflora

    Bloom: April

    Height: 12–15″

    Color: white

Pretty nodding white flowers with foliage that smells like onion when disturbed.

IXIA

Ixia

> Bloom: April
>
> Height: 8–12″
>
> Colors: yellow, orange, magenta, white and others

Flowers of many cheery colors form along a wiry stem.

ANEMONE

Anemones

> Bloom: March to June
>
> Height: 12″
>
> Colors: bright blue, red, white and purple

Two kinds are commonly sold: the single flowers of Anemones De Caen and the double flowers of Anemone St. Brigid. Both are hardy and exciting flowers. They will grow with special care in colder climates but bloom too late for use in an herbal lawn.

BULBS FOR COLD WINTER AREAS

WINTER
ACONITE

Winter Aconite (Eranthis)

> Bloom: January, February or March
>
> Height: 3–4″
>
> Color: bright yellow set against green leaves

Reseeds easily. Blooms before crocus. An old-time favorite.

Glory-of-the-Snow (Chionodoxia)

> Bloom: January, February or March
>
> Height: 4–6″
>
> Color: violet-blue with whitish centers

SNOWDROPS

Snowdrops (Galanthus nivalis)

> Bloom: January, February or March
>
> Height: 4″
>
> Color: white

Drooping white flowers do best in shade.

SQUILL

Squill (Scilla siberica)

> Bloom: March
>
> Height: 4–5″
>
> Color: blue

Short blooming but lovely flowers naturalize easily and will grow in partial shade.

Experimentation

We have talked with other people who have tried herbal lawn variations. All were happy with the lawn for the first year but then had one problem or another with the mixtures they tried. All felt that the right mix has yet to be found, but that finding it would be well worth the trouble. Until the mix is perfected this lawn is not for the average gardener or someone who needs certain results. You must be willing to experiment. For now it seems to be for the attentive gardener with some experience.

Some variation in the herbs used was noted. There are many varieties of creeping thyme, for example, going by the same name, some more aggressive than others. One idea is to plant herbs in sections or drifts to avoid the problem of one herb overpowering another. It is also hard to say that a given blend will perform the same under varying conditions. One person reported that chamomile took over; another clover; another yarrow, but only during certain times of the year! Perhaps it is just as Harding has noted in *Clover Lawns* that the plants alter to reach new equilibriums each year to match each new year's changing conditions. This is beautiful and much can be learned through observation. Just do not let the balance get out of hand. Chamomile seemed to need the most water (but still much less than grass) and to get more rangy unless grown in a cool moist climate such as England or San Francisco. The main area for work is balance. One person said that dwarf yarrow and creeping thyme together is marvelous when they are flowering but uneven at other times.

The mowing remains important as well. Except for the chamomile, mowing may only be needed about twice a year, but once a month is more usual. A height of 3 inches appears to be optimal, but we have yet to locate a mower that can be set that high.

Let us know of your problems, successes, and favorite combinations!

Sophisticated Low-Technology Tools

Plans for four "tools" that will help you get more out of your mini-farm

One of Ecology Action's goals has been to develop biointensive food-raising techniques that use as few procedures as possible, and as few tools as possible, preferably manual ones. Our philosophy has been to encourage the use of what we describe as sophisticated low-technology tools — tools that are inexpensive, simple, easy-to-build, yet highly functional. We wanted to avoid high initial capital investment and the high cost of running, maintaining and repairing complex mechnical equipment.

Cars have important purposes, but consider the true cost of running one, not to mention the pollution it creates. Ivan Illich, author of *Tools for Conviviality* and advocate of a simpler life, once remarked that if everyone added up all the time spent earning the money to purchase, maintain, fuel and drive an automobile, they would see that each person is really only traveling at four miles per hour in a car — the speed of the common bicycle! Recently, a study was made of the time the average housewife in the United States spends working in, around, and for the home

and family. It was discovered that, even with labor-saving tools, she spends the same amount of time that her counterpart spent 100 years ago! Why not look for ways to maximize simplicity, sophistication, and quality, yet get jobs done more quickly? This has been our goal in developing tools for mini-farming.

Early on in our research programs, we identified the need for four tools in particular that were available, but not quite in the form we needed. They were: 1) the *U-bar*, a large spading fork or kind of manual plow; 2) a versatile multi-use *mini-greenhouse* for temperature and pest control; 3) a *watering tool* that could water three times as rapidly and three times more gently (to avoid harming plants or compacting the soil) than any tool presently available; and 4) a *low-cost manual wheat thresher*. The U-bar and the mini-greenhouses are now a reality, and plans and specifications for these two tools are included in this chapter. In addition, there are plans for a special soil sifter, and instructions on building seedling flats.

We invite you to build these tools as presented

here, and to make your own modifications. Any modifications to the U-bar should be performed with special care, however, as it is the result of a special, lengthy research, development and testing process. Any modifications which make it less strong could be dangerous for the user. Currently we are trying to find a good durable design for a U-bar with detachable handles so it can be more easily transported. We also believe that the mini-greenhouse can be improved upon to make interchangeable panels fit into a single structure, rather than two. Your suggestions can help us with this ongoing design process.

U-BAR or "MANUAL PLOW"

Design:	William Burnett and Robert Clark
Drawing Development:	Dan Torjusen
Text:	Marion Cartwright
Illustrations:	Pedro J. Gonzalez

Deep soil preparation is of great importance in the biodynamic/French intensive method. Traditionally, the soil is loosened to a depth of 2 feet with a spade and spading fork in a process called the "double-dig." The first time a plot of ground is worked, the double-dig can take anywhere from 2 to 6 hours per 100-square-foot raised bed, depending on the soil's condition and the skill of the practitioner. After the ground has been double-dug and cropped once, it generally takes about 2 hours thereafter to double-dig and shape a raised bed using a spade and fork.

There is a less time-consuming and less tiring way to prepare raised beds while deeply aerating the soil. Once we have initially double-dug our beds, we often use a U-bar for subsequent cultivation in our test beds. Since the U-bar tines do not dig quite as deeply and do not aerate the soil as much as a double-dig with spade and fork, we still double-dig the soil periodically when significantly increased soil compaction is noticed. Another disadvantage of U-barring is that the gardener loses personal contact with the different strata of the soil and may not be aware of changes in soil quality due to different soil preparation techniques, crops grown, or soil amendments used. Yet the time saving the U-bar offers is significant. Each person will need to decide which factors are most important.

The U-bar is essentially a very large spading fork with two handles mounted on opposite ends of a rack of 18-inch long tines. The U-bar has cut our soil cultivation time from 2 hours per 100-square-foot bed to 10 to 30 minutes per bed. It is simple to use, and reduces the bending and lifting motions of digging. It loosens and aerates the soil with a minimum of soil strata mixing. Its only constraint is that it can only be used in well-loosened soil (usually soil that has been double-dug for at least one season).

Two undergraduate engineering students at Stanford University designed and built two types of U-bars for Ecology Action using two different designs as their starting point.[1] The design presented here is the one preferred by Ecology Action — both for ease

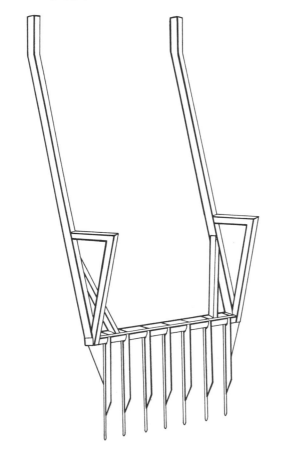

Figure 6. The U-bar.

---

[1]Case Study B9: Design of a simple agricultural implement— France/Canada: *A Handbook of Appropriate Technology*, The Canadian Hunger Foundations, Ottawa, Canada and the Brace Research Institute, Quebec, Canada, co-publishers, April 1976.

Maurice Franz, "Digging Without Pains and Aches," *Organic Gardening and Farming*, April 1976, pp. 76-77.

Figure 7. U-bar dimensions.

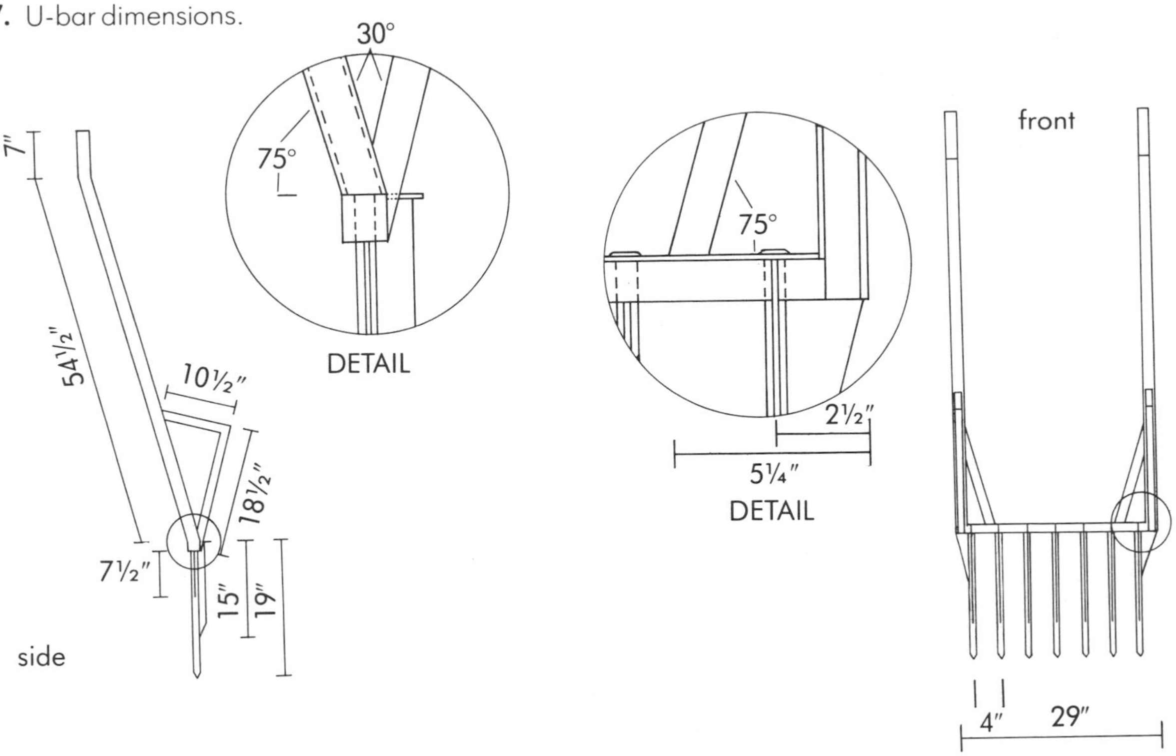

7"

54½"

10½"

18½"

7½"

15"

19"

side

30°

75°

DETAIL

75°

2½"

5¼"

DETAIL

front

4" 29"

of construction and for effectiveness in preparing the soil. The updated drawings should allow a competent welder to construct one with little difficulty. It is not intended to be a "do it yourself" project for someone without welding experience.

The designers of this U-bar found that a 2-foot wide tool with 18-inch long tines is as large as the U-bar can be made. Otherwise it becomes too difficult for a person of average size and strength to operate.

The *frame* of the U-bar is 1-1/4-inch square tubing with a wall thickness of 0.095 inches. The elbow and brace pieces are 1-inch square tubing of the same thickness. The frame material is hot-rolled, low carbon steel, also known as "mild" steel or 1010/1020 steel.

The *tines* of the U-bar are 1/2-inch round bar, plow steel stock. If plow steel is unavailable, use cold-rolled steel. The gussets on the back of the tines are 1/8-inch thick and 1 inch deep. The stand-up bar is made from the same 1/8-inch thick material and is welded to the tops of the gussets the whole width of the U-bar and is flush with the top of the square tubing.

Material costs are dependent upon the quantity ordered. If bought new from a dealer, steel is usually sold in 20-foot sections.

Figure 8. One easy carrying position. Be careful with tines, especially near your feet and others'. The U-bar is balanced so its weight will be evenly dispersed.

Figure 9. Using the U-bar.

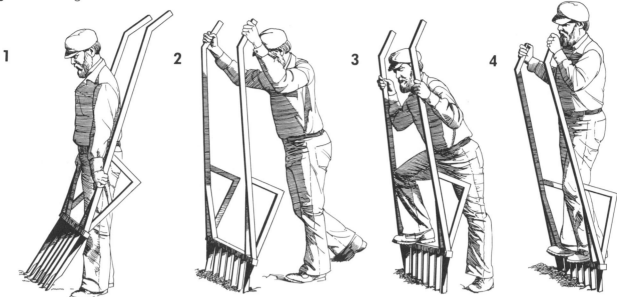

1. Place points of U-bar tines in soil at one corner of bed. You will be working your way backwards the length of the bed. (U-bar is 2 feet wide, but loosens a 2-1/2-foot wide strip of soil; two passes with U-bar are required to dig a 5-foot wide bed.)
2. Push U-bar into soil. Hands should be placed close to tines at first, then shifted to handles as you continue to fix tool firmly in soil. Wiggle the tool right and left if necessary.
3. Step onto U-bar, first with full weight on one foot.
4. Step onto U-bar with second foot, shifting body weight to make tool parallel with the soil. (Caution: U-bar should not be used on sloping areas.)

5. Shift body weight backwards to gain maximum leverage. The tines will rotate through the soil.
6. Just before you start to fall onto the ground, step off the U-bar. Continue to rotate the tines through the soil by alternately pulling the handles toward you, then pushing them down.
7. After you have rotated the tines completely through the soil, clods of soil may remain on the tines. Push the U-bar handles up and down rapidly until the clods break up and fall through the tines. Drag the U-bar back about 8 inches (do not lift the tool—it weighs about 40 pounds and lifting can wear you out or strain your back). Using the handles, tilt the U-bar back into position as shown in step 2. Continue the U-barring process.

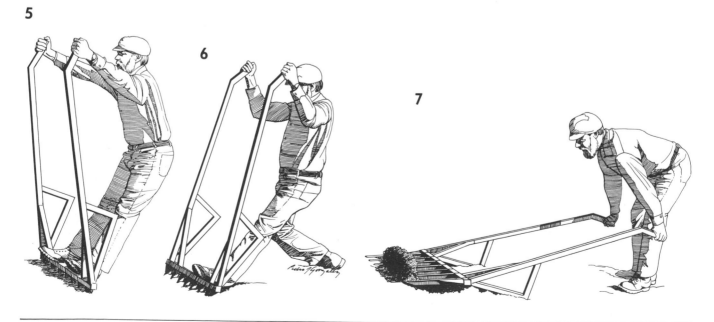

The U-bar makes a highly efficient form of personal food production possible. The design was kept simple so that the tool could be available to anyone. Often in this industrialized world, simple, efficient answers to problems are overlooked because they are thought of as *too* simple or not innovative enough. Yet, for us, the U-bar has been a breakthrough that makes biointensive minifarming more cost-effective.

We especially wish to thank William Burnett and Robert Clark for designing and constructing the prototype U-bar; the Stanford University Mechanical Engineering Department; ARLO (Stanford University's Action Research Liason Office); and Bill LeLand, who was instrumental in bringing us all together.

Mini-greenhouse on right, bush raspberries behind. At left is a newly prepared bed set out for planting.

MODULAR, MULTI-USE MINI-GREENHOUSE
(For Warmth, Shade and Pest Protection)

Design:	Dan Torjusen and Robert Clark
Drawing Development:	Patrick Long
Text:	Gaye Carlson
Illustrations:	Pedro J. Gonzalez

For many years, Ecology Action searched for a mini-greenhouse, shadenetting house, and birdnetting house to extend the growing season and to protect crops. The following design, created by Dan Torjusen, comes closest to what we have been looking for. While it is not intended for winter use in areas with great amounts of snowfall, the mini-greenhouse can be assembled early in the spring and placed over a 50-square-foot growing bed. This will increase the temperature of the soil and the air surrounding the plants and allow the gardener to get an early start on the growing season. The double-walled construction of the design can keep the inside temperature above the freezing point when the outside temperature falls as low as 20° F. This makes the unit a good season extender for crops.

The mini-greenhouse costs about $3 per square foot for materials, or $150 per 50 square feet. The wood can last for up to 12 years or more, the 6-year vinyl plastic sheeting can be replaced for about $50. The 12-year cost for the unit, then, would be about $150 or about $12.50 per year. Produce worth much more than this amount can be grown in the mini-greenhouse, even figuring on wholesale prices, so the unit is definitely cost-effective. (See Table 7, page 30 for more detailed produce income information.) Less expensive plastic sheeting may also be used. Monsanto 302 is another good plastic sheeting which lasts 2 to 3 years.

Figure 10. Final assembly of mini-greenhouse—exploded view.

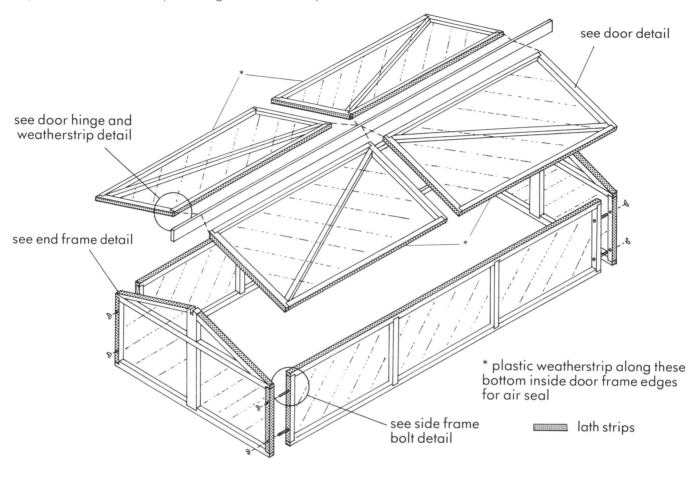

see door hinge and weatherstrip detail

see door detail

see end frame detail

see side frame bolt detail

* plastic weatherstrip along these bottom inside door frame edges for air seal

▦ lath strips

Tools

1. Hand saw or circular saw
2. Hammer
3. Staple gun
4. Drill and 3/16″, 3/8″, and 5/8″ wood bits
5. Chisel
6. Measuring tape
7. Straight edge or carpenter's square
8. Protractor
9. Table saw (optional)
10. Bar clamps (optional)

The tools required to build the mini-greenhouse are basic, with the exception of a table saw. The table saw is not really necessary, but it is useful since it allows one to purchase 2 × 4's and rip them in half. (Redwood 2 × 4's are less expensive than 2 × 2's, since 2 × 2's are generally sold as clear heart wood only.) With a table saw, it is also easier to make the necessary bevel cuts on the top rails of the doors.

Bar clamps are handy when cutting the joints as several pieces can be clamped together and cut at one time.

The shadehouse/birdnetting unit costs about $2.50 per square foot for materials. The shadenetting is rated to last up to 15 years with good care and comes in different thread densities which screen out 3%–98% of the sun's light. The 3% mesh can keep insects out while letting in most of the light; 30%, 45%, and 55% mesh fabric is used to grow cool-loving spring and fall crops in the summer. Experimentation will show which is best for your area at different times of the year and for different crops. Try a 30% mesh to begin with. Two or three meshes may be needed for one crop during the season as the weather gets hotter or cooler. Be careful not to overwater when using meshes 30% and over. The 90%+ meshes are reportedly used to let enough light in to keep the crops alive, but not enough to let them grow, for a three to five day period before marketing when more growth might involve their going to seed, bolting, or a general loss of crop quality.

Figure 11. Mini-greenhouse frame dimensions (lath omitted).

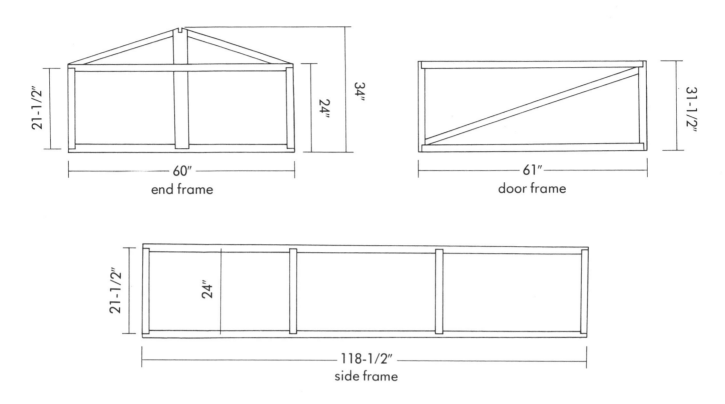

21-1/2"   24"   34"
60"
end frame

31-1/2"
61"
door frame

21-1/2"   24"
118-1/2"
side frame

If the entire 50-square-foot unit lasts for at least ten years, the per year cost would also be about $12.50 per year. This would be much less than the value of the produce grown or protected underneath.

There is also another advantage of this design — interchangeable panels. It is possible to mix or match the functions: a greenhouse panel on a side and an end to block out growth-inhibiting prevailing winds, shadenetting top doors to filter out excessive sunlight, and birdnetting (or 3% shadenetting) panels on the other side and end to keep out birds or insect pests.

It would also be possible to build a large greenhouse out of these panels by adding pegs and stacking panels on top of one another. Think of it as an adult appropriate technology tinker-toy set!

We hope you enjoy building and using this mini-greenhouse/shadenetting house/birdnetting house and look forward to learning about your results in using it, or any modifications you have made.

Materials

(Use redwood or other weather-resistant wood, well-seasoned to minimize warping.)

WOOD

6	$2'' \times 2'' \times 10'$
15	$2'' \times 2'' \times 8'$
or 3	$2'' \times 4'' \times 10'$
8	$2'' \times 4'' \times 8'$
	(if ripped to make 2 × 2's)
1	$2'' \times 4'' \times 8'$
1	$1'' \times 4'' \times 12'$
28	$1/4'' \times 8'$ lath strips
4	$3/8'' \times 3''$ dowels

FASTENERS

8	$3/16'' \times 2\text{-}1/2''$ machine screws (No. 10 size), with 8 nuts and 16 washers
4	$3/16'' \times 1\text{-}1/4''$ pan head wood screws (No. 10 size), with 4 washers
8	$3/8'' \times 5\text{-}1/2''$ completely threaded carriage bolts, with 8 nuts, 8 wing nuts, and 16 washers
1 lb.	8d galvanized box nails
1 lb.	3d galvanized box nails
	3/4''-wide nylon webbing, 8'
1 box	1/2'' staples

PLASTIC. 8 mm, 36″ × 312′ roll of 6-year, double-polished clear vinyl plastic film or other plastic sheeting. (Available from VJ Growers Supply, 500 W. Orange Blossom Trail, Apopka, FL 32703.) 100 5′ × 36″ pieces are needed for one double-glazed mini-greenhouse.

SHADENETTING. (Available from Jacobs Brothers Co., 8928 Sepulveda Blvd., Sepulveda, CA 91343.)

BIRDNETTING AND PESTNETTING. (Use 3% shade-netting from Jacobs Brothers Co.)

Procedure

1. If you purchased 2 × 4's for 2 × 2's, rip all except one 8-foot 2 × 4 in half.

2. Cut pieces as specified below. (Notches and bevels will be cut later.)

Side frames: (4) 2 × 2 × 118-1/2′ (will be
                   notched)
                   (8) 2 × 2 × 22-1/2″

Door frames: (4) 2 × 2 × 59-1/2″ (will be
                   beveled, see Figure 15)
                   (4) 2 × 2 × 59-1/2″
                   (8) 2 × 2 × 31-1/2″ (will be
                   notched)

End frames: (4) 2 × 2 22-1/2″
                 (4) 2 × 2 × 60″
                 (2) 2 × 4 × 36″

3. Cut notches. The joints of the 2 × 2 frame can be made by cutting a notch 3/4″ deep to fit the end of a 2 × 2. This can be done quickly by setting the circular saw to cut 3/4″ deep and making several cuts about 1/8″-1/4″ apart across the notch area. The remaining material in the notch can be removed with a hammer and chisel. Several 2 × 2's may be cut at the same time this way by clamping them together with bar clamps.

The joint between the 2 × 4 and the 2 × 2 in the end panels is a half-lapped joint where both pieces are continuous and notched to fit each other. Do this in the way indicated in step 3.

4. Assemble side frames with 8d nails. Install bolt assembly, locking carriage bolt in place with recessed nut.

5. Assemble door frames with 8d box nails. After nailing, but before cutting diagonals, be sure to check the doors for squareness by measuring across their diagonals. (When opposite diagonals are equal, then all corners will be 90°.) Once door is square, lay

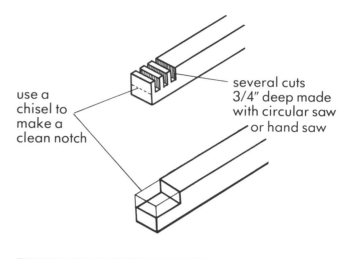

Figure 12. Making the notches.

use a chisel to make a clean notch

several cuts 3/4″ deep made with circular saw or hand saw

diagonal across frame in its position, mark and cut to length. (See Figure 11, Frame Dimensions Drawing.)

6. Assemble 2 × 2 end frame rectangle with 8d box nails. (Diagonals and center 2 × 4 are cut and installed in the next step.)

7. Make bevel cuts and roof of structure. Set 2 × 4 in its notched position on end frame, allowing it to extend longer than necessary. Two 18.5° angles now need to be cut in the 2 × 4's to form the roof peak. This angle can be determined with a protractor and then lay the 2 × 2 diagonal in place and mark where you will be cutting the 2 × 2 across the 2 × 4. The bevel angle for the other end of the 2 × 2 may be marked and cut in a similar manner. (The top edge of the doors where they will be hinged to the center ridge beam must also be bevel cut at an 18.5° angle for it to sit properly.) See Figures 13 and 15.

Finally, before nailing, cut a 3/4″ × 1-1/2″ notch in the 2 × 4 for the 1 × 4 roof ridge beam. See Figure 13, detail.

8. Wrap with plastic. The plastic is stretched tightly over the frame and stapled frequently (2 to 3 inches apart) *on the outside edges only*. Each frame is double glazed with plastic wrapped on both the inside and the outside. Excess plastic is trimmed after stapling. (See Figure 14 for more detail.)

9. Apply plastic weather strips on the top edge of the doors and where the doors meet in the middle. This is a simple 4-inch wide piece of plastic, folded and secured by a piece of lath. (See door frame detail in Figures 15 and 16.) Also apply plastic weather-strips along bottom inside door frame edges for air seal (see Figure 10).

Figure 13. End frame assembly.

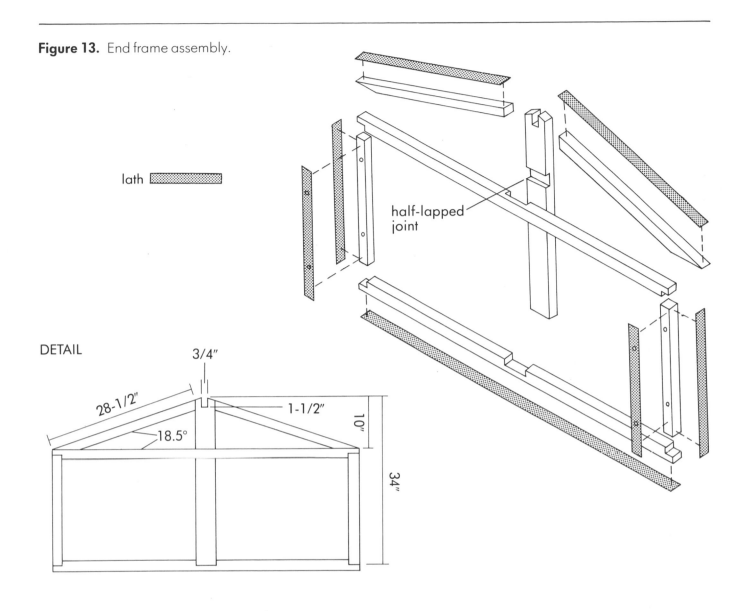

lath

half-lapped joint

DETAIL

3/4″

28-1/2″

18.5°

1-1/2″

10″

34″

10. Cut and nail lath strips over all stapled edges using 3d galvanized box nails.

11. Attach side to end frames with wing nuts. Set 1 × 4 × 12′ center ridge beam in slots in 2 × 4's but do not nail. This allows the mini-greenhouse to be quickly and easily disassembled for storage or changing of panels.

12. Assemble and install door hinges as shown in Figure 15.

13. Corner dowels. On each corner of the greenhouse there is a 3/8″ dowel which sets into a hole in the door (not shown in the diagrams). This is necessary for the structural rigidity of the greenhouse and prevents the 1 × 4 center ridge beam from sagging under the weight of the doors. It can be installed simply by drilling a 3/8″ hole in the corners of the end panel and tapping it halfway in with a hammer. Then the door is pressed onto the dowel, marking the position to be drilled on the door.

14. Spacers. It will be helpful during everyday operation of the greenhouse to attach a small piece of lath on *top* of the four bottom corners of each door to prevent the plastic from sticking together when the doors are open and laying upon the door opposite the open door.

Other Possibilities

We have made a second mini-greenhouse, but instead of enclosing it with plastic, we have used birdnetting as the covering of the panels. Shadenetting, which

Figure 14. Side frame bolt detail.

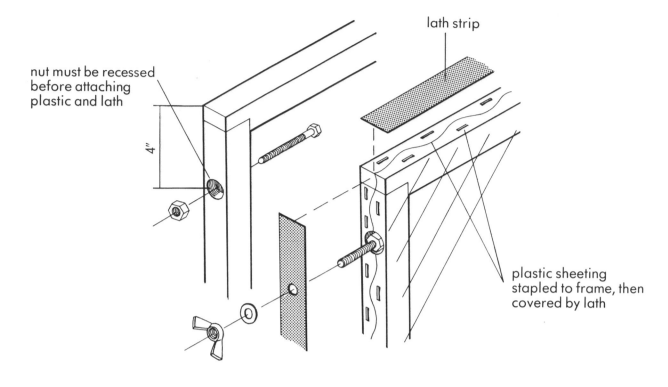

nut must be recessed
before attaching
plastic and lath

4"

lath strip

plastic sheeting
stapled to frame, then
covered by lath

Figure 15. Door hinge and weatherstrip detail.

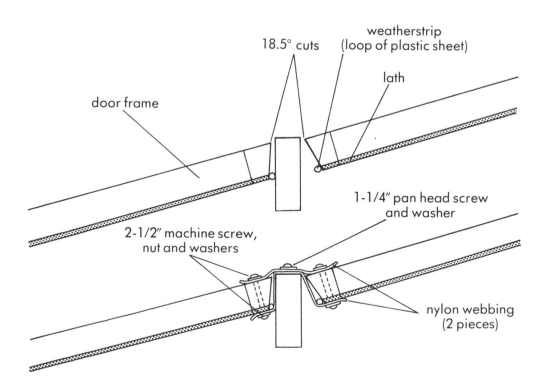

18.5° cuts

weatherstrip
(loop of plastic sheet)

lath

door frame

1-1/4" pan head screw
and washer

2-1/2" machine screw,
nut and washers

nylon webbing
(2 pieces)

screens out much more light than birdnetting or pest-netting, can then be placed on top of the birdnetting in order to control the amount of sunlight that the bed receives. (Shadenetting should be cut large enough to allow a 1"-1-1/2" hem to be sewn around the edges to prevent it from unraveling. It can then simply be attached with machine screws and washers.

Extra panels can be made so that plastic and net-ting panels can be combined in the same greenhouse to meet specific weather or horticultural require-ments.

Another possibility would be the routing out of the 2 × 2 frames and making removable panels instead of needing two separate structures.

Let us know your experiences building and growing with this mini-greenhouse/shadenetting house/birdnetting house/pestnetting house. Sugges-tions for improvements are welcome.

Figure 16. Door frame detail.

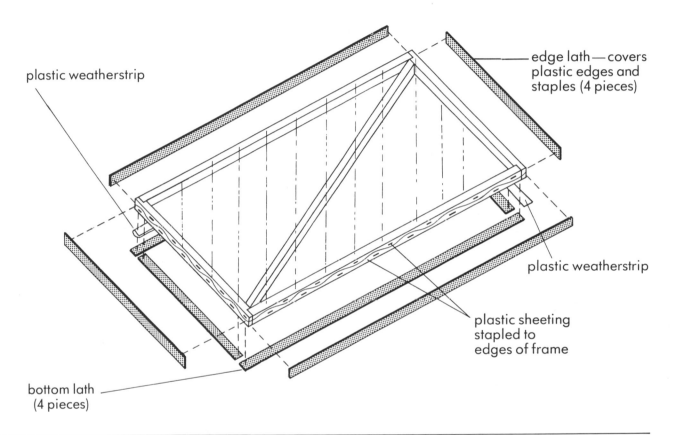

plastic weatherstrip

edge lath—covers plastic edges and staples (4 pieces)

plastic weatherstrip

plastic sheeting stapled to edges of frame

bottom lath (4 pieces)

WHEELBARROW SOIL AND COMPOST SIFTER

Design: Steve Shuck
Drawing Development: Pedro Klauder
Illustrations: Pedro J. Gonzalez

When we first started working the Common Ground Garden, Steve Shuck, a long-time Ecology Action member and supporter, saw we had a periodic need for large amounts of sifted soil and compost for seedling flats and sometimes for covering small seeds in the growing beds. As a result, he created a soil sifter for use with two 4-cubic-foot wheelbarrows. One wheelbarrow holds the soil to be sifted, while the second stands underneath the sifter to catch the refined soil.

The unsifted soil is placed on a screened "pan" that swings back and forth to speed the process. "Pans" with different mesh galvanized-wire "cloth" can be used depending on the size of the sifted particles needed. At the back of the "pan" is a hinged side which allows the clods which will not pass through the mesh to fall to the ground behind the sifter. The clods are later shoveled into the empty wheelbarrow and used as soil in the compost layering process. This tool made things a lot easier for us.

Figure 17. Wheelbarrow soil and compost sifter — support.

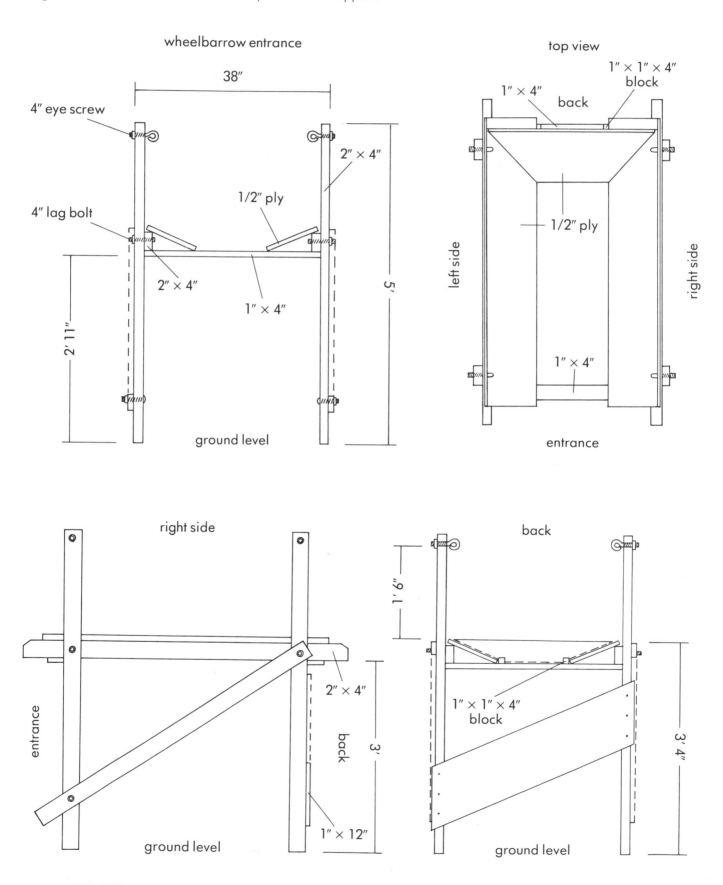

wheelbarrow entrance

38"

4" eye screw

2" × 4"

1/2" ply

4" lag bolt

2" × 4"

1" × 4"

2' 11"

5'

ground level

top view

1" × 1" × 4" block

1" × 4"

back

left side

right side

1/2" ply

1" × 4"

entrance

right side

entrance

2" × 4"

back

3'

1' 9"

ground level

1" × 12"

back

1" × 1" × 4" block

ground level

3' 4"

Figure 18. Sifter support—left side.

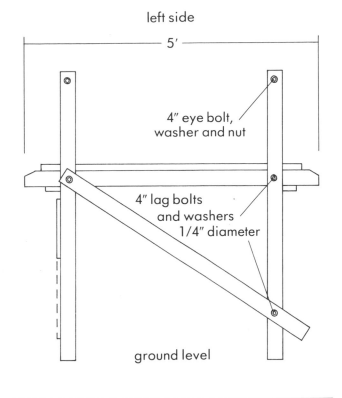

left side

5′

4″ eye bolt,
washer and nut

4″ lag bolts
and washers
1/4″ diameter

ground level

Materials

WOOD

6	2″ - 4″ × 8′
3	1″ × 4″ × 8′
1	1″ × 6″ × 3′
1	1″ × 12″ × 4′
1	1/2″ × 2′ × 4′ CDX plywood
2	1/4″ × 4′ × lath strips

HARDWARE

	1/2″ galvanized wire mesh*, 3′ × 3′
2	3″ × 3″ × 1/2″ "L" bends
2	small hook and eye sets
4	4″ eye screws
4	4″ eye bolts
6	4″ lag bolts with a 1/4″ diameter hole
20	washers for 4″ bolts (2 each for 4″ eye bolts and 4″ lag bolts)
4	1-inch pieces of chain
2	2″ hinge units
1 pkg.	3/8″ staples
1/2 lb.	3d galvanized nails
	* other mesh sizes optional

Figure 19. Soil sifter—swing bed.

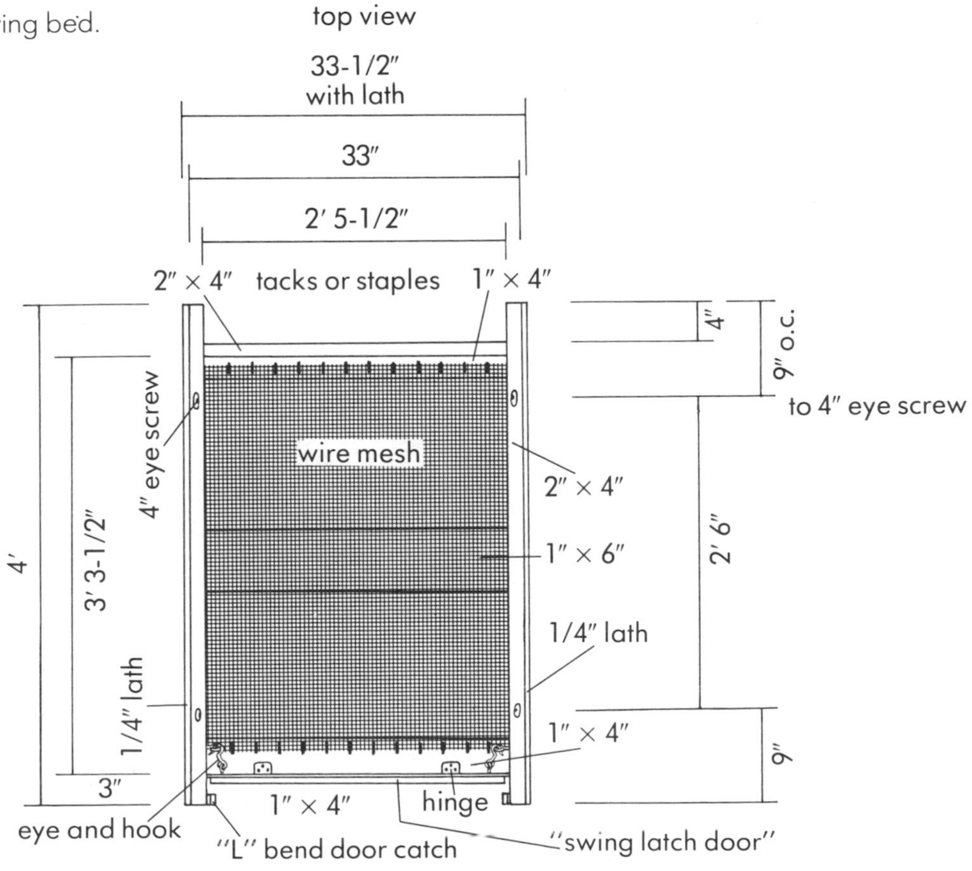

top view

33-1/2″
with lath

33″

2′ 5-1/2″

2″ × 4″   tacks or staples   1″ × 4″

4″ eye screw

wire mesh

2″ × 4″

1″ × 6″

1/4″ lath

1″ × 4″

4′

3′ 3-1/2″

1/4″ lath

3″

eye and hook

"L" bend door catch

1″ × 4″

hinge

"swing latch door"

4″

9″ o.c.

to 4″ eye screw

2′ 6″

9″

Figure 20. Soil sifter—swing bed (details).

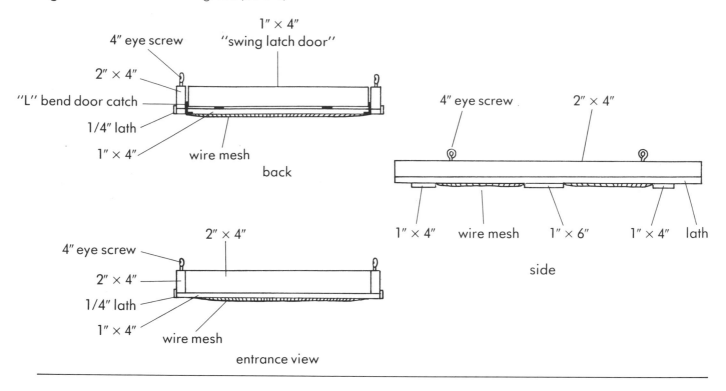

4" eye screw

1" × 4"
"swing latch door"

2" × 4"

"L" bend door catch

1/4" lath

1" × 4"

wire mesh

back

4" eye screw

2" × 4"

1" × 4"   wire mesh   1" × 6"   1" × 4"   lath

side

4" eye screw

2" × 4"

2" × 4"

1/4" lath

1" × 4"

wire mesh

entrance view

SEEDLING FLATS

We like to use wooden flats when raising seedlings. They offer seedlings a home that can breathe and drain easily, and are made of natural materials. The design given below is for a standard flat, 14 inches wide by 23 inches long by 3-1/4 inches deep (all outer dimensions). A flat this size will contain about 250 1-inch planting centers, or about 60 2-inch planting centers. You can make a flat any size that you like, but remember that the larger the flat, the heavier it will be (because of the soil contained within it) and some shapes are awkward to carry.

Figure 21. Seedling flat.

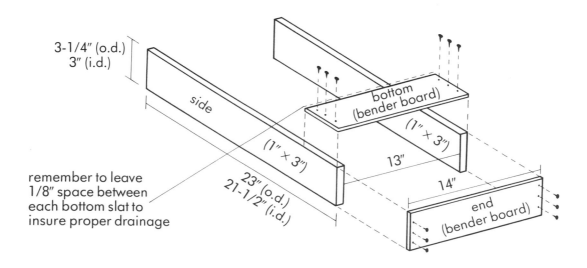

3-1/4" (o.d.)
3" (i.d.)

side

bottom
(bender board)

(1" × 3")

(1" × 3")

13"

23" (o.d.)
21-1/2" (i.d.)

14"

end
(bender board)

remember to leave
1/8" space between
each bottom slat to
insure proper drainage

PART TWO

Planning Your Garden and Keeping Records

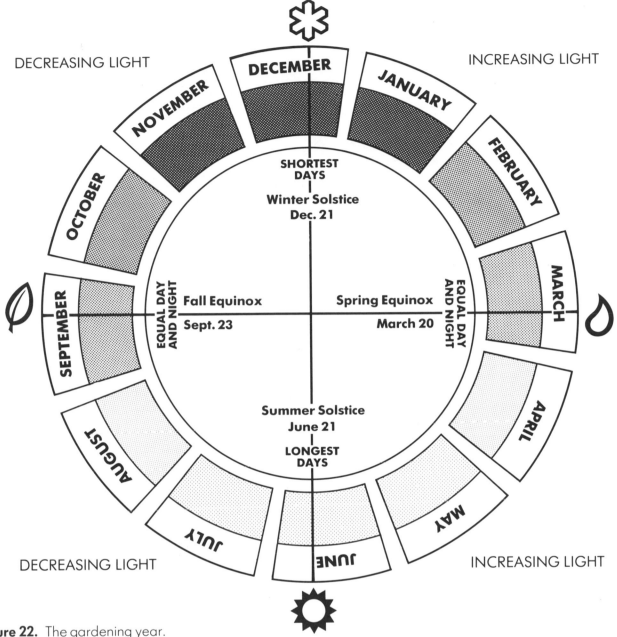

Figure 22. The gardening year.

The circle above portrays the general gardening year with increasing and decreasing light patterns, and increasing and decreasing day lengths. Generally, the best growing period is between March 21 and September 21, the spring and fall equinoxes. This is because the days are longer for 6 months and because the weather is warmer.

There are areas with both longer and shorter growing seasons, of course. To determine your general growing season, consult your local weather station to determine the:

☐ last frost date in spring _____

☐ first frost date in autumn _____

☐ point at which the night temperature begins to be 60°F or more _____

☐ point at which the night temperature begins to be less than 60°F _____

Then note these dates on this circle by drawing a line from the center of the circle to the approximate dates involved. This will give you a picture of your garden year and the key reference points you will need. If you cannot find the first and last frost date information easily, the maps on pages 148–150 will help you estimate them.

Figure 23. Average dates of last killing frost in spring.

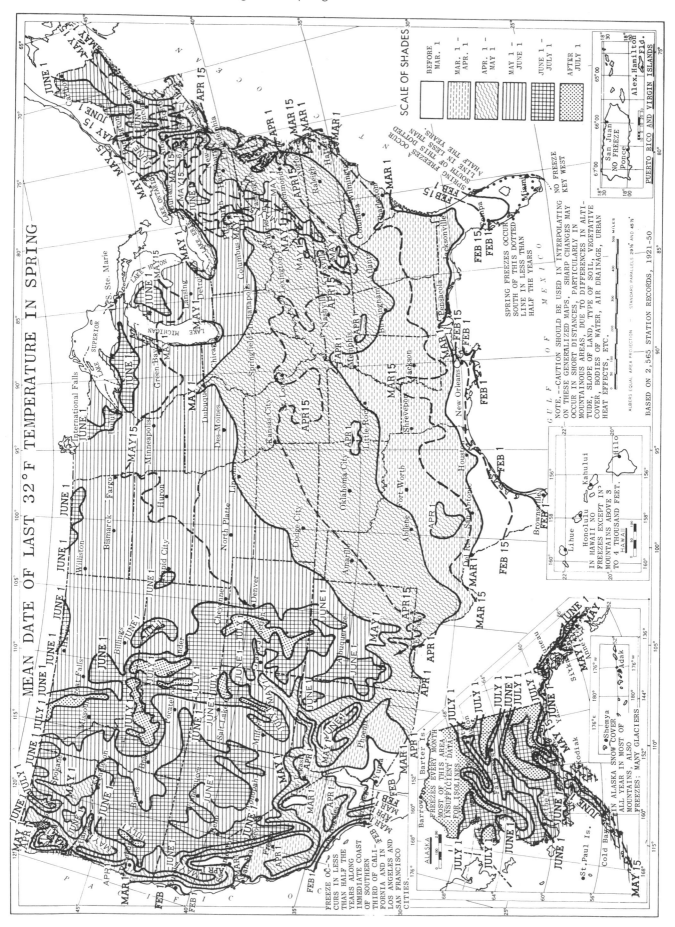

Figure 24. Average dates of first killing frost in autumn.

Figure 25. Average length of frost-free period (days).

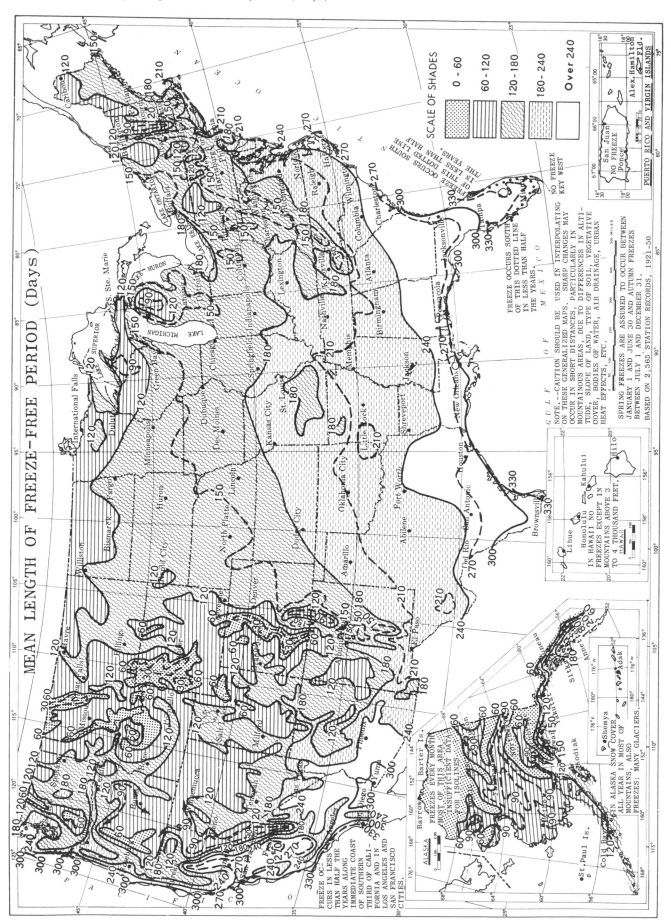

Figure 26. To determine the part of your yard which has the best potential for good crop growth, use the illustration below. A **minimum** of 4 hours of full sunlight is needed for any significant food plant growth, and 7 to 11 hours (**preferably the latter**) are normally required.

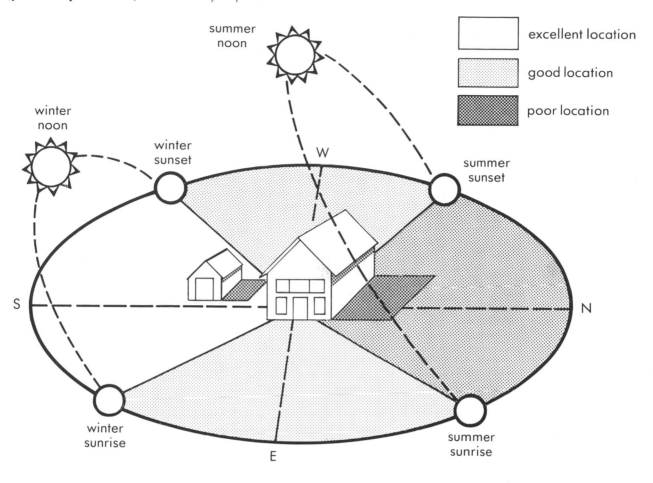

On the following pages you will find Annual Planning Calendars for many food crops. Six growing periods (determined by the dates of last and first frosts) are described:

90 Days (e.g. May 30-August 30)
130 Days (e.g. May 10-September 20)
150 Days (e.g. April 20-September 20)
170 Days (e.g. April 20-October 10)
190 Days (e.g. March 30-October 10)
240 Days (e.g. March 30-October 20)

Many crops, such as tomatoes and wheat, require a growing season of 4 months, or 120 days. A 90-day period can work if miniature greenhouses are used over the beds to extend the growing season 2 to 4 weeks at either end of the frost free period. Also, a 90-day season will allow one to grow short season crops, such as leaf lettuce and carrots. Crops can be grown in seasons less than 90 days, but generally special greenhouse growing skills are required for success. Planning Calendars for periods of more than 240 days are not included in this chapter. The temperature planning table on page 62 of *How to Grow More Vegetables* may be used to expand the 240-day Calendar into a longer growing period plan.

Choose the Planning Calendar closest to your situation. As you gain experience in your own particular region and with your own mini-climate, you will make adjustments to your Calendar. *Enter your own actual growing season ranges and dates on the Calendar to replace the theoretical ones provided.* Remember that seedlings begun in the summer for autumn transplanting need to be started in a partial shade environment, such as under 30%-45% shade netting. This is because these plants prefer cooler weather, rather than the heat of the summer.

Be sure to plant and grow vegetables in the summer and autumn, when possible. An expanded growing season with or without miniature greenhouses over your growing beds means a more abundant harvest and more fun!

Planning Calendar — 90 Day

90 DAY May 30– August 30	START IN FLATS (in Greenhouses, Cold-frames, or Mini- Greenhouses in Winter	SOW DIRECTLY in Soil	TRANSPLANT SEEDLINGS into Soil
FEBRUARY 15	Chives, Leeks, Onions, Parsley		
MARCH 1	Broccoli, Brussels Sprouts, Cabbage, Cauliflower, Collards, Eggplant, Kale, Kohlrabi, Peppers, Tomatoes		
APRIL 1	Annual Herbs, Garlic, Mustard, Shallots, Spinach, Spring Flowers	Prune Trees and Berries	
MAY 1 **Last Frost** ✽	Cucumbers, Lettuce, Melons, New Zealand Spinach, Pumpkins, Summer Squash Sunflowers, Winter Squash	Alfalfa, Beets, Buckwheat, Carrots, Chard, Clovers, Oats, Parsnips, Peas, Potatoes, Radishes, Rutabagas, Rye,* Salsify, Turnips, Wheat.* Plant Bare Root Trees and Berries. Build Spring Compost Pile.	Broccoli, Brussels Sprouts, Cabbage, Cauliflower, Chives, Collards, Garlic, Kale, Kohlrabi, Leeks, Mustard, Parsley, Shallots, Spinach
JUNE 1	Leaf Lettuce, Spinach (June 15)	Beans, Corn, Beets, Carrots, Chard, Radishes, Rutabagas, Turnips, Peanuts, Rice, Millet, Soybeans, Cotton	Cucumbers, Eggplant, Herbs, Lettuce, Melons, New Zealand Spinach, Sunflowers, Onions, Peppers, Pumpkins, Spring Flowers and Herbs, Summer Squash, Tomatoes, Winter Squash
JULY 1		Corn	Spinach (July 15), Lettuce
AUGUST 1		Radishes	
First Frost ✽ SEPTEMBER 1		Build Autumn Compost Pile	
OCTOBER 1	Flowering Spring Bulbs		
	(NOTE: Use shortest maturing varieties in this growing season.)	* Can also be started in flats one month earlier	

Planning Calendar — 130 Day

130 DAY May 10- September 20	START IN FLATS (in Greenhouses, Coldframes, or Mini-Greenhouses in Winter)	SOW DIRECTLY in Soil	TRANSPLANT SEEDLINGS into Soil
JANUARY 1	Celery, Chives, Leeks, Onions, Parsley		
FEBRUARY 10	Broccoli, Brussels Sprouts, Cabbage, Cauliflower, Collards, Eggplant, Kale, Kohlrabi, Okra, Peppers, Tomatoes		
MARCH 10	Annual Herbs, Garlic, Mustard, Shallots, Spinach, Spring Flowers, Tomatoes	Prune Trees and Berries	
APRIL 10 **Last Frost** �֍	Cucumbers, Lettuce, Melons, New Zealand Spinach, Pumpkins, Summer Squash, Sunflowers, Tomatoes, Winter Squash	Alfalfa, Beets, Buckwheat, Chard, Clovers, Oats, Parsnips, Peas, Potatoes, Radishes, Rutabagas, Rye*, Salsify, Turnips, Wheat*, Plant Bare Root Trees and Berries, Build Spring Compost Pile	Broccoli, Brussels Sprouts, Cabbage, Cauliflower, Celery, Chives, Collards, Garlic, Kale, Kohlrabi, Leeks, Mustard, Parsley, Shallots, Spinach
MAY 10	Cucumbers, Leaf Lettuce, Melons, New Zealand Spinach, Pumpkins, Summer Squash, Sunflowers, Tomatoes, Winter Squash	Beans, Beets, Carrots, Corn, Cotton, Millet, Parsnips, Peanuts, Potatoes, Radishes, Rice, Rutabagas, Salsify, Soybeans, Turnips	Cucumbers, Eggplant, Herbs, Lettuce, Melons, New Zealand Spinach, Okra, Onions, Peppers, Pumpkins, Spring Flowers, Summer Squash, Sunflowers, Tomatoes
JUNE 10	Leaf Lettuce, Cucumbers	Beans, Beets, Carrots, Corn, Parsnips, Peas, Radishes, Rutabagas, Salsify	Cucumbers, Leaf Lettuce, Melons, New Zealand Spinach, Pumpkins, Summer Squash, Sunflowers, Winter Squash
JULY 10	Broccoli, Brussels Sprouts, Cabbage, Cauliflower, Collards, Kale, Kohlrabi, Leaf Lettuce, Mustard, Spinach (July 24)	Corn	Leaf Lettuce, Cucumbers
AUGUST 10 **First Frost** ✤	Radishes	Broccoli, Brussels Sprouts, Cabbage, Cauliflower, Collards, Kale, Kohlrabi, Leaf Lettuce, Mustard, Spinach (August 24)	
SEPTEMBER 10		Radishes	
OCTOBER 10		Build Autumn Compost Pile	
NOVEMBER 10		Flowering Spring Bulbs	
	NOTE: Use shortest maturing varieties in this growing season	*Can also be started in flats one month earlier.	

Planning Calendar — 150 Day

150 DAY April 20– September 20	START IN FLATS (in Greenhouses, Coldframes, or Mini-Greenhouses in Winter)	SOW DIRECTLY in Soil	TRANSPLANT SEEDLINGS into Soil
NOVEMBER 20	Celery, Chives, Leeks, Onions, Parsley		
JANUARY 20	Broccoli, Brussels Sprouts, Cabbage, Cauliflower, Collards, Eggplant, Kale, Kohlrabi, Okra, Onions, Peppers, Tomatoes		
FEBRUARY 20	Annual Herbs, Garlic, Mustard, Shallots, Spinach, Spring Flowers, Tomatoes	Prune Trees and Berries	
MARCH 20	Cucumbers, Lettuce, Melons, New Zealand Spinach, Pumpkins, Spinach, Summer Squash, Sunflowers, Sweet Potatoes, Tomatoes	Alfalfa, Beets, Buckwheat, Chard, Clovers, Oats, Parsnips, Peas, Potatoes, Radishes, Rutabagas, Rye*, Salsify, Turnips, Wheat*, Plant Bare Root Trees, Build Spring Compost Pile	Broccoli, Brussels Sprouts, Cabbage, Cauliflower, Celery, Chives, Collards, Garlic, Kale, Kohlrabi, Leeks, Mustard, Parsley, Shallots, Spinach
Last Frost ❁			
APRIL 20	Cucumbers, Leaf Lettuce, Melons, New Zealand Spinach, Pumpkins, Summer Squash, Sunflowers, Winter Squash	Beans, Beets, Carrots, Corn, Cotton, Millet, Parsnips, Peanuts, Potatoes, Radishes, Rice, Rutabagas, Salsify, Soybeans, Turnips	Cucumbers, Eggplant, Lettuce, Melons, New Zealand Spinach, Okra, Onions, Peppers, Pumpkins, Spring Flowers and Herbs, Summer Squash, Sunflowers, Sweet Potatoes, Tomatoes, Winter Squash
MAY 20	Cucumbers, Leaf Lettuce, Melons, New Zealand Spinach, Pumpkins, Summer Squash, Sunflowers, Winter Squash	Beans, Beets, Carrots, Corn, Cowpeas, Parsnips, Potatoes, Radishes, Rutabagas, Salsify, Turnips	Cucumbers, Leaf Lettuce, Melons, New Zealand Spinach, Onions, Pumpkins, Summer Squash, Sunflowers, Winter Squash
JUNE 20	Leaf Lettuce	Beans, Beets, Carrots, Corn, Parsnips, Peas, Radishes, Rutabagas, Salsify	Cucumbers, Leaf Lettuce, Melons, New Zealand Spinach, Pumpkins, Summer Squash, Sunflowers, Winter Squash
JULY 20	Broccoli, Brussels Sprouts, Cabbage, Cauliflower, Collards, Kale, Kohlrabi, Lettuce, Mustard, Spinach (July 7)	Corn	Leaf Lettuce
	NOTE: Use shortest maturing varieties in this growing season for all **Spring** and **Autumn** crops.	*Can also be started in flats one month earlier	

150 DAY April 20– September 20	**START IN FLATS** (in Greenhouses, Coldframes, or Mini- Greenhouses in Winter)	**SOW DIRECTLY** in Soil	**TRANSPLANT SEEDLINGS** into Soil
AUGUST 20	Radishes	Broccoli, Brussels Sprouts, Cabbage, Cauliflower, Collards, Kale, Kohlrabi, Lettuce, Mustard, Spinach (August 7)	
First Frost ✳			
SEPTEMBER 20		Build Autumn Compost Pile	
OCTOBER 20		Flowering Spring Bulbs	

NOTE: Use shortest maturing
varieties in this growing season
for all **Spring** and **Autumn** crops.

Planning Calendar — 170 Day

170 DAY April 20– October 10	START IN FLATS (in Greenhouses, Coldframes, or Mini- Greenhouses in Winter)	SOW DIRECTLY in soil	TRANSPLANT SEEDLINGS into Soil
NOVEMBER 20	Celery, Chives, Leeks, Onions, Parsley		
JANUARY 20	Broccoli, Brussels Sprouts, Cabbage, Cauliflower, Collards, Eggplant, Kale, Kohlrabi, Okra, Onions, Peppers, Tomatoes		
FEBRUARY 20	Annual Herbs, Garlic, Mustard, Onions, Shallots, Spinach, Spring Flowers, Tomatoes	Prune Trees and Berries	
MARCH 20	Cucumbers, Lettuce, Melons, New Zealand Spinach, Pumpkins, Summer Squash, Sunflowers, Sweet Potatoes, Tomatoes, Winter Squash	Alfalfa, Beets, Buckwheat, Chard, Clovers, Oats, Parsnips, Peas, Potatoes, Radishes, Rutabagas, Rye*, Salsify, Turnips, Wheat*, Plant Bare Root Trees and Berries, Build Spring Compost Pile	Broccoli, Brussels Sprouts, Cabbage, Cauliflower, Celery, Chives, Collards, Garlic, Kale, Kohlrabi, Leeks, Mustard, Parsely, Shallots, Spinach
Last Frost	❀		
APRIL 20	Cucumbers, Leaf Lettuce, Melons, New Zealand Spinach, Pumpkins, Summer Squash, Sunflowers, Winter Squash	Beans, Beets, Carrots, Corn, Cotton, Millet, Parsnips, Peanuts, Potatoes, Radishes, Rice, Rutabagas, Salsify, Soybeans, Turnips	Cucumbers, Eggplant, Lettuce, Melons, New Zealand Spinach, Okra, Onions, Peppers, Pumpkins, Spring Flowers and Herbs, Summer Squash, Sunflowers, Sweet Potatoes, Tomatoes, Winter Squash
MAY 20	Cucumbers, Leaf Lettuce, Melons, New Zealand Spinach, Pumpkins, Summer Squash, Sunflowers, Winter Squash	Beans, Beets, Carrots, Corn, Cowpeas, Parsnips, Potatoes, Radishes, Rutabagas, Salsify, Turnips	Cucumbers, Leaf Lettuce, Melons, New Zealand Spinach, Onions, Pumpkins, Summer Squash, Sunflowers, Winter Squash
JUNE 20	Cucumbers, Leaf Lettuce, Melons, New Zealand Spinach, Pumpkins, Summer Squash, Sunflowers, Winter Squash	Beans, Beets, Carrots, Corn, Cowpeas, Parsnips, Potatoes, Radishes, Rutabagas, Salsify	Cucumbers, Leaf Lettuce, Melons, New Zealand Spinach, Onions, Pumpkins, Summer Squash, Sunflowers, Winter Squash
JULY 20	Lettuce, Autumn Flowers	Beans, Beets, Carrots, Corn, Parsnips, Peas, Radishes, Rutabagas, Salsify	Cucumbers, Leaf Lettuce, Melons, New Zealand Spinach, Pumpkins, Summer Squash, Sunflowers, Winter Squash

*Can also be started in flats one
month earlier

170 DAY April 20– October 10	START IN FLATS (in Greenhouses, Coldframes, or Mini- Greenhouses in Winter)	SOW DIRECTLY in soil	TRANSPLANT SEEDLINGS into Soil
AUGUST 20	Broccoli, Brussels Sprouts, Cabbage, Cauliflower, Collards, Kale, Kohlrabi, Lettuce, Mustard, Spinach (August 7)	Buckwheat, Corn, Fava Beans, Oats, White Cloer, Winter Hairy Vetch*	Autumn Flowers, Lettuce
SEPTEMBER 20		Radishes	Broccoli, Brussels Sprouts, Cabbage, Cauliflower, Collards, Kale, Kohlrabi, Lettuce, Mustard, Spinach (September 7)
First Frost ✳			
OCTOBER 10		Build Autumn Compost Pile	
NOVEMBER 20		Flowering Spring Bulbs	

Note: Using the shorter maturing varieties in this growing season for **second, or later plantings** will produce the best results.

*Winter Cover Crop which can withstand snow

Planning Calendar — 190 Day

190 DAY MARCH 30– OCTOBER 10	START IN FLATS (in Greenhouses, Coldframes, or Mini- Greenhouses in Winter)	SOW DIRECTLY in soil	TRANSPLANT SEEDLINGS into Soil
OCTOBER 30	Celery, Chives, Leeks, Onions, Parsley		
DECEMBER 30	Broccoli, Brussels Sprouts, Cabbage, Cauliflower, Collards, Eggplant, Kale, Kohlrabi, Okra, Onions, Peppers, Tomatoes		
JANUARY 30	Annual Herbs, Garlic, Mustard, Onions, Shallots, Spinach, Spring Flowers, Tomatoes	Prune Trees and Berries	
FEBRUARY 28	Cucumbers, Lettuce, Melons, New Zealand Spinach, Onions, Pumpkins, Summer Squash, Sunflowers, Sweet Potatoes, Tomatoes, Winter Squash	Alfalfa, Beets, Buckwheat, Chard, Clovers, Oats, Parsnips, Peas, Potatoes, Radishes, Rutabagas, Rye*, Salsify, Turnips, Wheat*, Plant Bare Root Trees and Berries, Build Spring Compost Pile	Broccoli, Brussels Sprouts, Cabbage, Cauliflower, Celery, Chives, Collards, Garlic, Kale, Kohlrabi, Leeks, Mustard, Parsley, Shallots, Spinach
MARCH 30 **Last Frost** ✺	Cucumbers, Lettuce, Melons, New Zealand Spinach, Pumpkins, Summer Squash, Sunflowers, Sweet Potatoes, Tomatoes, Winter Squash	Beans, Beets, Carrots, Corn, Cotton, Millet, Parsnips, Peanuts, Potatoes, Radishes, Rice, Rutabagas, Salsify, Soybeans, Turnips	Cucumbers, Eggplant, Lettuce, Melons, New Zealand Spinach, Okra, Onions, Pepper, Pumpkins, Spring Flowers and Herbs, Summer Squash, Sunflowers, Tomatoes, Winter Squash
APRIL 30	Cucumbers, Leaf Lettuce, Melons, New Zealand Spinach, Pumpkins, Summer Squash, Sunflowers, Winter Squash	Beans, Beets, Carrots, Corn, Cowpeas, Parsnips, Potatoes, Radishes, Rutabagas, Salsify, Turnips	Cucumbers, Leaf Lettuce, Melons, New Zealand Spinach, Onions, Pumpkins, Summer Squash, Sunflowers, Sweet Potatoes, Winter Squash
MAY 30	Cucumbers, Leaf Lettuce, Melons, New Zealand Spinach, Pumpkins, Summer Squash, Sunflowers, Winter Squash	Beans, Beets, Carrots, Corn, Cowpeas, Parsnips, Potatoes, Radishes, Rutabagas, Salsify, Turnips	Cucumbers, Leaf Lettuce, Melons, New Zealand Spinach, Onions, Pumpkins, Summer Squash, Sunflowers, Winter Squash
JUNE 30	Cucumbers, Leaf Lettuce, Melons, New Zealand Spinach, Pumpkins, Summer Squash, Sunflowers, Winter Squash	Beans, Beets, Carrots, Corn, Cowpeas, Parsnips, Potatoes, Radishes, Rutabagas, Salsify	Cucumbers, Leaf Lettuce, Melons, New Zealand Spinach, Onions, Pumpkins, Summer Squash, Sunflowers, Winter Squash

*Can be started in flats one month earlier

190 DAY MARCH 30– OCTOBER 10	START IN FLATS (in Greenhouses, Coldframes, or Mini-Greenhouses in Winter)	SOW DIRECTLY in soil	TRANSPLANT SEEDLINGS into Soil
JULY 30	Autumn Flowers, Lettuce	Beans, Beets, Carrots, Corn, Parsnips, Peas, Radishes, Rutabagas, Salsify	Cucumbers, Leaf Lettuce, Melons, New Zealand Spinach, Pumpkins, Summer Squash, Sunflowers, Winter Squash
AUGUST 30	Broccoli, Brussels Sprouts, Cabbage, Cauliflower, Collards, Kale, Kohlrabi, Lettuce, Mustard, Spinach (August 7)	Buckwheat, Corn (August 10), Fava Beans, Oats, White Clover*, Winter Hairy Vetch*	Autumn Flowers, Lettuce
SEPTEMBER 30		Radishes	Broccoli, Brussels Sprouts, Cabbage, Cauliflower, Collards, Kale, Kohlrabi, Lettuce, Mustard, Spinach (September 7)
First Frost ✿			
OCTOBER 10		Build Autumn Compost Pile	
NOVEMBER 10		Flowering Spring Bulbs	

NOTE: Using shorter maturing varieties in this growing season for **second, or later plantings** will produce the best results.

*Winter Cover Crop which can withstand snow

Planning Calendar — 240 Day

240 DAY MARCH 30– NOVEMBER 20	START IN FLATS (in Greenhouses, Coldframes, or Mini- Greenhouses in Winter)	SOW DIRECTLY in Soil	TRANSPLANT SEEDLINGS into Soil
OCTOBER 30	Celery, Chives, Leeks, Onions, Parsley		
DECEMBER 30	Broccoli, Brussels Sprouts, Cabbage, Cauliflower, Collards, Eggplant, Kale, Kohlrabi, Okra, Onions, Peppers, Tomatoes		
JANUARY 30	Annual Herbs, Garlic, Mustard, Onions, Shallots, Spinach, Spring Flowers, Tomatoes	Prune Trees and Berries	
FEBRUARY 28 **Last Frost** ✳	Cucumbers, Lettuce, Melons, New Zealand Spinach, Onions, Pumpkins, Summer Squash, Sunflowers, Sweet Potatoes, Tomatoes, Winter Squash	Alfalfa, Beets, Buckwheat, Chard, Clovers, Oats, Parsnips, Peas, Potatoes, Radishes, Rutabagas, Rye*, Salsify, Turnips, Wheat*, Plant Bare Root Trees and Berries, Build Spring Compost Pile	Broccoli, Brussels Sprouts, Cabbage, Cauliflower, Celery, Chives, Collards, Garlic, Kale, Kohlrabi, Leeks, Mustard, Parsley, Shallots, Spinach
MARCH 30	Cucumbers, Lettuce, Melons, New Zealand Spinach, Pumpkins, Summer Squash, Sunflowers, Sweet Potatoes, Tomatoes, Winter Squash	Beans, Beets, Carrots, Corn, Cotton, Millet, Parsnips, Peanuts, Potatoes, Radishes, Rice, Rutabagas, Salsify, Soybeans, Turnips	Cucumbers, Eggplant, Lettuce, Melons, New Zealand Spinach, Okra, Onions, Pepper, Pumpkins, Spring Flowers and Herbs, Summer Squash, Sunflowers, Tomatoes, Winter Squash
APRIL 30	Cucumbers, Leaf Lettuce, Melons, New Zealand Spinach, Pumpkins, Summer Squash, Sunflowers, Winter Squash	Beans, Beets, Carrots, Corn, Cowpeas, Parsnips, Potatoes, Radishes, Rutabagas, Salsify, Turnips	Cucumbers, Leaf Lettuce, Melons, New Zealand Spinach, Onions, Pumpkins, Summer Squash, Sunflowers, Tomatoes, Winter Squash
MAY 30	Cucumbers, Leaf Lettuce, Melons, New Zealand Spinach, Pumpkins, Summer Squash, Sunflowers, Winter Squash	Beans, Beets, Carrots, Corn, Cowpeas, Parsnips, Potatoes, Radishes, Rutabagas, Salsify, Turnips	Cucumbers, Leaf Lettuce, Melons, New Zealand Spinach, Onions, Pumpkins, Summer Squash, Sunflowers, Winter Squash
JUNE 30	Cucumbers, Leaf Lettuce, Melons, New Zealand Spinach, Pumpkins, Summer Squash, Sunflowers, Winter Squash	Beans, Beets, Carrots, Corn, Cowpeas, Parsnips, Potatoes, Radishes, Rutabagas, Salsify	Cucumbers, Leaf Lettuce, Melons, New Zealand Spinach, Onions, Pumpkins, Summer Squash, Sunflowers, Winter Squash

*Can be started in flats one month earlier

240 DAY MARCH 30– NOVEMBER 20	START IN FLATS (in Greenhouses, Coldframes, or Mini- Greenhouses in Winter)	SOW DIRECTLY in Soil	TRANSPLANT SEEDLINGS into Soil
JULY 30	Cucumbers, Leaf Lettuce, Melons, New Zealand Spinach, Pumpkins, Summer Squash, Sunflowers, Winter Squash	Beans, Beets, Carrots, Corn, Parsnhips, Potatoes, Radishes, Rutabagas, Salsify	Cucumbers, Leaf Lettuce, Melons, New Zealand Spinach, Onions, Pumpkins, Summer Squash, Sunflowers, Winter Squash
AUGUST 30	Autumn Flowers, Lettuce	Beans, Beets, Carrots, Corn, Parsnips, Peas, Radishes, Rutabagas, Salsify	Cucumbers, Leaf Lettuce, Melons, New Zealand Spinach, Pumpkins, Summer Squash, Sunflowers, Winter Squash
SEPTEMBER 30	Broccoli, Brussels Sprouts, Cabbage, Cauliflower, Collards, Kale, Kohlrabi, Lettuce, Mustard, Spinach (September 7)	Buckwheat, Corn (September 10), Fava Beans, Oats, White Clover*, Winter Hairy Vetch*	Autumn Flowers, Lettuce
OCTOBER 30		Radishes	Broccoli, Brussels Sprouts, Cabbage, Cauliflower, Collards, Kale, Kohlrabi, Lettuce, Mustard, Spinach (October 7)
First Frost ✻			
NOVEMBER 20		Build Autumn Compost Pile	
DECEMBER 20		Flowering Spring Bulbs	
	NOTE: Using shorter maturing varieties in this growing season for **second, or later plantings** will produce the best results.	*Winter Cover Crop which can withstand snow	

To Plan Your Garden:

1. Measure your growing area and map it on a photocopy (or hand-drawn facsimile) of the Garden Map. Indicate the scale you decide to use: the number of feet represented by an inch.

2. Decide what and how much you would like to eat each year for the crops you want to grow. (Add the figures up, divide them by 365 days for your projected daily average consumption. Then check to see if this amount is enough for your family.) Use a photocopy (or facsimile) of the Planning Guide to enter the amounts on.

3. Refer to pages 63-93 of the 1982 edition of *How to Grow More Vegetables . . .* and note those crops you chose. Take the amount you would like to eat of each crop and *divide* it by the first figure in COLUMN E if you are just beginning the biointensive method (the second figure if you have been using the method for a while, the third figure if you have been using the method for a long time on the same plot of ground). Then *multiply* these results by 100 square feet to arrive at the approximate space you will need to grow each crop. Enter the results on the Planning Guide. If you do not have enough space, modify your wants until they fit the growing area you do have. (Also remember if you are first starting out that as soon as both your soil and skill improve, the yields will go higher, allowing you to grow more in the same amount of space. It is alright to grow less during the first year(s) and put your energy into a smaller space.) Finally, add these area amounts together and continue to modify your results until you can grow all you wish to grow in your given area.

4. Note COLUMN K in *How to Grow More Vegetables . . .* ('Plant Initially in Flats or Beds') to see which seeds will be started in flats and which will be planted directly into the ground.

5. Now that you know approximately how many square feet you will need for each crop, you should figure the approximate number of plants you will need, the approximate number of flats you will have to make, and the approximate ounces of seed you will need. The results will also be entered on the Planning Guide.

> For example: I am just starting to use the method and I have decided to raise 100 pounds of zucchini and have already divided this by the first figure in COLUMN E (160-319-478+). 100 ÷ 160 = 62.5 square feet.
>
> $$\left(\text{Or } \frac{100 \text{ lbs.}}{1} \times \frac{100 \text{ sq. ft}}{160 \text{ lbs.}} = 62.5 \text{ sq. ft.}\right)$$
>
> Now to find out the number of plants I will need to grow my 100 pounds of zucchini, I take this COLUMN F figure ('Possible Pounds Yield Per Plant') on page 72 and *divide* this into the 100 pounds. Zucchini will yield 3 to 9 pounds per plant. As a beginner, I assume the smaller figure of 3 pounds, *divide* it into 100 pounds, find I need 33.3 plants, and round it up to 34 plants.
>
> Seeing that I should start my zucchini in flats in COLUMN K, I take the number of plants that I will need and *divide* it by the COLUMN M figure. (34 plants ÷ 45 plants to a flat = .755 flats). Therefore, I will need to plant a little over 3/4 of a flat of zucchini on 2-inch centers (COLUMN L). (The figures in COLUMN M have already been adjusted for each particular seed's germination rate and assumes

the flat's *inside* dimensions are 13 inches by 21 inches (or 273 square inches). More seeds may sprout than you need and you should pick those that are healthiest at transplanting time.)

Finally, the amount of seed I will need to get my 100 pounds of zucchini can be found by *multiplying* the number of square feet I will need to grow that amount by the figure in COLUMN D.

$$\left(\frac{62.5 \text{ square feet}}{1} \times \frac{.24 \text{ ounces}}{100 \text{ square feet}} = .15 \text{ ozs.}\right)$$

This figuring process should be done for each crop you are going to plant in order to determine the number of flats you will need to make and the amount of seed you will need to obtain.

6. You can now decide where to place your crops on the map you have outlined on the Garden Map according to the square feet which are needed for each crop.

Planning Guide

LINE 1 Crop	Beets, regular				
LINE 2 Desired annual yield in pounds	40				
LINE 3 Desired daily yield in pounds	.11				
LINE 4 Desired weekly yield in pounds	.77				
LINE 5 Possible yield/100 sq. ft. (Col. E, 1st figure*)	55				
LINE 6 Area to be planted (Line 2 ÷ Line 5 × 100)	$\frac{40}{55} \times 100$ = 72.7				
LINE 7 No. plants needed (Line 2 ÷ Col. F, 1st figure*)	40 ÷ .02 = 2,000				
LINE 8 No. of flats needed (Line 7 ÷ Col. M*)	NO FLATS				
LINE 9 Seed needed (Col. D* × Line 6 ÷ 100)	$\frac{2.4 \times 72.7}{100}$ = 1.7 oz.				

*Refer to *How to Grow More Vegetables . . .*, pages 68ff for the appropriate figures for Columns D, E, F, and M. Where multiple figures are given, use the first figure.

Additional Planning Guide

LINE 1 Crop					
LINE 2 Desired annual yield in pounds					
LINE 3 Desired daily yield in pounds					
LINE 4 Desired weekly yield in pounds					
LINE 5 Possible yield/100 sq. ft. (Col. E, 1st figure*)					
LINE 6 Area to be planted (Line 2 ÷ Line 5 × 100)					
LINE 7 No. plants needed (Line 2 ÷ Col. F, 1st figure*)					
LINE 8 No. of flats needed (Line 7 ÷ Col. M*)					
LINE 9 Seed needed (Col. D* × Line 6 ÷ 100)					

*Refer to *How to Grow More Vegetables . . .*, pages 68ff for the appropriate figures for Columns D, E, F, and M. Where multiple figures are given, use the first figure.

Garden Map, Monthly Calendars and Logs

On the following pages appear a Garden Map (a blank grid to help you plan your garden space), twelve Monthly Calendars and 12 Monthly Log Sheets. The Calendars will allow you to enter your daily planned activities, such as when to prepare a bed, plant a crop section in a bed, or transplant seedlings. Use the appropriate Annual Planning Chart to help you determine which things you should be doing on which days. Use a pencil while planning. There may be too many things to do on a given day, and a rescheduled compromise may have to be worked out. Also, weather changes and job schedules may force you to alter your plans. The Planning Guide will help you figure out how many flats and/or beds of which crops to plant for the season. Eventually you will work out a satisfactory approach!

On the Monthly Log Sheets, enter information about what actually happened: when a crop was planted, on what spacing, in which bed, and so on. This information will be an invaluable aid in planning the next year's crop and timing!

It may be useful to use a photocopy of these pages so you will have forms to use year after year.

January

Codes for the Calendar

PF = Plant Flats
TP = Transplant into Soil
P = Plant Seeds in Soil

January
Log Sheet

Types of Things to Note in Log

CROP—name, source, bed number, spacing, date planted, yields

BED—bed number, date dug, date fertilized, kinds and amounts of fertilizers, organic matter and amendments added

SOIL TESTS—date, bed number, results

WEATHER CONDITIONS—temperature ranges, humidity, rainfall amount, wind speeds and directions, sunlight duration

February

Codes for the Calendar

PF = Plant Flats
TP = Transplant into Soil
P = Plant Seeds in Soil

February
Log Sheet

Types of Things to Note in Log

CROP — name, source, bed number, spacing, date planted, yields

BED — bed number, date dug, date fertilized, kinds and amounts of fertilizers, organic matter and amendments added

SOIL TESTS — date, bed number, results

WEATHER CONDITIONS — temperature ranges, humidity, rainfall amount, wind speeds and directions, sunlight duration

March

Codes for the Calendar

PF = Plant Flats
TP = Transplant into Soil
P = Plant Seeds in Soil

March
Log Sheet

Types of Things to Note in Log

CROP — name, source, bed number, spacing, date planted, yields

BED — bed number, date dug, date fertilized, kinds and amounts of fertilizers, organic matter and amendments added

SOIL TESTS — date, bed number, results

WEATHER CONDITIONS — temperature ranges, humidity, rainfall amount, wind speeds and directions, sunlight duration

April

Codes for the Calendar

PF = Plant Flats
TP = Transplant into Soil
P = Plant Seeds in Soil

April
Log Sheet

Types of Things to Note in Log

CROP — name, source, bed number, spacing, date planted, yields

BED — bed number, date dug, date fertilized, kinds and amounts of fertilizers, organic matter and amendments added

SOIL TESTS — date, bed number, results

WEATHER CONDITIONS — temperature ranges, humidity, rainfall amount, wind speeds and directions, sunlight duration

May

Codes for the Calendar

PF = Plant Flats
TP = Transplant into Soil
P = Plant Seeds in Soil

May
Log Sheet

Types of Things to Note in Log

CROP — name, source, bed number, spacing, date planted, yields

BED — bed number, date dug, date fertilized, kinds and amounts of fertilizers, organic matter and amendments added

SOIL TESTS — date, bed number, results

WEATHER CONDITIONS — temperature ranges, humidity, rainfall amount, wind speeds and directions, sunlight duration

June

Codes for the Calendar

PF = Plant Flats
TP = Transplant into Soil
P = Plant Seeds in Soil

June
Log Sheet

Types of Things to Note in Log

CROP — name, source, bed number, spacing, date planted, yields

BED — bed number, date dug, date fertilized, kinds and amounts of fertilizers, organic matter and amendments added

SOIL TESTS — date, bed number, results

WEATHER CONDITIONS — temperature ranges, humidity, rainfall amount, wind speeds and directions, sunlight duration

July

July
Log Sheet

Types of Things to Note in Log

CROP—name, source, bed number, spacing, date planted, yields

BED—bed number, date dug, date fertilized, kinds and amounts of fertilizers, organic matter and amendments added

SOIL TESTS—date, bed number, results

WEATHER CONDITIONS—temperature ranges, humidity, rainfall amount, wind speeds and directions, sunlight duration

Codes for the Calendar

PF = Plant Flats
TP = Transplant into Soil
P = Plant Seeds in Soil

August
Log Sheet

Types of Things to Note in Log

CROP — name, source, bed number, spacing, date planted, yields

BED — bed number, date dug, date fertilized, kinds and amounts of fertilizers, organic matter and amendments added

SOIL TESTS — date, bed number, results

WEATHER CONDITIONS — temperature ranges, humidity, rainfall amount, wind speeds and directions, sunlight duration

September

Codes for the Calendar

PF = Plant Flats
TP = Transplant into Soil
P = Plant Seeds in Soil

September
Log Sheet

Types of Things to Note in Log

CROP—name, source, bed number, spacing, date planted, yields

BED—bed number, date dug, date fertilized, kinds and amounts of fertilizers, organic matter and amendments added

SOIL TESTS—date, bed number, results

WEATHER CONDITIONS—temperature ranges, humidity, rainfall amount, wind speeds and directions, sunlight duration

October

Codes for the Calendar

PF = Plant Flats
TP = Transplant into Soil
P = Plant Seeds in Soil

October
Log Sheet

Types of Things to Note in Log

CROP — name, source, bed number, spacing, date planted, yields

BED — bed number, date dug, date fertilized, kinds and amounts of fertilizers, organic matter and amendments added

SOIL TESTS — date, bed number, results

WEATHER CONDITIONS — temperature ranges, humidity, rainfall amount, wind speeds and directions, sunlight duration

November

November
Log Sheet

Types of Things to Note in Log

CROP — name, source, bed number, spacing, date planted, yields

BED — bed number, date dug, date fertilized, kinds and amounts of fertilizers, organic matter and amendments added

SOIL TESTS — date, bed number, results

WEATHER CONDITIONS — temperature ranges, humidity, rainfall amount, wind speeds and directions, sunlight duration

Codes for the Calendar

PF = Plant Flats
TP = Transplant into Soil
P = Plant Seeds in Soil

December
Log Sheet

Types of Things to Note in Log

CROP — name, source, bed number, spacing, date planted, yields

BED — bed number, date dug, date fertilized, kinds and amounts of fertilizers, organic matter and amendments added

SOIL TESTS — date, bed number, results

WEATHER CONDITIONS — temperature ranges, humidity, rainfall amount, wind speeds and directions, sunlight duration

Resource Guide

In this section we have listed the resources that have been cited in this book, and some basic reference material that you might find helpful if you need additional information or wish to pursue a particular topic more thoroughly. The material has been grouped under several different headings. Following the general bibliography are special lists of books on food and nutrition, greenhouse culture, herbal lawns, livestock, soils, and trees. In addition, there are listings of periodicals, seed catalogs, sources for seeds, plants, tools and films, and a list of some places that conduct learning/apprenticeship programs.

Before going on to the Resource Guide, we would like to call special attention to two books that we feel are indispensable to your success as a minifarmer, and to the series of booklets which formed the basis for this book.

How to Grow More Vegetables Than You Ever Thought Possible on Less Land Than You Can Imagine, by John Jeavons. Ten Speed Press, Berkeley, CA. 1982. Everything you need to know to grow the most on the least. *The* primer on the biodynamic/French intensive method.

The Vegetable Garden, by M. M. Vilmorin-Andrieux. Paperback edition: Ten Speed Press, Berkeley, CA. 1981, 620 pp. Hardcover edition: Jeavons-Leler Press, Willits, CA. 1976, 620 pp. Very detailed reprint of the excellent 1885 English edition by John Murray. This classic is still one of the most useful works on vegetable gardening in existence today.

Self-Teaching Mini-Series. Ecology Action of the Mid-Peninsula, 2225 El Camino Real, Palo Alto, CA 94306.

#1 *Cucumber Bonanza*
#2 *One-Crop Test Booklet: Soybeans*
#3 *Self-Fertilizing Herbal Lawn*
#4 *Food from your Backyard Homestead*
#5 *U-Bar Booklet*
#6 *Beginning to Mini-Farm*
#7 *Miniature Green- and Shade-Houses*
#8 *Ten-Crop Learning and Test Booklet: A Five-Year Workbook*
#9 *A Biointensive Mini-Farming Perspective*
#10 *Grow Compost Materials at Home*
#11 *Examining the Tropics*

GENERAL BIBLIOGRAPHY

Berry, Wendell. *The Unsettling of America: Culture and Agriculture.* Sierra Club, San Francisco, CA. 1977, 226 pp. Eloquent and passionate view of the sociological aspects of farming.

———. "Wendell Berry's Adventures With South American Potatoes." *Organic Gardening Magazine,* January 1979. Some overlooked advantages of "peasant wisdom" in growing many varieties.

Borsodi, Ralph. *Flight From the City: The Story of a New Way to Family Security.* Harper and Brothers, New York. 1933, 194 pp. Although the statistics and figures cited are not up-to-date, Mr. Borsodi's analysis is as pertinent today as when he wrote the book. We have been told that it was reprinted in paperback around 10 years ago by Harper & Row, but are unable to find it in the current paperback catalogs. Local libraries may have it.

Bromfield, Louis. *Malabar Farm.* Ballantine Books. 1970. Personal experience with worn-out soil brought back to life.

Bronson, William. "The Lesson of a Garden." *Cry California,* Winter, 1970–71.

Brown, Lester R. *The Twenty-Ninth Day.* W. W. Norton & Co., New York. 1978, 363 pp.

Buchanan, Keith. *The Transformation of the Chinese Earth.* Praeger Publishers, New York. 1970, 336 pp.

Burns, Scott. *The Household Economy.* Beacon Press. 1974. A totally new and simply explained perspective on the value of work done at home.

Burrage, Albert C. *Burrage on Vegetables.* Houghton Mifflin, New York. 1975, 224 pp. Good note on scheduling for continuous harvest. Can be ordered from Ecology Action.

Carter, Vernon Gill and Dale, Tom. *Topsoil and Civilization.* University of Oklahoma Press, Norman, OK. 1974. The historical perspective. Should be required reading.

Chittenden, Fred J., ed. *Dictionary of Gardening.* Three volumes (second edition). Royal Horticultural Society, Clarendon Press, Oxford. 1977, 2,316 pp.

Cocannouer, Joseph A. *Water and the Cycle of Life.* Devin-Adair. 1962. Easy reading from a soil scientist.

Council on Environmental Quality and the Department of State. *The Global 2000 Report to the President: Entering the Twenty-First Century, Volume 2, Technical Report.* Gerald O. Barney, Study Director. U.S. Government Printing Office, Washington, DC. 1980, 766 pp.

Creasy, Rosalind. *The Complete Book of Edible Landscaping.* Sierra Club. 1982, 400 pp. Excellent book for the backyard gardener.

DeCrosta, Anthony. "The Real Scoop on the Plant Patent Controversy." *Organic Gardening Magazine,* May 1980. Outlines well the important issue of our dwindling genetic base. Balanced presentation.

Food and Agriculture Organization of the United Nations. *1976 FAO Production Yearbook, Volume 30.* United Nations, F.A.O., Rome. 1977, 296 pp.

Foster, Catherine. *The Organic Gardener.* Random House, New York. 1972. Excellent, chatty, experienced. New England area especially.

Fukuoka, Masanobu. *The One Straw Revolution.* Rodale Press. 1978. One farmer's approach to natural farming.

Howard, Sir Albert. *The Soil and Health: A Study of Organic Agriculture.* Devin-Adair. 1956. A classic that stands undisputed today on the long-term advantages of the organic approach.

Hyams, Edward. *Soil and Civilization.* Harper & Row, New York. 1976, 312 pp. Reprint from 1952.

King, F. H. *Farmers of Forty Centuries.* Rodale Press, Emmaus, PA. 1972, 441 pp. Firsthand observations of Chinese agriculture. Reprinted from 1911.

Koepf, Herbert H., Bo. D. Peterson and Wolfgang Schauman. *Bio-Dynamic Agriculture: An Introduction.* Anthroposophic Press, Spring Valley, NY. 1976, 429 pp.

Kohr, Leopold. *The Breakdown of Nations.* E. P. Dutton, New York. 1978, 250 pp.

_____. *The City of Man: The Duke of Buen Consejo.* University of Puerto Rico Press, San Juan, PR. 1976, 71 pp.

_____. *Development Without Aid.* Schocken Books, New York. 1973, 227 pp.

_____. *The Overdeveloped Nations: The Diseconomics of Scale.* Schocken Books, New York. 1978, 185 pp.

(Economist Dr. Kohr brings life and common sense to his historical, physical, and metaphysical analysis of the present, unmanageable state of the world. Excellent!)

Langer, William L., ed. *An Encyclopedia of World History.* Houghton Mifflin Co., Boston, MA. Fifth edition, 1972, 1270 pp.

Mowat, Farley. *People of the Deer.* Jove/Harcourt, Brace, Jovanovich, New York. 1977, 303 pp.

_____. *The Desperate People.* Little, Brown & Co., Boston/Toronto. 1959, 305 pp.

National Agricultural Lands Study. "Where Have the Farm Lands Gone?" U.S. Government Printing Office, Washington, DC. 1981, 26 pp.

Nearing, Helen. *The Good Life Album of Helen and Scott Nearing.* E. P. Dutton, New York. 1974, 127 pp.

Nearing, Helen and Scott. *Living the Good Life: How to Live Sanely and Simply in a Troubled World.* Schocken Books, New York. 1970, 213 pp.

_____. *Continuing the Good Life: Half a Century of Homesteading.* Schocken Books, New York. 1980, 208 pp.

O'Brien, R. Dalziel. *Intensive Gardening.* Faber & Faber, London. 1956, 183 pp. Useful for potential mini-farmers.

Osborn, Fairfield. *Our Plundered Planet.* Little, Brown & Co., Boston, MA. 1948, 217 pp.

Philbrick, John and Helen. *Gardening for Health and Nutrition.* Rudolph Steiner Publications, Blauvelt, NY. 1971, 93 pp. Harper & Row, New York. 1980, 96 pp.

Rateaver, Bargyla and Gylver. *The Organic Method Primer.* Published by the authors, Pauma Valley, CA 92061. 1975, 257 pp. Packed with information!

Robinson, William. *The Wild Garden.* Reprinted by the Scolar Press, Ikley, Yorkshire, England from the 1894 edition. 1977, 305 pp.

Root, Waverly. *Food: An Informal Dictionary.* Simon & Schuster, New York. 1980, 602 pp.

Schumacher, E. F. and Gillingham, Peter N. *Good Work.* Harper & Row, New York. 1980, 223 pp.

Seshadri, C. V. *Biodynamic Gardening: Monograph Series on Engineering of Photosynthetic Systems, Volume 4.* Shri AMM Murugappa Chettiar Research Centre, Photosynthesis & Energy Division, Tharamani, Madras 600 042, India. 1980, 38 pp. Available through Ecology Action for $2.25 postpaid.

Seymour, John. *The Book of Self-Sufficiency.* Hearst Publishing. 1976. Brief information on each of a wealth of topics. Good planning guide.

Smith, Marney. *Growing Your Own Food.* Save the Children Federation, 48 Wilton Road, Westport, CT 06880. 1980, 35 pp.

Storl, Wolf. *Culture and Horticulture: A Philosophy of Gardening.* Bio-dynamic Literature, Wyoming, RI 02898. 1979, 435 pp.

Sunset Editors. *Sunset Western Garden Book.* Lane Publishing Co., Menlo Park, CA. 1979, 512 pp.

Thomas, William L. Jr., ed. *Man's Role in Changing the Face of the Earth, Volume I & II.* University of Chicago Press, Chicago, IL. 1956, 1,193 pp.

United States Department of Agriculture. *A Time to Choose: Summary Report on the Structure of Agriculture.* U.S. Government Printing Office, Washington, DC. 1981, 164 pp.

_____. *Report and Recommendations on Organic Farming.* Office of Government and Public Affairs, Washington, DC 20205. 1980, 94 pp.

FOOD AND NUTRITION

Hur, Robin. *Food Reform: Our Desperate Need.* Heidelberg Publishers, 3707 Kerbey Lane, Austin, TX 78731. 1975, 260 pp. Examines food and disease of "advanced" nations.

Katzen, Mollie. *Moosewood Cookbook.* Ten Speed Press, P.O. Box 7123, Berkeley, CA 94707. 1977. Undisputed favorite vegetarian cookbook. Also see her new cookbook, *The Enchanted Broccoli Forest.* Ten Speed Press. 1982.

Robertson, Laurel et al. *Laurel's Kitchen: A Handbook for Vegetarian Cookery and Nutrition.* Nilgiri Press. 1976. Excellent nutritional information and vegetarian recipes. Also in paperback. Includes charts of Recommended Daily Allowances for various nutrients.

USDA, Agricultural Research Service. *Composition of Foods.* Agricultural Handbook No. 8. U.S. Government Printing Office, Washington, DC. 1963, 190 pp.

GREENHOUSE CULTURE

Anderson, Phyllis. "Gardening Under a Roomy Tent You Make with Shadecloth or Plastic over PVC Pipe." *Sunset,* Southern California edition. March 1980, pp. 200–201.

Antill, David. *Gardening Under Protection.* EP Publishing, Ltd., East Ardsley, Wakefield, West Yorkshire, WF3 2JN, England. 1978, 72 pp.

Bailey, L. H. *The Forcing Book: A Manual of the Cultivation of Vegetables in Glass Houses.* MacMillan, New York. 1903, 259 pp.

Browse, Philip McMillan. *Step-by-Step Guide to Plant Propagation.* Simon & Schuster, New York. 1979, 96 pp.

Chase, J. L. H. *Cloche Gardening.* Faber & Faber, London. 1948, 195 pp.

Colebrook, Binda. *Winter Gardening in the Maritime Northwest.* Tilth Association, Rt. 2, Box 190-A, Arlington, WA 98223. 1977, 128 pp.

Dremann, Craig. *Vegetable Seed Production.* Redwood City Seed Co., Box 360, Redwood City, CA 94064. 1974, 6 pp. For moderate climates; expanded version planned.

Johnston, Robert Jr. *Growing Garden Seeds.* Johnny's Selected Seeds, Albion, ME 04910. 1976, 32 pp. Culture of plants for saving seed.

Lawrence, William J. C. and J. Newell. *Seed and Potting Composts.* George Allen & Unwin, Ltd., London. 1942, 136 pp.

Lawrence, William J. C. *Science and the Glasshouse.* Oliver and Boyd, London. 1950, 175 pp.

McCullagh, James C., ed. *The Solar Greenhouse Book.* Rodale Press, Emmaus, PA. 1978, 328 pp.

Miller, Douglas C. *Vegetable and Herb Seed Growing for the Gardener and Small Farmer.* Bullkill Creek Publishing, Hershey, MI. 1977, 46 pp. A good book to start with.

Nearing, Helen and Scott. *Building and Using Our Sun-Heated Greenhouse: Grow Vegetables All Year Round.* Garden Way Publishing, Charlotte, VT. 1977, 148 pp.

Reilly, Ann. *Park's Success with Seeds.* Geo. W. Park Co., Greenwood, SC. 1978, 364 pp.

Rieke, Dr. Paul E., and Dr. Darryl D. Warncke. *Greenhouse Soils.* LaMotte Chemical Products Co., Chestertown, MD. 1975, 36 pp.

Rivers, Thomas. *Miniature Fruit Garden.* Orange Judd & Company, New York. 1866, 133 pp. Espaliered dwarf trees under mini-greenhouses!

HERBAL LAWNS

Foster, Catherine Osgood. *Organic Flower Gardening.* Rodale Press, Emmaus, PA. 1975, 305 pp. Good bulb section.

Harding, W. F. W. "Clover Lawns." *Journal of the Royal Horticultural Society.* 1952, pp. 377–80.

Hatfield, Audrey Wynne. *How to Enjoy Your Weeds.* Sterling Publishing Company, New York. 1971, 192 pp.

Hylton, William H., ed. *The Rodale Herb Book: How to Use, Grown and Buy Nature's Miracle Plants.* Rodale Press, Emmaus, PA. 1974, 653 pp.

Levy, Juliette de Bairacli. *Common Herbs for Natural Health.* Schocken Books, New York. 1974, 200 pp.

Robinson, William. *The Wild Garden.* Reprinted by the Scolar Press, Ikley, Yorkshire, England from the 1894 edition. 1977, 305 pp.

Sunset Editors. *How to Grow Herbs.* Lane Publishing Company, Menlo Park, CA. 1972, 80 pp.

———. *Lawns and Ground Covers.* Lane Publishing Company, Menlo Park, CA. 1979, 96 pp.

LIVESTOCK

Belanger, Jerry. *Raising Milk Goats the Modern Way.* Garden Way Publishing. 1975, 151 pp. Simple and practical.

Grout, Roy A. *The Hive and the Honey Bee.* Dadant. 1949. Excellent, complete text. Many editions; all are good buys.

Hills, Lawrence. *Comfrey: Fodder, Food and Remedy.* Universe. 1976, 254 pp. A plant with many uses as animal feed and healing herb. Its use as a human food is being challenged currently, the issue remains unresolved.

Kelly, Walter T. *How to Keep Bees and Sell Honey.* 1978. Best of the many inexpensive beginners' handbooks.

Tetrault, Jeanne and Sherry Thomas. *Country Women: A Handbook for the New Farmer.* Doubleday, New York. 1976. The best on chickens, goats and sheep. Good information on rabbits, turkeys and pigs. Also covers related homestead subjects.

SOILS

Brady, Nyle C. *The Nature and Properties of Soils.* MacMillan, New York. 1974, 8th edition, 672 pp. (See also: first edition, T. Lyttleton Lyon & Harry O. Buckman, 1929, 428 pp.; and fourth edition by the same authors, revised by Harry O. Buckman, 1949, 499 pp.).

Brooklyn Botanic Garden. *Handbook on Soils*. Brooklyn, NY. 1956, 81 pp. Some photos of root systems in the soil.

California Department of Conservation. *California Soils: An Assessment*. April 1979, draft report.

Faulkner, Edward H. *Plowman's Folly*. University of Oklahoma Press, Norman, OK. 1943, 154 pp. A classic.

Pauli, F. W. *Soil Fertility: A Biodynamical Approach*. Adam Hilger, Ltd., 98 St. Pancras Way, London NW1, England. 1976, 204 pp. Supplemental.

TREES

Baker, Richard St. Barbe. *My Life My Trees*. Findhorn Publications, The Park, Forres IV36 OTZ, Scotland. 1979, 167 pp. Autobiography of "The Man of the Trees." May be purchased from Ecology Action.

———. *Dance of the Trees*. Oldbourne Press, London. 1956, 192 pp.

———. *Green Glory: The Forests of the World*. A. A. Wyn, Inc., New York. 1949, 253 pp.

———. *Sahara Challenge*. Lutterworth Press, London. 1954, 152 pp.

Brooks, Harold and Claron Hess. *Western Fruit Gardening*. University of California Press, Berkeley, CA. 1953, 287 pp. Older, but still good.

Douglas, J. Sholto and Robert A. de J. Hart. *Forest Farming*. Rodale Press. 1976. Detailed.

Foster, Ruth. *Landscaping That Saves Energy Dollars*. David McKay Co. 1978. Clear information.

Giono, Jean. *The Man Who Planted Hope and Grew Happiness*. Friends of Nature, Winchester, MA 01890. 1967, 17 pp. An account of a one-man tree planting program that is very inspirational. May be ordered from Ecology Action.

Kraft, Ken and Pat. *Grow Your Own Dwarf Fruit Trees*. Walker & Company, New York. 1975, 218 pp. Good beginning book.

Martin, R. Sanford. *How to Prune Fruit Trees*. Pub. by author, 10535 Las Lunitas Ave., Tujunga, CA 91042. 1978, 90 pp. Best and simplest book on pruning for West Coast gardeners.

Ray, Richard and Walheim, Lance. *Citrus*. H P Books, Tucson, AZ. 1980, 176 pp.

Smith, J. Russell. *Tree Crops*. Harper & Row, New York. 1978. Good ideas.

Sunset Editors. *Sunset Pruning Handbook*. Lane Books, Menlo Park, CA. 1972, 96 pp.

Tukey, Harold Bradford. *Dwarfed Fruit Trees*. Comstock. 1978, 576 pp. Definitive work on the subject.

United States Department of Agriculture. *Trees: The Yearbook of Agriculture*. 1949, 944 pp.

Walheim, Lance and Stebbins, Robert L. *Western Fruit, Berries and Nuts: How to Select, Grow and Enjoy*. H P Books, Tucson, AZ. 1981, 192 pp. An *excellent* planning book with many uses outside the West. Detailed charts and beautiful photographs.

Weiner, Michael A. *Plant A Tree: A Working Guide to Regreening America*. MacMillan, New York. 1975, 277 pp. Very good!

Wheatly, Margaret Tipton. *Joy of a Home Fruit Garden*. Doubleday, New York. 1975. How to raise fruit in the smallest spaces. Detailed pruning tips.

Yepsen, Roger B. Jr., ed. *Trees for the Yard, Orchard and Woodlot*. Rodale Press, Emmaus, PA. 1976, 305 pp. Introduction to the different uses of trees.

Note: Your local agricultural extension agent is usually an excellent source of fruit tree information. The address and/or phone number for your agent is available from your county administration. Pamphlets are usually available free or at minimal cost.

PERIODICALS

Acres, U.S.A. P.O. Box 9547, Raytown, MO 64133. Monthly newspaper on different organic approaches. $9/12 issues.

Alan Chadwick Society Newsletter. Green Gulch Farm, Star Rt., Sausalito, CA 94965. Quarterly publication with articles on Alan Chadwick's teachings, the work sites which have developed as the result of his work, learning opportunities, and other good information. $15/2 issues.

Bio-Dynamics. Bio-Dynamic Farming and Gardening Association, Inc., P.O. Box 253, Wyoming, RI 02898. Quarterly journal with in-depth articles on bio-dynamic cultivation. $12/4 issues.

Biological Agriculture and Horticulture. International Institute of Biological Husbandry, A.B. Academic Publishers, Box 97, Berkhamsted, Herts HP4 2PX, England. Scientific journal dedicated to alternative systems of agriculture. $75/4 issues to institutions. $33/4 issues to individuals.

The Christian Science Monitor. P.O. Box 125, Astor Station, Boston, MA 02123. An international daily newspaper (5 days/week) that provides in-depth but concise reporting of the news in the US and elsewhere. Delivered every day by your postman. $90/year (saves about $40 over newsstand price). Toll-free number is: 800-225-7090.

Co-Evolution Quarterly. P.O. Box 428, Sausalito, CA 94966. Articles cover soft technology, economic reporting, environmental issues, community activism, plus reviews of useful books, magazines and tools. $14/4 issues.

Countryside. Hwy. 19 East, Waterloo, WI 53594. Monthly magazine about farming and homesteading skills.

The Dump Heap. 2950 Walnut Blvd., Walnut Creek, CA 94598. One of our favorites for home-grown growing-edge ideas and information. $6/4 issues.

East-West Journal. P.O. Box 1200, Brookline Village, MA 02147. Monthly publication on health care, natural agriculture, alternative energy and the quality of life. $18/12 issues.

The Ecologist. 73 Molesworth Street, Wadebridge, Cornwall, PL27 7DS, England. Wide array of articles dealing with the world environment. $16/10 issues.

The Green Revolution. School of Living, P.O. Box 3233, York, PA 17402. Started in 1943, it is one of the longest running publications reporting on contemporary society from the human-scale point of view. $8/6 issues, or $12 if you want to become a member giving you 10% discount on books and workshops.

Harrowsmith. Camden East, Queen Victoria Road, Ontario K0K 1J0, Canada. Magazine with taste and style for homesteaders. $13.50/6 issues.

Henry Doubleday Research Association Newsletter. Convent Land, Bocking, Braintree, Essex, England. Very interesting grass-roots research efforts for backyard enthusiasts in England. $15/at least 4 issues—also many different reports.

International Federation of Organic Agriculture Movements (IFOAM) Newsletter. Caretaker Farm, Hancock Road, Williamstown, MA 01267. Send for current membership information. Good periodic newsletters.

The Land Report. The Land Institute, Route 3, Salina, KS 67401. Good periodical on alternatives in agriculture, energy, shelter, and waste management. $5/about 3 issues.

Maine Organic Farmer and Gardener. Maine Organic Farmers and Gardeners Association, P.O. Box 187, 110 Water St., Hallowell, ME 04347. Respectable and relevant newspaper format with good basic and regional information. $5/6 issues.

MANAS. P.O. Box 32112, Los Angeles, CA 90032. Weekly journal presenting ideas and viewpoints (unsigned) which seeks to study the principles that move world society and in so doing provide a vision for the future. For the 35 years of its existence, this aquifer has never run dry. Write for a sample copy (include two stamps). $10/44 issues per year!

The Mother Earth News. P.O. Box 70, Hendersonville, NC 28791. Huge issues with good growing-edge reporting of new and old urban and rural homesteading approaches. $18/6 issues.

The Natural Farmer. P.O. Box 335, Antrim, NH 03440. One of the very good newsletters with basic and relevant contents. $10/4 issues.

The New Farm. 33 E. Minor St., Emmaus, PA 18049. Organic farming newsletter that is the "natural" outgrowth of Rodale's previous *Organic Gardening and Farming Magazine.* $24/12 issues.

Organic Gardening. 33 E. Minor St., Emmaus, PA 18049. Diverse and increasingly in-depth articles on gardening and self-reliance. The most read magazine on gardening. $10/12 issues.

Practical Self-Sufficiency. Broad Leys Publishing Co., Widdington, Saffron, Waldon, Essex CB11 3SP, England. Homesteading skills from gardening to small livestock management. $10.50 surface, $18 air/6 issues.

RAIN. 2270 N.W. Irving, Portland, OR 97210. Good coverage of appropriate technology and publications. $15/6 issues.

The Soil Association Quarterly Review. Walnut Tree Manor, Haughley, Stow Market, Suffolk, IP14 3RS, England. Journal with good articles and reviews about natural farming methods. About $16/4 issues—write for their U.S. price.

Tilth. Rte. 2, Box 190-A, Arlington, WA 98223. Good publication on organic culture by an active group. $10/4 issues.

SEED CATALOGS AND SOURCES FOR SEEDS AND PLANTS

Abundant Life Seeds Foundation, P.O. Box 772, Port Townsend, WA 98368. Small seed exchange for residents of the Pacific Northwest and California only. Catalog: $2.00.

Charles Hart Seed Company, 304 Main Street, Wethersfield, CT 06109. Largest selection of old-fashioned and non-hybrid vegetables. Many hard-to-find varieties available on request.

Dave Wilson Nursery, Hughson, CA 95326. Good selection of fruit trees. Recommended.

DeGiorgi Co., P.O. Box 413, Council Bluffs, IA 51501. Forage crops, old-fashioned lettuce and other vegetables, open-pollinated corn. Catalog: 66¢.

Hillier Nurseries Ltd., Ampfield, Ramsey, Hants S05 9PA, England. Excellent tree and plant supplier.

J.L. Hudson Seed Company, P.O. Box 1058, Redwood City, CA 94064. One of the world's largest selections of flower and herb seed. Catalog: $1.00.

Johnny's Selected Seeds, Albion, ME 04910. Small seed company with integrity. Carries native American crops, select oriental vegetables, grains, short-maturing soybeans. Catalog: $1.00.

Redwood City Seed Co., P.O. Box 361, Redwood City, CA 94064. Basic selection of non-hybrid, untreated vegetable and herb seeds. Catalog: $1.00.

R.H. Shumway, Rockford, IL 61101. Good selection of grains, fodders and cover crops.

Sassafras Farms, P.O. Box 1007, Topanga, CA 90290. Two dozen organically grown vegetable varieties and miscellaneous roots. Send $1.00 for poster-catalog.

Stark Brothers, Louisiana, MO 63353. Specializes in fruit trees, especially dwarfs and semi-dwarfs. Carries many developed by Luther Burbank.

Stokes Seeds, P.O. Box 548, Buffalo, NY 14240. Carries excellent varieties of many vegetables, especially carrots.

Sutton Seeds, London Road, Earley, Reading, Berkshire RG6 1AB, England. For gourmet gardeners. Excellent, tasty varieties, hot-house vegetables.

Tree Crops Nursery, Rt. 1, Box 44-B, Covelo, CA 95428. Excellent fruit tree stock — known and rare.

HERB SEEDS

J.L. Hudson Seed Company (see listing above). Probably most extensive herb listings in the world.

Meadowbrook Herb Garden, Whispering Pines Rd., Wyoming, RI 02898. Bio-dynamically grown herbs and seeds. Catalog: 50¢.

Nichols Garden Nursery, 1190 North Pacific Highway, Albany, OR 97321. Many novelty items.

Redwood City Seed Company (see listing above). Petalless Roman Chamomile, Creeping Thyme and Yarrow Seeds, if you cannot locate plants.

CLOVER AND TREFOIL SEEDS

Nitragin Company, 3101 West Custer Ave., Milwaukee, WI 53209. Rhizobia inoculant for *Lotus corniculatus* (Birdsfoot Trefoil) and clovers.

P.L. Rohrer, Smoketown, PA 17576. Five-pound minimum.

POTATO SUPPLIERS

Note: If your nursery does not carry seed potatoes, you may contact these companies listed below. Ask for price with a stamped, self-addressed return envelope.

Irish potatoes: White Rose and Red La Sol varieties (and probably Russet). 100-pound orders or more — go in with 2 or 3 friends. Order in September *untreated* for next spring from: *Cal-Ore Seed Company,* 1212 Country Club Blvd., Stockton, CA 95204.

Sweet potatoes: Jewel, Centennial, Garnett, Jersey varieties. Order in September *untreated,* number two size, for following summer. 40-pound boxes from: *Joe Alvernaz,* P.O. Box 474, Livingston, CA 95334.

BULBS

K. Van Bourgondien Brothers, P.O. Box A, 245 Farmingdale Road, Rt. 9, Babylon, NY 11704. Low prices, large orders only (25 or more of each bulb).

Burpee Seed Co., Clinton, IA 52732. Fall bulb catalog.

P. deJager & Sons, South Hamilton, MA 01982. Fine selection, beautiful color catalog.

French's, P.O. Box 87, Center Rutland, VT 05736.

Messelaar, County Rd., Rt. 1A, P.O. Box 269, Ipswich, MA 01938.

Michigan Bulb Co., 1950 Waldorf, Grand Rapids, MI 49550. Inexpensive young bulbs.

Charles H. Mueller, River Road, New Hope, PA 18939.

Plants Alive, 2603 Third Ave., Seattle, WA 98121. Their "Spring Bulb Guide" includes list of 40+ mail-order bulb suppliers and basic cultural information. $2.00.

John Schleepers, 63 Wall Street, New York, NY 10005.

White Flower Farm, Litchfield, CT 06759. Their *Garden Book* costs $5.00 (refundable with your first order), but has invaluable detailed information on bulbs and other plants (selections not illustrated).

TOOLS

Chemplast, Inc., 150 Dey Road, Wayne, NJ 07470. For constructing mini-greenhouses. Sold in 60-inch wide, 50 foot rolls. Longer lengths available. 5 and 7 millimeter thicknesses.

Ecology Action, 2225 El Camino Real, Palo Alto, CA 94306. Mail order books. Also LaMotte soil test kits.

Hersey Products, Inc., Water Meter and Controls Division, 250 Elm Street, Dedham, MA 02026. Good water meter that measures in tenths of a gallon. Order no.: Q0H0201-MVR-30A-COMPACT-10-SCG-B-L/CONN-RZ-BOTTOM.

Jacobs Brothers Company, 8928 Sepulveda Boulevard, Sepulveda, CA 91343. 15-year shade-netting in various percentages of shading capacity; use 3% type for bird and pest netting.

LaMotte Chemical Company, P.O. Box 329, Chestertown, MD 21620. The best soil kits we have found.

Organic Farm and Garden Center, 840 Potter Street, Berkeley, CA 94710. Mail order fertilizers.

Smith and Hawken Tool Co., 68 Homer Ave., Drawer 52, Palo Alto, CA 94301. Superbly crafted D-handled spades and forks from England. Also other tools. Send for catalog.

Walter Nicke's Garden Talk, Box 667G, Hudson, NY 12534. Catalog of small tools — including min/max thermometers and Spyn-guides (which guide hoses easily around corners of growing areas).

VJ Grower's Supply, 500 W. Orange Blossom Trail, Apopka, FL 32703. 36 inch × 312 foot rolls of double-polished, clear, 6-year rated, 8 millimeter vinyl film for covering miniature greenhouses. Also carries Monsanto 302 plastic sheeting.

MINI-FARM (Learning/Apprentice)

Note: While the written word can be a great aid in helping learn things, many people find it rewarding to work with others. This list contains a few places that either have programs themselves or can direct you to others who will be able to provide you with people or groups that conduct programs. Remember when you write to any of these people, it is always considerate to include a self-addressed and stamped envelope to help them cover the costs, and possibly even a dollar or two. Tell whom you are writing to a little about yourself and give them, at least, a general idea of what you are looking for. This will help them help you. If you make an agreement and commit yourself for a period of time, make every effort to keep your commitment.

* indicates that these sites have biointensive *teaching* programs.

* *Camp Joy,* 131 Camp Joy Road, Boulder Creek, CA 95006. Biointensive apprenticeships and special classes at a successful "homestead."

Center for Rural Affairs, P.O. Box 405, Walthill, NE 68067. Provides information on opportunities in their area.

* *Community Environmental Council,* 924 Anacapa Street, Santa Barbara, CA 93101. Offers apprenticeships, six-week courses, five-day courses, three-day and one-day seminars in biointensive training.

* *Farallones Institute—Integral Urban House,* 1516 5th Street, Berkeley, CA 94710. Offers various programs which show the potential for an ecological lifestyle in an urban environment.

* Farallones Institute—Rural Center, 15920 Coleman Valley Road, Occidental, CA 95465. Offers various programs and has horticultural apprenticeship or internship positions in biointensive gardening and edible landscaping with a focus on tree crops. These are residential 6 to 12 month commitments.

Mary Jurinko—Apprenticeships, Organic Gardening, Emmaus, PA 18049. Has a list of over 100 places around the U.S. to live and learn at.

Land Trust Homesteading Farm, Jon Towne, Director, R.R. 2, Box 311, Bangor, MI 49013, (616) 427-8791. Room for seven students beginning May 1. Learn by experience under supervision with freedom to pursue individual reading and informal discussions. 38-acre general farm with livestock and emphasis on market vegetable production. Fees range from $125, first month, to $75 for the fifth and sixth months.

MOFGA (Maine Organic Farmers and Gardeners Association), Farm Apprentice Placement Service, Box 2176, Augusta, ME 04330. Refers people to various members of MOFGA.

* *Mother Earth News,* Food Raising Classes, P.O. Box 70, Hendersonville, NC 28791.

The Mountain School, Eliot Coleman, Vershire, VT 05079. Summer seminars where school heads and administrators can learn how to make their schools almost food self-sufficient as well as give their students hands-on gardening experience.

New Alchemy Institute—East, 237 Hatchville Road, East Falmouth, MA 02536. Offers detailed alternative technology learning programs in energy, aquaculture and food raising.

NOFA (Natural Organic Farmers Association), Apprentice Program, P.O. Box 335, Antrim, NH 03440. Refers people to various members of NOFA.

* *The Rural Development Programme,* Emerson College, Forest Row, Sussex, RH18 5JX, England. Good one, two and three year apprenticeships in biointensive practices. Especially for those intending to do work in the Third World.

School of Homesteading, Sally and Maynard Kaufman, R.R. 2, Box 316, Bangor, MI 49013. (616) 427-8986. Room for 5 students on their 100-acre general farm with livestock and emphasis on dairy production. Learning by experience under supervision with more structured reading and discussion. Term is May 1 to September 1. Try to apply by March. Four-month program: $400. College credit can also be earned.

* *Saratoga Community Gardens,* 14500 Fruitvale Ave., Box 756, Saratoga, CA 95070. A 10-acre biointensive garden offering a one-year apprentice training program.

School of Living, P.O. Box 3233, York, PA 17402. This is, of course, the great grandparent of the whole "New Age" movement, whose founder, Ralph Borsodi, influenced J.I. Rodale of *Prevention* and *Organic Gardening* magazines and Lyman Wood of *Garden Way.* The School of Living has five centers which offer programs in all aspects of homesteading and have been around since the 1930's.

* *University of California, Santa Cruz,* Provost Robert Curry, College 8/Farm & Garden Program, Santa Cruz, CA 95064. Offers apprenticeship training in the biodynamic/French intensive method. This garden was begun by the late Alan Chadwick.

VIISA, P.O. Box 6790, Santa Barbara, CA 93111. Offers participation in small-scale, personal self-help projects in the Third World for one, two, twelve or twenty-four months. Write for details.

Western WOOF (Workers on Organic Farms), 13201 Harding, Sylmar, CA 91342. Networking people who list farmers in California, Hawaii, and Colorado for those who would like to "get their feet wet." $6/6 issues per year.

FILMS AND VIDEOTAPES

Bullfrog Films. Dept. G., Oley, PA 19547. Good selection of films on food/farming/land use/nutrition/solar and other renewable energy sources. They have PBS Special on Alan Chadwick and the biodynamic/French intensive method (also containing the work of Ecology Action), entitled "Gardensong." Ask for their catalog and include a few stamps to help cover their postage.

National Video Portrait Library. Linda Maslow, Director, 1869 Kirby Road, McLean, VA 22101. Has a 55-minute, black and white 3/4" videocassette of a spontaneous philosophical interview with the late Alan Chadwick available for sale or rental entitled "Portrait of Alan Chadwick: Master Horticulturalist." Please enclose a few stamps when inquiring.

Order Form

The **Redwood City Seed Company** is offering the particular seed varieties recommended for crop-testing in the proper amounts required. You can purchase single packets of each of the test crops or purchase them as kits. If there is a shortage of any seed, they will substitute the closest variety recommended by Ecology Action. You can also send for their Seed Growing Guide or their Catalog of Useful Plants.

   Please note that, when ordering from outside the United States, there may be restrictions on the importation of some seeds. Make sure you check with your local Department of Agriculture.

SINGLE TEST SEED PACKETS	PRICE	AMOUNT
WHEAT	$1.00 ea.	
CHERRY TOMATOES	$1.00 ea.	
SOYBEANS (6″ centers)	$2.00 ea.	
LETTUCE, Romaine	$1.00 ea.	
BEETS, Cylindra	$1.00 ea.	
KIT #1 (one each of above)	**$5.00 ea.**	
ALFALFA	$1.00 ea.	
COLLARDS	$1.00 ea.	
SOYBEANS (9 & 12″ centers)	$1.50 ea.	
CUCUMBERS	$1.00 ea.	
KIT #2 (one each of above)	**$4.00 ea.**	
SEED GROWING GUIDE	$1.00 ea.	
CATALOG OF USEFUL PLANTS	$1.00 ea.	

All items postpaid via airmail worldwide.
Prices effective January, 1983.

**Grand Total
Enclosed** $

Mail this form to: Redwood City Seed Co.
P.O. Box 361
Redwood City, California 94064
U.S.A.

Ship to:

NAME _____

ADDRESS _____

TOWN _____ STATE _____

COUNTRY _____ POSTAL CODE _____

*May we introduce
other Ten Speed books
you will find useful . . .*

HOW TO GROW MORE VEGETABLES
than you ever thought possible
on less land than you can imagine

by John Jeavons

". . . the best plain-language explanation of Biodynamic/French Intensive gardening techniques we've yet seen." — *Mother Earth News*

This new edition has thoroughly updated the planting charts, information and plans needed to develop a garden rich and abundant in food, fruit and grains — enough to feed a family of four in the space of the average lawn.

8½ × 11 inches, 144 pages,
$7.95 paper, $10.95 cloth

THE VEGETABLE GARDEN

by MM. Vilmorin-Andrieux

First published in English in 1895, this book describes cultivation techniques that pre-date the days in chemical gardening.

". . . a monumental work for the serious or inquisitive gardener, this book is a treasure."
— *Co-Evolution Quarterly*

6 × 9 inches, 620 pages,
Illustrated with over 650 drawings, $11.95 paper

THE SEED FINDER

by John Jeavons and Robin Leler

This unique seed catalog lists thousands of the best plant varieties from an assortment of fine seed houses. Illustrated with engravings from the classic THE VEGETABLE GARDEN, as well as helpful planting tips — Every gardener should have one!

6 × 9 inches, 176 pages, $4.95 paper

You will find them in your bookstore or library, or you can order directly from us.
Please include $1.00 additional for each book's shipping and handling.

TEN SPEED PRESS
P.O. Box 7123   Berkeley, California 94707